3

39.55
8CE

D0203336

AMERICAN
WOMEN
SONGWRITERS

AMERICAN WOMEN SONGWRITERS

A Biographical Dictionary

VIRGINIA L. GRATTAN

GREENWOOD PRESS
Westport, Connecticut · London

Library of Congress Cataloging-in-Publication Data

Grattan, Virginia L.
    American women songwriters : a biographical dictionary / Virginia
L. Grattan.
        p. cm.
    Includes bibliographical references and indexes.
    ISBN 0-313-28510-1
    1. Songs—United States—Bio-bibliography—Dictionaries.   2. Women
composers—United States—Biography—Dictionaries.   I. Title.
ML106.U3G73   1993
782.42′092′273—dc20
[B]   92-32211

British Library Cataloguing in Publication Data is available.

Copyright © 1993 by Virginia L. Grattan

All rights reserved. No portion of this book may be
reproduced, by any process or technique, without the
express written consent of the publisher.

Library of Congress Catalog Card Number: 92-32211
ISBN: 0-313-28510-1

First published in 1993

Greenwood Press, 88 Post Road West, Westport, CT 06881
An imprint of Greenwood Publishing Group, Inc.

Printed in the United States of America

The paper used in this book complies with the
Permanent Paper Standard issued by the National
Information Standards Organization (Z39.48-1984).

10 9 8 7 6 5 4 3 2 1

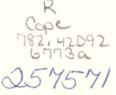

Copyright Acknowledgments

"Luka" lyrics by Suzanne Vega. Copyright 1987 Waifersongs Ltd./WB Music Corp. Used by permission. All rights reserved.

"The Way We Were" by Alan Bergman, Marilyn Bergman and Marvin Hamlisch. © 1973 COLGEMS-EMI MUSIC INC. All rights reserved. International copyright secured. Used by permission.

"A Fine Romance" by Dorothy Fields and Jerome Kern. Copyright © 1936 PolyGram International Publishing, Inc. Copyright renewed.

"Little Boxes," words and music by Malvina Reynolds. © Copyright 1962 Schroder Music Co. Renewed 1990 N. Schimmel. Used by permission. All rights reserved.

"Moonshine Blues" by Ma Rainey, by permission of John Steiner.

"Louisiana Hoodoo Blues" by Ma Rainey, by permission of John Steiner.

"Jolene" by Dolly Parton. Copyright 1973 by Velvet Apple Music. Used by permission. All rights reserved.

"That's Enough," words and music by Dorothy Love Coates. © Copyright 1956 by ATV MUSIC. All rights controlled and administered by MCA Music Publishing, A Division of MCA Inc., New York, NY 10019, under license from ATV MUSIC. Copyright renewed. Used by permission. International copyright secured. All rights reserved.

Epigraph from Lalo Schifrin's "Cantos Aztecas" based on the poetry of Nezahualcoyotl. Used by permission.

It cannot be in vain why we come to this earth;
  Let us leave some flowers;
  Let us leave some song.

—Nezahualcoyotl, 1432–1472

CONTENTS

PREFACE

Women have written songs in America since the early years of the nation. Some of their songs are national treasures, like "The Battle Hymn of the Republic" and "America the Beautiful." Even though women have written songs for motion pictures, for the theater, gospel songs and hymns, blues, jazz, folk songs, every kind of song, little recognition has been given to them in the literature of American popular song.

This book has been written to acknowledge the contribution of women to American popular song. It is not intended to be a history of women songwriters, nor a critical evaluation of their contribution. The purpose is simply to provide biographical information about the key American women who have written popular songs.

Not surprisingly many of the women included here are well-known singers, such as Barbra Streisand and Carly Simon. Since they are always looking for new songs, many singers have tried their hand at songwriting, and some have been very successful. Of course, in the days of vaudeville, performers often wrote their own songs for their acts. Performers in musical revues, also, had the opportunity to contribute songs and sketches. The early classical blues women frequently wrote their own songs. Bessie Smith sometimes wrote songs at recording sessions when she needed something to record. Today singer-songwriters are common. In fact, if a songwriter wants to succeed in the business, she had better become a singer as well and record her own songs. The all-important record contract is what makes songwriting viable.

There was a time, however, when songwriters just wrote songs, and many women made their living as songwriters. Some women, like Dorothy Fields, had long careers writing songs for the theater or for motion pictures. Some, like Fanny Crosby, made their living writing hymns. Many women were second- or third-generation songwriters. That is, they were the daughters or granddaughters of songwriters. Although it was usually the father who had been the songwriter, in the case of Sylvia Dee it was her mother and grandmother who had been songwriters. Some women were married to songwriters and wrote with their husbands, as did country songwriter Felice Bryant. Other women had access to the songwriting business through their jobs as band pianists or music arrangers.

Women songwriters were more likely to be lyricists than composers. In fact, in the nineteenth century writing lyrics was so much a woman's job that at least one man, Septimus Winner, wrote under the pseudonym of a woman, Alice Hawthorne. It was not so common for women to compose music. It is interesting to note, however, that many of the women who did compose songs were very well educated; they were graduates of the Juilliard School of Music, the New England Conservatory of Music, the Curtis Institute of Music, or the like. Some women had studied privately abroad. Obviously, many of the women who composed popular songs had originally aspired to careers in classical music as singers, concert pianists, or composers.

Much can be learned from the lives of these women. It is apparent that despite the brilliant success of a few women, many found the songwriting business difficult and unprofitable. There are many examples here of women who sold their song or their lyrics outright for a few dollars and never received any royalties, which sometimes amounted to a substantial amount of money. Particularly those who were poor and unsophisticated were often denied a fair share of the profit from their songs. Folk songwriter Aunt Molly Jackson apparently never received any money for her songs, even though they were widely recorded and produced revenue for someone. The blues singer-songwriters usually were paid a flat fee and did not receive royalties. It is disturbing to see how hard the lives of many of these women were, and what short life spans many of the blues women had. These hardships are not unrelated to wages, gender, and race.

However, those readers who hope to pursue a songwriting career should not despair. There are also examples here of women who became songwriters against all odds through sheer tenacity. Carrie Jacobs Bond, widowed and with a child to support, wrote, self-published, sang, and promoted her own songs until they sold in the millions. There is also the example of the two kindergarten teachers who wrote a song that still produces a million dollars in royalties each year, "Happy Birthday to You."

A few notes on the structure of the book.

This book was designed to be used not only for locating information about an individual but also for reading more widely about those who wrote in a particular style of music or era. Thus, the songwriters have been grouped by the type of music they wrote, such as country music or blues, or by the period of time in which they wrote, such as early women songwriters. Chapter introductions have been added to provide a brief historical background for each type of music.

The scope of the book has been limited to native-born American women. A name in **bold type** indicates that there is a biographical sketch of that person elsewhere in the book, which can be located by referring to the General Index. Women who worked in more than one field are profiled in the area where they did the majority of their work.

I

POP ROCK

INTRODUCTION

For years Tin Pan Alley was the center of the music-publishing business in New York. It was located on West Twenty-eighth Street between Fifth and Sixth Avenues. There, songwriters worked at pianos in small cubicles, plunking out tunes. The sound of the tinkling pianos gave rise to the street's nickname, Tin Pan Alley. The songs were designed for the white, middle- and upper-class audience, prosperous enough to own a piano and buy sheet music. Music publishers believed that people would buy songs that were entertaining and optimistic, and they encouraged their songwriters to create such songs. Unlike blues, folk, and country songs that liked to dwell on the world's problems, Tin Pan Alley songs were cheerful, romantic, and upbeat. Over the years the songs of Tin Pan Alley became more sophisticated, but they continued to be the same pleasant, noncontroversial songs directed to the same mainstream audience.

In the 1920s and 1930s Tin Pan Alley, Broadway, and Hollywood produced some of the finest in American popular song. It was the era of Irving Berlin, Jerome Kern, George Gershwin, Cole Porter, Richard Rodgers, and Dorothy Fields. Songs were romantic and melodic; the lyrics were clever and witty. These were the songs of the Fred Astaire–Ginger Rogers musicals.

The music industry was greatly aided by the advent of radio in the 1920s. Radio helped to disseminate popular songs, to advertise them, to make them hits, but the networks also restricted songs and promoted conformity.

Songs were carefully selected to avoid offending the listening audience. Profanity and references to drinking or sex, including such words as "necking" and "petting," were prohibited. Songs were also rejected for their political content. NBC's 1939 manual banned songs that had to do with "labor, national and political propaganda." In one year alone NBC banned 200 songs they considered unsuitable.

The restrictions applied by the radio networks had a powerful impact on what songs were produced by the recording industry. In the 1930s NBC and CBS together were so large that they controlled 88 percent of what was broadcast. Because the recording industry profited from having their records broadcast, they were willing to follow the networks' restrictions. Consequently, for the most part, popular songs of this period were clean, pleasant, and noncontroversial.

With the advent of World War II, big band music became popular. On the home front servicemen and women danced to the music of Tommy Dorsey, Harry James, Duke Ellington, Count Basie, and Benny Goodman and listened to the voices of Billie Holiday, Ella Fitzgerald, Peggy Lee, and Jo Stafford.

The event that broke the dominance of Tin Pan Alley music on radio occurred in 1940. That year the radio networks refused to sign the costly new contract with ASCAP—the American Society of Composers, Authors and Publishers—which permitted their stations to broadcast the music of ASCAP members, who were primarily the top songwriters of Tin Pan Alley and Broadway. The networks simply stopped broadcasting ASCAP music. They played old songs in the public domain, like those of Stephen Foster, while they formed their own agency, Broadcast Music Incorporated (BMI), and signed as many new songwriters as they could find, including many black and many country-western songwriters. Then the networks signed with BMI and began broadcasting this music. ASCAP later gave in, but this dispute ended the monopoly of ASCAP and brought a greater diversity to the music broadcast on the radio networks.

Many independent regional stations for years had been broadcasting specialized music, rhythm and blues, or country music over various regions of the country. The Grand Ole Opry in Nashville, Tennessee, for instance, had been broadcasting country music since the 1920s, and other stations like WLAC had broadcast rhythm and blues (R&B) over 21 states from Chicago to Florida. The specialized regional stations and the new BMI sound on the networks advanced the move toward greater diversity in popular music.

In the meantime the music-publishing companies of Tin Pan Alley were being purchased by the motion picture industry and moved to Hollywood. A large part of the recording industry was also located there. As popular music began to fragment into many different styles, the music industry became more decentralized—country music became centered in Nashville, for example, and Motown in Detroit. Philadelphia and Chicago also became important centers.

The most radical change in popular music came in the 1950s with the advent of rock and roll. It came from the influence of black rhythm and blues and white country music. It was the flip side of the witty, clever, romantic music Tin Pan Alley had produced for so many years. It could be characterized by rasping or shouting vocals, suggestive lyrics, and a heavy rhythmic beat for dancing; it was also loud. Not surprisingly, young people loved it and bought the records. Rock and roll radically changed the course of popular music. The record that introduced the new style was "Sh-Boom" by a black R&B group, the Chords. It was soon "covered" by a white group, the Crew Cuts, whose record outsold the original group.

National events influenced the course of popular music in the 1960s, the civil rights movement, and the war in Vietnam. Folk music, which had always been more political, became the accompaniment for civil rights marches and rallies. It was also the music of opposition to the war in Vietnam. With the influence of the civil rights movement, black music changed from rhythm and blues (R&B) to Soul, and Motown blossomed in Detroit. Rock became the new style, a combination of jazz, folk, rhythm and blues, and country. And the Beatles dominated the popular music scene.

Disco music was big in the 1970s, and punk and new wave in the 1980s.

In the decades since rock and roll began, popular music has been directed primarily toward the youth market. Its leading characteristic has been diversity. From heavy metal to reggae, Cajun, hip hop, and new wave, there have been a wide variety of styles. Rock has become the music of the white, affluent, mainstream audience of young people, the children of those who listened to the songs of Tin Pan Alley.

During the rock era it became customary for rock groups to write their own music. As a result, contemporary vocalists are often singer-songwriters, as are many of the women included here.

The earlier generation of women in this chapter wrote in the style of Tin Pan Alley and show tunes. A great many of them began their careers as songwriters in the 1940s during World War II, replacing their male counterparts who had gone to war. The songs they wrote are a reflection of that era. Yet even in some of today's rock music, the influence of Tin Pan Alley can still be heard.

BAEZ, JOAN   *See* Folk.

BAKER, ANITA (1957–   )   "Sweet Love"

Born January 26, 1957, Anita Baker grew up in Detroit's inner city. Because her mother was unable to care for her, she was raised by an aunt and uncle from the time she was two years old.

Even with her considerable talent, becoming a successful popular singer was difficult and often discouraging. She began as the lead singer for a local band, Chapter 8. With them she cut a single. However, the experience was not encouraging. The record company didn't promote the record, and one executive told her that she couldn't sing. Discouraged, Anita Baker took a job as a word processor. Two years later, however, a record producer signed her to an exclusive contract and cut an album, *The Songstress*. The album sold well, but the producer wouldn't pay her her royalties. She finally found a new record company that helped her sue to break the exclusive contract. After that, she was on her way. But these early experiences in the music business caused her to take control of the business side of her work as well as the artistic. She now produces her own albums.

Her first album with Elektra Records, *Rapture* (1986), sold 5 million copies; her second, *Giving You the Best That I've Got*, sold 3 million copies in just two months. For her recordings she has won five Grammys. In 1990 she won a Grammy for Best Rhythm and Blues Female Vocal Performance for "Compositions."

Besides making recordings, Anita Baker has given concerts in the United States and in Europe and has made guest appearances on television. She sang at the inauguration of President George Bush.

Anita Baker has written a number of hits, among them "Giving You the Best That I've Got," written with Skip Scarborough and Randy Holland, and "Sweet Love," written with Louis A. Johnson and Gary Bias. With Michael Powell and Vernon Fails she wrote "Talk to Me," "More Than You Know," and "Fairy Tales." "Perfect Love Affair" was written with Joel Davis. With Gerald Levert and Marc Gordon she wrote "Whatever It Takes," and with James McBride she wrote "Good Enough." Other Anita Baker songs include "Lonely," "You Better Watch Your Step," and "No One to Blame," the latter written with Vernon Fails.

Although Anita Baker is only four foot eleven inches tall, she has a commanding presence. She also has a remarkable three-octave vocal range. She is married and lives in a suburb of Detroit.

SOURCES
Allen, Bonnie. "Hot Voice, Cool Head." *Ms*, June 1989, pp. 42–45.
Who's Who of American Women, 1991.

BELLE, BARBARA (1922–   )   "A Sunday Kind of Love"

A writer, producer, and theatrical agent for many years as well as a songwriter, Barbara Belle was born Barbara Einhorn in Brooklyn, New York, on November 22, 1922. She was educated at New York University and later she worked as a personal manager for such performers as Fran Warren, Louis Prima, Jose Ferrer, Keely Smith, and Morgana King. At one time or another she wrote for television, worked as an executive in a music-publishing company, and was an associate producer for the film *Hey Boy– Hey Girl*. She married Lee Newman in 1951.

Some of the songs Barbara Belle has written include "My Possession," "I Wanna," "You Broke the Only Heart That Ever Loved You," and "William Didn't Tell." Her biggest hit, "A Sunday Kind of Love," was written with Anita Leonard, Stan Rhodes, and Louis Prima.

SOURCES
Dahl, Linda. *Stormy Weather*.
Lynn Farnol Group. *ASCAP Biographical Dictionary*.
Who's Who of American Women, 1989.

BERGMAN, MARILYN   *See* Motion Pictures.

CAREY, MARIAH (1970–   )   "Emotion"

One of the rising stars of today's popular music is singer-songwriter Mariah Carey. She made her debut album in 1990.

Mariah grew up in a household filled with music. Her mother, as a young woman, studied classical music and sang with the New York Opera Company before becoming a vocal teacher. As a youngster, Mariah liked to listen to the recordings of Aretha Franklin and Gladys Knight, which her brother and sister played, and it was this music that influenced her own vocal style. Even in childhood Mariah Carey knew she would become a singer someday.

After graduating from high school in Huntington, Long Island, she moved to Manhattan to pursue a singing career. There she worked as a waitress at night and wrote songs during the day. She sang backup vocals for pop singer Brenda K. Starr. At a party of the record company, Brenda handed Mariah's demo tape to the president of CBS Records. As a result Mariah Carey was signed to a contract.

At the age of 20, she made her debut album, *Mariah Carey* (1990). Columbia records promoted her as their new superstar. The accompanying video had Mariah Carey in a form-fitting black dress singing "Vision of Love." The album subsequently reached number five on the charts. All the songs on the album were co-written by Mariah Carey and Ben Margulies. For "Vision of Love" she won two Grammys for Best Pop Vocal by a Female and for Best New Artist.

In the meantime she was invited to sing "America the Beautiful" at the finals of the National Basketball Association and to be a guest on the "Arsenio Hall Show."

Her album *Emotions* (1991) did well on the charts, appearing in the top ten. Her single of the title song reached three on the R&B chart. Some of the songs from the album she and Ben Margulies co-wrote are "Love Takes Time," "Prisoner," "All in Your Mind," "Vanishing," and, of course, "Emotions."

Mariah Carey seems to be on her way.

SOURCES

Gates, David. "Starting Out at No. 1." *Newsweek,* August 6, 1990, p. 63.
"In Person: Mariah Carey." *Seventeen,* October 1990, p. 64.
"Pop's New Vision," *New York,* May 28, 1990, p. 26.
Tannenbaum, Rob. "Building the Perfect Diva." *Rolling Stone,* August 23, 1990,
        p. 33.

CARLISLE, UNA MAE (1918–1956)   "I See a Million People"

Una Mae Carlisle was born in Xenia, Ohio, on December 16, 1918, and began playing the piano and singing at the age of three.

When she was 14, Fats Waller discovered her and hired her to play with his band. After several years with Waller she decided to work solo playing in clubs in the United States and in Europe. She recorded from 1937 to 1939 in Europe, but the threat of war caused her to return to the United States. In the late 1940s Una Mae Carlisle had her own radio and television series; however, in 1954 ill health forced her to retire.

Una Mae Carlisle wrote approximately 500 songs. Two of them, "Walkin' by the River" and "I See a Million People," the latter with words by Robert Sour, became very popular. Some of her other songs were "Where the River Meets the Sea," "Glory Day," "You're on Your Own," and "Who Kisses Who."

She died in New York on November 7, 1956, at the age of 38.

SOURCES
Chilton, John. *Who's Who of Jazz.*
Dahl, Linda. *Stormy Weather.*
Handy, D. Antoinette. *Black Women in American Bands and Orchestras.*
Shapiro, Nat. *Popular Music.*

CARPENTER, IMOGEN (1919–   )   "If Winter Comes"

Composer Imogen Carpenter was born in Hot Springs, Arkansas, on February 2, 1919. She won a scholarship to the Chicago Musical College, where she studied to be a concert pianist.

For a time she led her own orchestra. Then she became a singer-pianist playing in theaters and night clubs. In 1941 she appeared in the *Ziegfeld Follies* and in *Mexican Hayride.*

As a songwriter she has collaborated with Lenny Adelson and Kim Gannon. Among the songs she composed are "Anytime, Anywhere," "If Winter Comes," "Say So," "Born to Sing the Blues," and "Don't Change Your Mind about Me."

SOURCE
Lynn Farnol Group. *ASCAP Biographical Dictionary.*

CHAPMAN, TRACY (1964–   )   "Fast Car"

The remarkable young singer-songwriter Tracy Chapman was born in Cleveland, Ohio, in 1964. When Tracy Chapman was four, her parents separated. Alone, her mother struggled to support Tracy and her sister. They were often very poor. However, her mother could play the guitar and often sang to her young daughters. When Tracy was in the first grade, she was given a ukelele. By the time she was eight, she was playing the organ and beginning to write songs. In school she took clarinet lessons. Finally, though, she got a guitar. She wrote her first social commentary song, "Cleveland '78," when she was 14.

Tracy Chapman was shy and serious, and she always read a lot. She did well at school and as a result was awarded a scholarship to Wooster, a private prep school in Danbury, Connecticut. At home while she was growing up, she used to listen to gospel music and the Motown sound, but at Wooster she began listening to folk singers like Joni Mitchell, Jackson Browne, and Bob Dylan. Their songs seemed more like the songs she was trying to write. At the same time she began to develop a greater political awareness of issues like nuclear weapons and the draft. A good athlete, she participated on the girls' basketball, softball, and soccer teams. While at Wooster she played her songs at the school's coffee house. The chaplain at the school started a collection and bought her a new Fender guitar to replace her old one.

After prep school Tracy Chapman enrolled at Tufts University in Medford, Massachusetts. At first she planned to become a veterinarian, but she changed her major to cultural anthropology with an emphasis on West Africa and ethnomusicology. She also began to sing in coffee houses and clubs around the Cambridge area. Part of the time she was a street musician, playing on Harvard Square.

A fellow student whose father was in the music business helped her obtain an audition at Elektra Records. Elektra offered her a contract, but she wanted to complete her studies first. At the age of twenty-four she recorded her first album, *Tracy Chapman* (1988), singing a collection of her own songs. Among them was "Fast Car," which became an enormous hit that sold an estimated 10 million copies around the globe.

In 1989 Tracy Chapman was awarded three Grammys, one as the Best New Artist of the year.

Invited to England for a celebration of Nelson Mandela's birthday, Tracy sang to a huge audience in a sports stadium. The event was televised to many countries around the world. After that she toured with Bruce Springsteen, Sting, and Peter Gabriel on the Amnesty International *Human Rights Now!* tour. They played in 15 nations on five continents.

Crossroads, her second album, came out in 1989. It included such songs as "Subcity," "Material World," and "All That You Have Is Your Soul." After the record came out, she toured the United States and also made a guest appearance on Arsenio Hall's television show.

Among the songs she has written are "Mountains o' Things," "She's Got Her Ticket," "Why?" "For My Lover," "If Not Now," "For You," "Talkin' 'bout a Revolution," "Fast Car," "Across the Lines," "Subcity," "Behind the Wall," "This Time," "Born to Fight," "Material World," "Freedom Now," "Bridges," "All That You Have Is Your Soul," "Crossroads," and "Baby Can I Hold You."

Her 1992 album was *Matters of the Heart.*

Tracy Chapman is a shy, modest person who seems reluctant to be in the spotlight. She plays an acoustic guitar and in a haunting voice sings poignant and moving songs, many of which are about people who live in America's underclass.

Tracy Chapman talked about her work in an interview with Robert Hilburn in the *San Francisco Chronicle* (Datebook, July 1, 1990, p. 39): "I just write about what I see going on . . . about what life is right now. . . . The conditions around us speak for themselves."

Tracy Chapman lives in San Francisco.

SOURCES
Gareffa, Peter. *Newsmakers,* 1989.
Givens, Ron. "The Pick of the Crop." *Newsweek,* October 16, 1989, pp. 65–66.
Hilburn, Robert. "Tracy Chapman's Next 'Crossroads,' " *San Francisco Examiner-Chronicle,* Datebook, July 1, 1990, p. 39.
Moritz, Charles. *Current Biography,* 1989.

COLLINS, JUDY   *See* Folk.

DANZIG, EVELYN (1902–   )   "Scarlet Ribbons"

Composer Evelyn Danzig was born on January 16, 1902, in Waco, Texas, but she grew up in Albany, New York, and was educated there.

She began her musical career as a pianist performing on the radio; later she turned to composing music.

Over the years she has written many songs, collaborating with Gordon Jenkins, Jack Segal, Sylvia Dee, and Sammy Gallop. Among her songs are "Warm Hearted Woman," "Teddy Bear," "Simple, Simple, Simple," "I Miss the Boy," "Where I May Live with My Love," "Half a Heart," "Midnight in Manhattan," "A Face in the Crowd," "We're All Kids at Christmas," and "Rippling Stream."

Her most famous song was "Scarlet Ribbons," with the lyrics of Jack Segal. It was made famous by singer Harry Belafonte.

SOURCES
Dahl, Linda. *Stormy Weather.*
Shapiro, Nat. *Popular Music.*
Wilder, Alex. *American Popular Song.*

DE SHANNON, JACKIE (1944–   )   "Bette Davis Eyes"

Actress, singer, and songwriter Jackie De Shannon was born Sharon Myers
in Hazel, Kentucky, on August 21, 1944. She grew up in Chicago and
made her singing debut at the age of six. By the time she was 12, she was
singing on her own radio show on a station in southern Illinois.

After being offered a contract in Los Angeles, she moved there. She sang
on the televisions shows of Ed Sullivan, Andy Williams, and Johnny Cash.
She also had straight dramatic acting roles on television. In addition to
singing and acting, she continued to write songs as she had since she was
a youngster.

When her acting-singing career declined, she gave up performing to concentrate on songwriting. She has written more than 500 songs in the pop
and folk vein, among them "Don't Doubt Yourself Babe," "Dum Dum,"
"When You Walk in the Room," and "Come Stay with Me." Her song "Put
a Little Love in Your Heart" was a hit in 1969 and became a gold record.
She has collaborated on songs with Randy Newman, Sharon Sheeley, and
Jimmy Page. Her song "When You Walk in the Room" was on the top 30
chart in 1981. In that year, her song "Bette Davis Eyes," co-written with
Donna Weiss, became a smash hit and won a Grammy.

SOURCES
Clarke, Donald. *Penguin Encyclopedia of Popular Music.*
Mattfeld, Julius. *Variety Music Cavalcade.*
Stambler, Irwin. *Encyclopedia of Pop, Rock and Soul.*

DEE, SYLVIA (1914–1967)   "Too Young"

Born Josephine Moore Proffitt on October 22, 1914, in Little Rock, Arkansas, Sylvia Dee became a short story writer, a novelist, and a lyricist.
She grew up in a family of musicians and songwriters. Her mother was the
songwriter Evelyn Moore, who had published 400 songs, and her grandmother had written a hit song in the 1890s. Sylvia's stepfather was a concert violinist. Although she grew up in a musical environment, Sylvia Dee
was primarily interested in writing. After attending the University of Michigan, she worked as a newspaper copywriter.

In 1945 a song Sylvia Dee had written with Sidney Lippman when she
was 18 became a huge hit and sold a million records. It was the novelty
song "Chickery Chick." The song remained on the "Hit Parade" for 14
weeks.

Giving the musical theater a try, she and Sidney Lippman wrote the stage score for the musical *Barefoot Boy with Cheek* (1947). Although the show had a short run, one of their songs, "After Graduation Day," became a hit.

Sylvia Dee wrote many short stories, which were published in magazines, and several novels. Her books include *And Never Been Kissed* (1949), *Dear Guest and Ghost* (1950), and *There Was a Little Girl* (1951).

In 1951 she and Sidney Lippman had another huge hit with their song "Too Young." It became the only song in the 23-year history of the "Hit Parade" to remain number one for 12 weeks.

Some of Sylvia Dee's other songs include "My Sugar Is So Refined," "Laroo Laroo Lili Balero," "A House with Love in It," and "It Couldn't Be True."

She was married to Jere B. Falson and had a son.

SOURCES

Burke, W. J. *American Authors and Books.*
Davis, Sheila. *Craft of Lyric Writing.*
Ewen, David. *Panorama of American Popular Music.*
Lynn Farnol Group. *ASCAP Biographical Dictionary.*
Spaeth, Sigmund. *History of Popular Music in America.*
Warfel, Harry R. *American Novelists of Today.*

DUNHAM, KATHERINE (1910–   )   "New Love, New Wine"

Katherine Dunham is primarily associated with the field of dance. She is an authority on Afro-American dance and has had considerable influence on the development of modern dance. For many years she was a dancer, a choreographer, and the director of her own dance company. In addition to her work in dance, she was a collector of folk songs and a songwriter.

She was born on June 22, 1910 in Joliet, Illinois. At the University of Chicago she earned a degree in social anthropology. Beginning her career as a dancer, she toured the world in a dance company. In 1931, she formed her own dance company, Ballet Negre. When this group disbanded, she founded the Negro Dance Group.

Interested in the origins of black popular dances, she received a fellowship in 1935 to study these dances in the West Indies. With her dance troupes she toured throughout the world, and at different times lived in Europe, Haiti, Japan, and West Africa. She has been artist-in-residence at various universities in the United States.

She performed in many Broadway musicals, among them *Cabin in the Sky* (1940) and *Carib Song* (1945). In films she worked as a choreographer and dancer in movies such as *Star Spangled Rhythm* (1942), *Stormy Weather* (1943), *Casbah* (1948), and *Mambo* (1954). Some of the songs she has written are "New Love, New Wine" and "Coco da Mata."

In the late 1960s she settled in East St. Louis, Illinois, where she supervised the Katherine Dunham Center for the Performing Arts at Southern Illinois University. For her contributions to the field of dance she has received many awards and honorary doctorates.

She was married to John Pratt.

Public television did a documentary about her life and work in 1980.

SOURCES
Lanker, Brian. *I Dream a World.*
Lynn Farnol Group. *ASCAP Biographical Dictionary.*
New York Times Film Reviews.
Southern, Eileen. *Biographical Dictionary of Afro-Americans and African Musicians.*

EDWARDS, CLARA (1887–1974)
"With the Wind and the Rain in Your Hair"

Singer, pianist, and songwriter, Clara Edwards was born Clara Gerlich on March 18, 1887, in Mankato, Minnesota. She attended the Mankato State Normal School and the Cosmopolitan School of Music. She also studied in Europe, preparing for a career as singer. She began her career by giving concerts in both the United States and Europe.

Clara Edwards later turned her efforts to composing songs. Her most successful song was "With the Wind and the Rain in Your Hair," which had lyrics by Jack Lawrence. Although it was first published in 1930, ten years passed before it became a hit.

Clara Edwards composed more than 50 songs, including "Into the Night," "Sing Softly," "The Fisher's Widow," "Stars of the Night," and "By the Bend of the River." The latter was composed as a setting for a Bernhard Haig poem. She also wrote sacred songs, among them "When Jesus Walked on Galilee," "27th Psalm," and "Dedication."

In addition to writing songs, Clara Edwards composed music for animated films and for children's plays like *Alice in Wonderland.*

She died in New York on January 17, 1974.

SOURCES
Anderson, E. Ruth. *Contemporary American Composers.*
Hitchcock, H. Wiley. *New Grove Dictionary of American Music.*
Lynn Farnol Group. *ASCAP Biographical Dictionary.*
Spaeth, Sigmund. *History of Popular Music in America.*

EDWARDS, JOAN (1919–1981)   "Anytime"

Joan Edwards, born on February 13, 1919, in New York City, grew up in a family of songwriters. Her uncles Gus and Leo and her brother, Jack, were songwriters, and her father was a music publisher. She became an accomplished pianist, arranger, singer, and songwriter.

Joan Edwards studied music at Hunter College, after which she was a pianist and vocalist with the orchestras of Paul Whiteman and Rudy Vallee in the late 1930s and 1940s. For a time she sang in hotels and clubs, and then from 1941 to 1946 was featured with Frank Sinatra on "Your Hit Parade," singing the week's top tunes on the radio. She also appeared in the movie *Hit Parade of 1947*.

In 1950 she and Lyn Duddy tried their hand at writing a Broadway revue, *Tickets Please* (1950). It was a success, running 245 performances. Two years later she did the music and lyrics for *Godfrey's Calendar Show*. That year she had her own radio show, "At Home with Joan."

Joan Edwards also worked as a pianist, arranger, and composer for television shows, as well as a writer of television advertising jingles.

Some of the songs Joan Edwards wrote include "Darn It Baby," "That's Love," "Anytime," "You Can't Take It with You When You Go," "And So It Ended," and "Do You Still Feel the Same?"

She was married to Jules Schachter, a violinist in Paul Whiteman's Orchestra, and they had three children. She died in New York City on August 27, 1981, at the age of 62.

SOURCES

Lewine, Richard. *Songs of the American Theater.*
Lynn Farnol Group. *ASCAP Biographical Dictionary.*
Moritz, Charles. *Current Biography*, 1953.
New York Times Film Reviews.
New York Times, Obituaries, August 29, 1981, p. 11.

FITZGERALD, ELLA (1918–   )   "A-Tisket, A-Tasket"

Ella Fitzgerald has been one of the great vocalists of jazz and popular song for more than 50 years.

She was born in Newport News, Virginia on April 25, 1918, and raised by an aunt in New York after her mother died.

Ella Fitzgerald got her start at the age of 16 by winning an amateur contest at the Apollo Theater in Harlem. Her prize was a short engagement with the Chick Webb Band, but the engagement was extended for more than five years. Unfortunately, Chick Webb died in 1939, and the band stayed together only another year. When the band broke up, Ella continued to perform solo in clubs, theaters, and concert halls in the United States and abroad.

Her first hit record came in 1938, when she was 20; it was a recording of her own song "A-Tisket, A-Tasket," written with Van Alexander. She went on to record more than 250 albums and sell over 50 million records. She won 11 Grammy Awards and for 18 consecutive years was named Best Female Singer by *Down Beat* magazine.

The films in which Ella Fitzgerald has appeared include *Pete Kelly's Blues* (1955), in which she sang "Hard-Hearted Hannah," and *St. Louis Blues* (1958) with Nat "King" Cole, Pearl Bailey, Cab Calloway, and Mahalia Jackson. She also appeared in *Let No Man Write My Epitaph* (1960).

Among the songs she has written are "You Showed Me the Way," "Spinnin' the Web," "Chew, Chew, Chew," "Please Tell the Truth," "I Fell in Love with a Dream," and "Just One of Those Nights." She has worked with many collaborators, including Chick Webb, Josef Myrow, and Lupin Fien.

Ella Fitzgerald has received numerous awards, among them the Kennedy Center Honors from the White House for a lifetime of achievement in the performing arts.

She was married first to Benny Kornegay and later to Ray Brown, a bass player, with whom she had a son, Ray, Jr., who became a drummer.

In the 1970s she sang with various symphony orchestras in the United States. She continues to perform to this day.

SOURCES
Berendt, Joachim. *Jazz Book.*
Gourse, Leslie. *Louis' Children.*
Kinkle, Roger. *Complete Encyclopedia of Popular Music and Jazz.*
Lynn Farnol Group. *ASCAP Biographical Dictionary.*

FRANKLIN, ARETHA (1942–   )   "Think"

Known as the Queen of Soul, Aretha Franklin was born in Memphis, Tennessee on March 25, 1942. When Aretha was six, her mother left the family; she died four years later. Aretha Franklin's father, C. L. Franklin, moved the family to Detroit, where he became the pastor of the New Bethel Baptist Church. As a child Aretha Franklin learned to play the piano, and by the age of 14 she had joined her father on the gospel circuit.

Although she had been singing mostly gospel music, she had always enjoyed listening to rhythm and blues, and she decided to try for a career in popular music. In the early 1960s she was offered a record contract. She made several recordings but was not happy with the way the record company wanted to change her style. In 1966 she joined Atlantic Records, where she had more success. The title song from her album *I Ain't Never Loved a Man (the Way I Love You)* hit the top of the charts. *Billboard* chose her the top vocalist of 1967. From then on she had a string of hits.

In 1968 Aretha toured the United States and Europe and performed on television. But it was all too much. For the next two years she took time out to recover her strength.

Then in 1970 she began recording again. Her rendition of "Bridge over Troubled Waters" made the top 40 charts. The following year she had a gold record and a Grammy for her album *Aretha Live at Fillmore West* (1971). In 1972 she won two Grammys, one for rhythm and blues, the other for soul-gospel for her recording of the hymn "Amazing Grace." It was recorded at the Reverend James Cleveland's church in Los Angeles.

Throughout the 1970s Aretha continued to record approximately one album a year, for which she invariably won a Grammy. After the 1970s, however, her soul records didn't sell. Her record company believed a change of image was needed. So she changed her hair color to blond and selected songs more in the pop vein. All this was done in an attempt to capture the market again.

In 1980 she sang in the motion picture comedy *The Blues Brothers*, with Dan Aykroyd and John Belushi.

Dissatisfied with her record company, in 1980 she moved to a new label, Arista, which brought her success again. She won a Grammy in 1981 and had gold record albums (500,000-copy sellers) in 1982 and 1985.

By 1986 she had accumulated 24 gold records and 14 Grammy awards. Her album *Who's Zoomin' Who?* also sold a million copies. That year she did a television special "Aretha!" and her album *Aretha* succeeded on both pop and R&B charts. The album also won a Grammy.

In 1987 Aretha Franklin returned to her roots and recorded her first gospel collection in 15 years.

Aretha Franklin's personal life has been filled with difficulties. She has been married three times and has four children. Her father, who was a friend of Martin Luther King's and had been active in the civil rights movement, was shot and lay in a coma for five years. Aretha took care of him until he passed away in 1984.

In 1989 Public Television broadcast a documentary of Aretha Franklin's life and music on "American Masters."

Among the songs she has written are "He'll Come Along," "He's the Boy," and "Think," the latter written with Ted White.

SOURCES
Berendt, Joachim. *Jazz Book.*
Jones, Hettie. *Big Star Fallin' Mama.*
Stambler, Irwin. *Encyclopedia of Pop, Rock and Soul.*

GENTRY, BOBBIE   *See* Country.

GOETSCHIUS, MARJORIE (1915–   )   "I Dream of You"

Composer-lyricist Marjorie Laura Goetschius was born on September 23, 1915, in Raymond, New Hampshire. She was the daughter of Percy Goetschius, who taught at the Juilliard School of Music.

Marjorie Goetschius attended Georgian Court College, Tufts University, and the Juilliard School of Music, where she studied composition. She began her career by playing the piano and singing on the radio. For a time she wrote background music and scripts for network programs.

Marjorie Goetschius has written a number of popular songs, often collaborating with Edna Osser. In 1944 they wrote the hit song "I Dream of You (More Than You Dream I Do)." They also wrote "The Last Time I Saw You," "I'll Always Be with You," "You're Different," and "Can I Canoe You up the River?" Other songs by Marjorie Goetschius include "Green Grass and Peaceful Pastures," "So Much in Love," "This Is My Confession," and "When You Make Love to Me."

Besides writing popular songs, Marjorie Goetschius also composed classical music for piano, voice, violin, and small orchestra.

She married Emery Deutsch in 1940 and has two children.

SOURCES
Anderson, E. Ruth. *Contemporary American Composers.*
Lynn Farnol Group. *ASCAP Biographical Dictionary.*
Mattfeld, Julius. *Variety Music Cavalcade.*

HOLIDAY, BILLIE   *See* Jazz.

IAN, JANIS (1951–   )   "At Seventeen"

Janis Ian was born Janis Eddy Fink on April 7, 1951, in New York City. Musical from an early age, she played the piano when she was only three. She also learned to play the guitar as a child. In her teens when she was offered a recording contract, Janis Ian dropped out of high school to become a singer and songwriter.

It was a song that she recorded in her 1967 album, *Janis Ian,* that made her famous. The song, "Society's Child," which she had written when she was 13, became a million seller. After this Janis Ian did several concert tours, but her career seemed to falter, so she retired at the age of twenty.

Three years later she was back with a new album, *Stars* (1974). Her song "Jesse" from this album became a hit for Roberta Flack. Janis Ian followed this success with another album, *Between the Lines,* which contained the hit song "At Seventeen," another song she had written while still in her teens. Tremendously successful, the song won her a Grammy.

She has been recording since the age of 16 and has cut a dozen albums. From those, she has seven gold records and one platinum. Her album *Night Rains* (1979) included her hit song "Fly Too High," which she wrote with Giorgio Moroder.

Some of the other songs Janis Ian has written are "In the Winter," "Stars," "Hello Jerry," "Love Is Blind," "Watercolors," "Present Company," and "The Other Side of the Sun." With Michelle Wright she wrote "As Far as Love Goes," and with Kye Fleming, "What about the Love." She has also collaborated with Albert Hammond.

In addition to songwriting, Janis Ian writes poetry. In 1969 she published a collection of her poems, *Who Really Cares.*

SOURCES

Davis, Sheila. *Craft of Lyric Writing.*
Hitchcock, H. Wiley. *New Grove Dictionary of American Music.*
Jacques Cattel Press. *ASCAP Biographical Dictionary,* 4th ed.
Locher, Frances. *Contemporary Authors,* vol. 105.
Stambler, Irwin. *Encyclopedia of Pop, Rock and Soul.*

JACKSON, JANET (1966–   )   "Control"

Sister of superstar Michael Jackson and the youngest of the nine children of Joe and Katherine Jackson, Janet Jackson was born on August 16, 1966, in Gary, Indiana. Her father worked as a crane operator for a steel company. Both parents encouraged their children to be musical, and by the time Janet was three years old her older brothers had already become famous as the Jackson Five. After her brothers signed a contract with Motown Records, the family moved to Los Angeles.

Janet Jackson made her debut in 1974, at the age of eight, appearing with her other brothers and sisters in a Jackson family show in Las Vegas. She did an impression of Mae West.

The following year Janet Jackson began working as an actress on television. She was hired to play Penny on producer Norman Lear's television show "Good Times." After three years with the show, she moved to the role of Charlene on "Diff'rent Strokes," in 1980. Later she appeared on television's "Fame."

Her recording debut occurred in 1983 with the album *Janet Jackson*, which had moderate success. It was followed the next year by *Dream Street*, which did not do as well as the first album. Both were aimed at the teeny-bopper audience.

In 1984, when she was 18, Janet Jackson eloped with James DeBarge, whom she had known since childhood. He was a singer with another group, and the demands of their separate careers put a strain on their relationship. So in 1985 the marriage was annulled, and Janet Jackson moved back to the family home.

It was her third album, *Control* (1986), that established Janet Jackson as a performer in her own right. Besides singing and playing the keyboards, she co-wrote and co-produced the album. Several songs from the album hit the top ten charts: "What Have You Done for Me Lately," "Nasty," "Control," and "When I Think of You." The album went to number one on the charts and sold 7 million copies.

Rhythm Nation 1814, which she recorded in 1989, included songs dealing with social issues such as homelessness, illiteracy, and prejudice. It not only sold well but also received critical approval. A hit single from the album was "Miss You Much."

To promote the record Janet Jackson did a national tour. Her mother accompanied her. After each performance mother and daughter would board the bus. Janet Jackson would have a massage, then eat. In the early hours of the morning the touring company would reach the hotel, where she would sleep until the next afternoon. She would then have lunch and take the bus to the arena by 4 P.M. There she would do her makeup, dress, greet people backstage, and perform her show. After that she would board the bus to continue the long, hard grind of being on the road.

Janet Jackson's first hit, "Young Love," came in 1982. Other hits, including "What Have You Done for Me Lately," "Nasty," "When I Think of You," "Control," "Let's Wait Awhile," and "The Pleasure Principle," followed.

A number of Janet Jackson's songs were written with James Harris III, and with Terry Lewis, who produced her albums. Together they collaborated on "What Have You Done for Me Lately," "Control," "Someday Is Tonight," "You Can Be Mine," "When I Think of You," "Funny How Time Flies," and "Nasty." Janet wrote "Let's Wait Awhile" with Harris, Lewis, and Reginald Andrews. "Black Cat" was written entirely by Janet Jackson, both the words and the music. For her work she has won a Grammy and two American Music awards.

Janet Jackson lives in Los Angeles.

SOURCES
Jackson, Katherine. *My Family the Jacksons.*
Mooney, Louise, ed. *Contemporary Newsmakers.*

JOPLIN, JANIS (1943–1970)   "Move Over"

Janis Joplin was one of the great personalities of the rock era. She was a stunning blues and rock singer whose career developed amidst the Haight-Ashbury hippie scene. In a few brief years she achieved rock music superstardom, before a drug overdose ended it all.

She was born Janis Lyn Joplin on January 19, 1943, in Port Arthur, Texas, which is in the eastern corner of Texas bordering Louisiana. She grew up loving Bessie Smith, Odetta, and all the great blues singers. Alienated from the standards of her family and the community, she carried the pain and resentment of their disapproval all of her life.

In the early 1960s the West Coast rock music scene was beginning. Shortly after high school and a brief try at college at the University of Texas (where she was nominated the ugliest man on campus), Janis Joplin moved to San Francisco to become a singer. Her career took off when she joined Big Brother and the Holding Company, a group she sang with from 1966 until 1969. Her performance at the first Monterey International Pop Festival in 1967 astounded the music scene. (A documentary film of this festival shows Cass Elliot of the Mamas and Papas watching Janis Joplin sing, and Mama

Cass's mouth falls open in amazement.) Appearances on television followed. Then another triumph in New York City and one at the Newport Folk Festival in 1968 established her as a force to be reckoned with. In 1968 she recorded the album *Cheap Thrills*. After this she made her debut in London, toured the United States, and finished off 1969 with a concert in Madison Square Garden.

For two years Janis Joplin performed with Big Brother at Fillmore West in San Francisco at the height of the Haight-Ashbury flower-children, drug-scene, hippie era. Wearing her outrageous feathers and driving a psyche-delic-colored Porsche, she blended into the scene. Her singing was described in *Cashbox* magazine as "a mixture of Leadbelly, a steam engine, Calamity Jane, Bessie Smith, an oil derrick, and rot-gut bourbon funnelled into the 20th century somewhere between El Paso and San Francisco" (*Cashbox*, 1966, as quoted in Harris, *Blues*, 1979, p. 296). Columbia recorded her, and television beamed her frenetic blues-rock to millions through appearances on the "Ed Sullivan Show," the "Tom Jones Show," and "60 Minutes." Still looking for the right backup sound, she formed a new band, the Full Tilt Boogie Band, which debuted with her in Louisville in 1970.

On stage she maintained the appearance of a hard-living, hard-drinking, hard-loving woman; indeed she was all that, drinking too much, sleeping with a lot of people, both men and women, and shooting up on drugs. But an interview with Dick Cavett on television revealed another side of her personality—a wit as quick as Cavett's, and a charm and vulnerability hidden during her raucous performances. She told Cavett of her intention to go back to her high school reunion in Texas to make a triumphant return to the town that had rejected her. Some weeks later she did just that.

Her career, however, did not have a long run. Just three years after her triumph at the Monterey Pop Festival, she had gone to her room after a long day at the recording studio. There she injected an unintentional overdose of heroin and died. It was all over for Janis Joplin at the age of 27.

When Janis Joplin had begun to make a name for herself as a singer, she learned that the grave of her idol, Bessie Smith, had been left unmarked. Together with other admirers of Bessie, Janis helped arrange for a headstone that was placed on Bessie Smith's grave in 1970. October 4 of the same year, Janis Joplin died and her ashes were scattered over the Pacific Ocean.

The songs Janis Joplin wrote were mostly blues, among them "Comin' Home," "Down on Me," "Mary Jane," "Kozmic Blues," "No Reason for Livin'," "One Good Man," "What Good Can Drinkin' Do," "Turtle Blues," and "Move Over." She co-authored "I Need a Man to Love," "Oh, Sweet Mary," and "Mercedes Benz."

A 1975 film documentary, *Janis,* captures the magnetism of Janis Joplin in performance.

SOURCES

Friedman, Myra. *Buried Alive.*
Harris, Sheldon. *Blues Who's Who,* 1989.
Sicherman, Barbara. *Notable American Women, The Modern Period.*
Stambler, Irwin. *Encyclopedia of Pop, Rock and Soul.*

KING, CAROLE (1942–   )   "You've Got a Friend"

She was born Carol Klein on February 9, 1942, in Brooklyn, New York. By the age of 16 she was writing songs. At Queens College she met chemistry major Gerry Goffin, who was a promising lyricist. They got married, dropped out of college, and went to work writing songs for a music publisher. In a tiny room in the Brill Building on Broadway, they pounded out their tunes on a piano, while in adjoining rooms Neil Sedaka, Barry Mann, **Cynthia Weil,** Howard Greenfield, and others did the same. This continuous effort produced a number of hits.

The first hit for Goffin and King came in 1960 with "Will You Love Me Tomorrow?" By 1963 more than 200 of Carole King's songs had been recorded by other artists; this success made her more inclined to begin performing her own songs. In 1967 Gerry Goffin, Carole King, and Jerry Wexler had another hit in "(You Make Me Feel like) a Natural Woman."

Carole's marriage, however, broke up in 1965, and she moved to Los Angeles with her daughter; she nonetheless continued to collaborate on songs with Gerry Goffin. She performed with James Taylor in concert and worked with an LA group, The City, where she met her second husband, Charles Larkey, a bass player. But Carole King's personal life has had a lot of difficulties. The marriage to Larkey did not last, and she subsequently married Rick Evers. Unfortunately, Evers died. Later she married Rick Sorensen.

Finally Carole went solo and began performing in public. She sang at Carnegie Hall and did a free Central Park concert for 70,000 people.

She found a new lyricist, Toni Stern, and began to have tremendous success with her albums. Her second album, *Tapestry* (1973), sold 14 million copies. She received a Grammy in 1971 for Best Song. In 1972 she received four Grammys for Best Album, Best Song, Best Record, and Best Female Pop Vocalist.

Some of her songs include "Chains," "Take Good Care of My Baby," "Will You Love Me Tomorrow?," "Up on the Roof," "Child of Mine," "I

Can't Stay Mad at You," "One Fine Day," "Hey Girl," "I Feel the Earth Move," "So Far Away," "It's Too Late," "Go Away Little Girl," "City Streets," and "You Light Up My Life." She has collaborated on songs not only with Gerry Goffin but also with Howard Greenfield, Toni Stern, and Phil Spector.

She lives with her husband and four children in Southern California.

SOURCES
Davis, Sheila. *Craft of Lyric Writing.*
Hamm, Charles. *Yesterdays.*
Mattfeld, Julius. *Variety Music Cavalcade.*
Moritz, Charles. *Current Biography,* 1974.
Stambler, Irwin. *Encyclopedia of Pop, Rock and Soul.*
Steward, Sue. *Signed, Sealed, and Delivered.*
Taylor, Paul. *Popular Music since 1955.*
Who's Who of American Women, 1986.

LEE, PEGGY (1920–   )   "I Don't Wanna Leave You Now"

Peggy Lee is an elegant, sultry vocalist, an actress, an author, and a songwriter. She has been one of the top song stylists for more than 50 years.

She was born Norma Deloris Egstrom on May 27, 1920, in Jamestown, North Dakota, one of seven children. Her mother died when she was still a child, and after her father remarried, her stepmother beat her continually. Consequently, as soon as she was old enough, she left home. She sold her high school graduation watch, bought a bus ticket, and set off to become a singer. By the age of 16 she had a job singing and touring with a local band. Her salary of $15 a week also helped support her brother and sisters.

For a time she sang in Los Angeles and then in Chicago, using her new name Peggy Lee. In 1941 Benny Goodman hired her as a vocalist with his band. With them she recorded **Lil Green**'s song, "Why Don't You Do Right?" which became her first hit. For this she was paid a flat fee of $10 and no royalties. Backed by Benny Goodman's orchestra, she sang in two films, *The Powers' Girl* and *Stage Door Canteen,* both in 1942.

The following year she left the band to marry guitarist Dave Barbour. They settled in Hollywood and had a daughter. Peggy Lee had expected to retire from the music world, but she and her husband began writing songs together, and their songs turned into hits: "It's a Good Day," "I

Don't Know Enough about You," and "Mañana." Peggy was brought in to record the songs, and her vocal career took off again.

Offers for movies came in. She appeared in *Mister Music* (1950), *The Jazz Singer* (1953), and *Pete Kelly's Blues* (1955). Usually she sang, but in *Pete Kelly's Blues* she had an acting role that brought her a nomination for an Academy Award.

In 1955 Walt Disney hired her for the cartoon film *Lady and the Tramp*. She wrote the lyrics, performed the songs, and did four of the voices. For her work on this film she was paid a flat fee of $3,500. Years later with the advent of VCRs, the Disney studios released the film on video and made $72 million in profit. Peggy Lee sued for compensation, as other performers had, and won more than $3 million.

Some of the songs Peggy Lee has written were commissioned for motion pictures. She wrote the lyrics of the title song for *Johnny Guitar* (1954) and *Anatomy of a Murder* (1959), the theme song for *About Mrs. Leslie* (1954), and with Sonny Burke all the songs for *Tom Thumb* (1958). She also sang the title song "Johnny Guitar" in the film. She wrote the lyrics to the song "The Shining Sea" for the film *The Russians Are Coming, the Russians Are Coming!*

Although her professional life has been very successful, Peggy Lee has had many difficulties in her personal life. Her marriage to Dave Barbour ended in 1952. She married again three more times, but all her marriages ended in divorce. In addition she has had severe health problems since 1978. Her ailments have caused her to perform from a wheelchair at recent engagements.

Peggy Lee also wrote and performed in a Broadway show, the 1983 autobiographical one-woman show *Peg*. She wrote the lyrics; and Paul Horner wrote the music. Among the songs were "Daddy Was a Railroad Man," "One Beating a Day," "That's How I Learned to Sing the Blues," and "Sometimes You're Up." The show, however, ran only a few performances.

Over the years Peggy Lee has written more than 200 popular songs, including "I Don't Wanna Leave You Now," "Where Can I Go without You," "He's a Tramp," "How Strange," "I Love Being Here with You," "In Love Again," "What More Can a Woman Do?," "Bella Notte," "So What's New?" and "You Was Right Baby."

Besides songwriting and performing in motion pictures and supper clubs and on radio and television, Peggy Lee has recorded more than 700 songs. In her album *The Peggy Lee Songbook* (1990) she sang many of the songs she has written. For her work she has been given many awards, numerous Grammys, and an honorary doctorate from the University of North Dakota.

She lives in Bel Air, California, and paints for a hobby.

SOURCES
Clarke, Donald. *Penguin Encyclopedia of Popular Music.*
Kinkle, Roger. *Complete Encyclopedia of Popular Music and Jazz.*
Lee, Peggy. *Miss Peggy Lee.*
Lewine, Richard. *Songs of Theater.*
Lynn Farnol Group. *ASCAP Biographical Dictionary.*
Simon, George. *Best of Music Makers.*
Spaeth, Sigmund. *History of Popular Music in America.*

MADONNA (1958–   )   "Like a Virgin"

Madonna Louise Veronica Ciccone was born in Bay City, Michigan, on
August 16, 1958, into a large family of eight children. She was given the
same name as her mother, who died when Madonna was just five. Three
years later her father, a design engineer for Chrysler, married a woman
who had been the family housekeeper.

Madonna attended a Catholic school, where she was a superior student.
Interested in acting and dancing, she appeared in school plays and after
school took piano and ballet lessons. She won a dance scholarship to the
University of Michigan. However, after two years she left college to go to
New York, arriving there with only $35. To support herself she did figure
modeling for artists, appeared in an underground film, and finally was accepted into the third company of the Alvin Ailey dance company.

Through her boyfriend, who was a rock musician, she became interested
in rock music. He taught her to play drums, and she subsequently became
a drummer and vocalist for a rock group called the Breakfast Club. It was
at this time that she began to write songs. However, when she wasn't advanced to lead singer, she left the group and with a former boyfriend formed
her own band, Madonna. Together they also wrote songs. She persuaded
a disc jockey (DJ) at a disco to play her demo tape, and the crowd liked it.
The DJ then helped her get a contract with Sire Records.

Her debut album, *Madonna* (1983), consisted of disco and pop tunes. It
was not an instant success, but in time three songs from the album became
hits: "Holiday," "Lucky Star," and "Borderline." The latter reached number one on the charts in 1984. By 1985 the album had sold 3 million copies.
The accompanying video helped the sales.

The same year, Madonna had a brief role in the film *Vision Quest*, singing "Crazy for You."

It was her second album, *Like a Virgin* (1984), and the accompanying
video, that made her a pop idol. For the next year she dominated the
record charts with songs from the album such as "Like a Virgin," "Touched,"

and "Material Girl." The title song was a number one single, and the album sold over 6 million copies. The *Material Girl* video was Madonna's version of Marilyn Monroe singing "Diamonds Are a Girl's Best Friend." It was mainstream rock with a Marilyn Monroe image. The song "Material Girl," about being proud of materialistic values, reached a sympathetic audience in the materialistic 1980s and went to number two on the charts.

Although she had achieved great success with her videos and her recordings, Madonna still wanted to have a film career. In 1985 she had an opportunity to co-star in the punk detective comedy *Desperately Seeking Susan.* The film was moderately successful, and she received praise for her acting ability. The video in which she sang "In the Groove" helped popularize that song from the movie.

In 1985 Madonna ranked number one as Billboard's Top Pop Female Artist, and she was nominated for a Grammy.

That year, she and motion picture star Sean Penn decided to marry. In August, several weeks before the wedding, *Penthouse* magazine ran nude photos of Madonna that had been taken years before when she was trying to get into show business. The magazine saw an opportunity to cash in on Madonna's popularity. Since she had built so much of her fame on her erotic dancing and suggestive songs, she seemed to be fair game for the more sensational press. But the photo incident got lost in all the publicity about the wedding, which went on without further complications.

After her marriage Madonna took on a new persona. She had already gone through her punk and her Marilyn Monroe phases; now she cut her hair short and developed an innocent, feminine image.

Her third album, *True Blue,* came out in 1986 and sold more than two and a half million copies. The album had nine songs co-written by Madonna. Two hit songs were "Papa Don't Preach" and "Live to Tell," which came from Sean Penn's film *At Close Range.*

However, Madonna's movie career was not doing well. She co-starred with Penn in *Shanghai Surprise* (1986), which turned out to be a flop. The following year she starred in a screwball comedy, *Who's That Girl?* (1987), with Griffin Dunne, but the critics thought the film had neither charm nor humor. After the film, she did a *Who's That Girl* concert tour. Her marriage to Sean Penn fell apart, and they divorced in 1989.

Then Warren Beatty offered her a role co-starring in his film *Dick Tracy* (1990). Madonna played Breathless Mahoney to Beatty's Dick Tracy. They also had an off-camera romance.

With the completion of the movie Madonna went on her third world tour, her Blond Ambition tour. It was filmed, on stage and off, and released as the documentary *Truth or Dare* (1991). The title was apt. Critics questioned how much was true about the off-stage behavior of Madonna and how much was put on for the camera.

Always industrious, Madonna completed the album *The Immaculate Collection* in 1991 as well as a new movie, *A League of Their Own.*

Whether it is solely for publicity or for some other reason, Madonna seems to focus her creative energies primarily on challenging sexual mores and creating situations that shock people. In her productions on stage she has used religious symbols in a profane manner, putting a cross between her legs, for instance. She has also dressed her male dancers in bras and simulated masturbation on stage. Her off-stage manner has also been provocative. For example, she arrived at a film festival wearing a cloak, which she opened to reveal that she was dressed in only a bra and girdle. Yet she was offended when her video "Justify My Love" was banned from MTV and when two of her concerts were canceled in Italy through the influence of the Vatican. In interviews Madonna justifies what she does by suggesting that male rock stars are not criticized for similar behavior. (For another point of view see Susan McClary's *Feminine Endings.*)

If success is measured in money, then Madonna is certainly successful. *Forbes* magazine estimated that she earns $39 million a year and has earned close to $125 million since 1986. However, in interviews Madonna often speaks of the things she hasn't achieved, particularly in her personal life. She would like to marry and have a child, but she hasn't found the right man yet.

She works hard at her career, keeps herself fit with two hours of exercise each day, and subsists on a vegetarian diet. Constantly working, she goes from recording sessions to concert tours to films with barely a break. In the last ten years she has taken only three short vacations.

Madonna has written many of the songs she has recorded, among them "Lucky Star," "Burning Up," "I Know It," "Think of Me," and "Everybody." Two of the songs Madonna wrote with Patrick Leonard are "Who's That Girl" and "Live to Tell." With Stephen Bray she wrote "Causing a Commotion," "Angel," and "Can't Stop." She also co-authored "Papa Don't Preach" with Brian Elliot, and "Dress You Up" with Peggy Stanziale and Andrea La Russo.

Madonna has a home in Los Angeles and a seven-room apartment in New York City.

SOURCES
Arrington, Carl. "Madonna in Bloom," *Time,* May 20, 1991, pp. 56–58.
Evory, Ann. *Contemporary Newsmakers,* Issue 2.
Hirschberg, Lynn. "The Misfit," *Vanity Fair,* April 1991, pp. 158–68.
Hitchcock, H. Wiley. *New Grove Dictionary of American Music.*

Moritz, Charles. *Current Biography,* 1986.
Stambler, Irwin. *Encyclopedia of Pop, Rock and Soul.*
Stuessy, Joe. *Rock and Roll.*

MIDLER, BETTE (1945–   )   "You're Movin' Out Today"

Singer, songwriter, and motion picture comedienne, Bette Midler was born in Honolulu, Hawaii, on December 1, 1945. Her mother named her after the film star Bette Davis. Bette Midler also has two sisters and a brother. Her parents had moved to Hawaii from New Jersey in 1940. In Hawaii her father worked as a house painter for the U.S. Navy. In the first grade Bette won a prize for singing "Silent Night." She attended the University of Hawaii but left after one year and supported herself by working in a pineapple factory and later in a radio station.

When the motion picture *Hawaii* was being filmed in the islands in 1965, Bette got a small acting part in the movie playing a missionary's wife who was always seasick. When the motion picture crew returned to Los Angeles to finish the film, Bette went with them. Six months later with her work in the film completed, she took her savings and left for New York to get into show business. There she worked at various jobs—as a typist, a sales-clerk, a hat check girl, and a go-go dancer—while auditioning for Broadway shows.

In 1966 she got a part in the chorus of *Fiddler on the Roof.* From understudy she moved into a supporting role, that of the eldest daughter. She remained with the show for three years. Often after work she would sing at the Improvisation Club, which showcased new talent. The owner of the club became her manager. After this she had guest appearances singing on the television shows of Merv Griffin and David Frost. In 1970 she appeared in the off-Broadway show *Salvation,* which had a short run.

Looking for work, she learned that the Continental Baths, a gay bathhouse, wanted a singer, and she took the job. It was at the baths that Bette Midler's zany, outrageous humor had room to develop. Singing to an audience of men wrapped in towels, she wore her most eccentric garb and sang a mixture of crazy novelty songs, show tunes, blues, and rock. Red-haired, green-eyed, and of ample proportions, she was so popular that the management decided to admit both men and women to the show. As a wider New York audience saw her work, offers began to come in from record companies and television shows. She appeared on Johnny Carson's "Tonight Show" several times and later performed with Carson when he did a show in Las Vegas.

In 1971 Bette went to Seattle to appear in the rock opera *Tommy*. Returning to New York, she performed at Downstairs at the Upstairs, where she was held over. The following year she made a return to the Continental Baths. She continued singing at sold-out performances at clubs and also sang in the 1972 Schaefer Music Festival in Central Park.

A record contract for Bette Midler's first album came in 1973. Determined to make her debut album a success, she put in ten months of hard work to finish *The Divine Miss M* for Atlantic Records. The work paid off. The album sold 100,000 copies in one month alone.

One of the highlights of 1973 was her New Year's Eve performance at Lincoln Center's Philharmonic Hall singing with her trio, the Harlettes. The evening was noteworthy for her midnight appearance wrapped in a diaper like Baby New Year sporting a 1973 sash and rising like Venus on a seashell through an opening in the stage floor, all the while singing "Lullaby of Broadway." It brought down the house.

Bette Midler was awarded a Grammy for Best New Artist in 1975; that year she also won a special Tony Award for her stage work.

Her first film, *The Rose* (1979), was based on the life of a Janis Joplin–like rock star. Her performance in the movie earned her an Academy Award nomination. After that, she had a flop with the film *Jinxed*. Finally under contract to Disney, she began to find her niche in films as a comedienne. With Disney she made a number of funny films, including *Down and Out in Beverly Hills* (1986) with Richard Dreyfus, *Ruthless People* (1986) with Danny De Vito, *Outrageous Fortune* (1987) with Shelley Long, and *Big Business* (1988) with Lily Tomlin. Only her film *Scenes from a Mall* with Woody Allen was unsuccessful. Her role in the motion picture *Beaches* (1988) demonstrated her considerable ability as an actress. Her film, *For the Boys* (1991), was set in the 1940s, which gave her a chance to sing the music she likes best. In recent years she has formed her own company, All Girl Productions, and now co-produces some of her own films, such as *For the Boys* and *Beaches*.

On television she has performed in her own revues: "Clams on the Half Shell" and "The Fabulous Bette Midler Show." Her show "Ol' Red Hair Is Back" won her an Emmy.

In her personal life Bette Midler has had two family tragedies. Her sister was killed in a traffic accident while on her way to see Bette in *Fiddler on the Roof*, and in 1979 her mother died of cancer. Her personal life took a happier turn in 1985 when she married Martin von Haselberg. They now have a young daughter. Motherhood has changed her somewhat: She no longer smokes, drinks, or uses bad language. She and her family live on a hillside above Beverly Hills.

In addition to all her other activities Bette Midler also writes songs. She co-authored two for the movie *Beaches* (1988): "Otto Titsling," with Wendy Waldman; and "Oh Industry," with Jerry Blatt, Charlene Seeger, and Marc Shalman. For her album *Thighs and Whispers,* she wrote "Hurricane" with Randy Kerber. Her best song to date is "You're Movin' Out Today," written with **Carole Bayer Sager** and Bruce Roberts.

SOURCES

Davis, Sheila. *Craft of Lyric Writing.*
Gareffa, Peter. *Newsmakers,* 1989.
Moritz, Charles. *Current Biography,* 1973.
Scott, V. "Bette." *Good Housekeeping,* March 1991, p. 64.
Who's Who of American Women, 1981.

NICHOLS, ALBERTA (1898–1957)
" 'Till the Real Thing Comes Along"

Alberta Nichols composed popular songs and songs for Broadway.

She was born in Lincoln, Illinois, on December 3, 1898, and studied at the Louisville Conservatory. After this she worked as a writer of special material for vaudeville, wrote radio theme songs, and composed musical commercials.

She married Mann Holiner, and together they formed a successful songwriting team, with Mann writing the lyrics to her music. Their most successful songs were "A Love like Ours" and " 'Till the Real Thing Comes Along," written with Sammy Cahn, Saul Chaplin, and L. E. Freeman.

On Broadway, Nichols and Holiner had songs in the show *Gay Paree* (1926). In 1928 they wrote the musical *Angela,* which starred Jeanette MacDonald. Some of their songs from the musical were "I Can't Believe It's True," "Maybe So," and "The Regal Romp." That same year they had one song in the musical *Luckee Girl.*

They also wrote for the movies. In 1931 they collaborated with Sammy Cahn, Saul Chaplin, and L. E. Freeman on songs for the film *Rhapsody in Black.* After that they wrote songs for the Broadway show *Blackbirds of 1934.*

One of their best songs, "A Love like Ours," appeared in the Van Johnson–June Allyson film *Two Girls and a Sailor* (1944). The film featured the orchestras of Harry James and Xavier Cugat and the singing of Helen Forrest.

Alberta Nichols and Mann Holiner composed over 100 songs, among them "There Never Was a Town like Paris," "Sing a Little Tune," "You Can't Stop Me from Loving You," "Why Shouldn't It Happen to Us?" "I'm

Walkin' the Chalk Line," "Your Mother's Son-in-Law," "I Just Couldn't
Take It Baby," and "Sing a Little Tune."

Alberta Nichols died in Hollywood on February 4, 1957.

SOURCES
Anderson, E. Ruth. *Contemporary American Composers.*
Dahl, Linda. *Stormy Weather.*
Kinkle, Roger. *Complete Encyclopedia of Popular Music and Jazz.*
Lewine, Richard. *Songs of Theater.*
Lynn Farnol Group. *ASCAP Biographical Dictionary.*
Wilder, Alex. *American Popular Song.*

PETKERE, BERNICE (1906–   )   "Close Your Eyes"

Bernice Naomi Petkere was born in Chicago on August 11, 1906, and by
the age of five was touring in vaudeville. At 12 she won a scholarship to
study voice at the Hinshaw Conservatory of Music in Chicago. When she
was older, she worked in Irving Berlin's music-publishing company as a
song demonstrator playing and singing songs. During this time she began
to write songs.

In the early 1930s she and lyricist Joe Young wrote several popular songs,
among them "Starlight," and the lovely "Lullaby of the Leaves." In 1933
she wrote both the words and music to "Close Your Eyes," which became
a standard.

She also wrote for motion pictures, composing the score for the film *Ice
Follies of 1938* and writing the screenplay for the film *Sabotage Squad*
(1942).

In 1941 she married Frederick Norbert Berrens.

Bernice Petkere has written over 100 songs, among them "By a Rippling
Stream," "The Lady I Love," "Stay Out of My Dreams," "It's All So New
to Me," "Dancing Butterfly," "Tell the Truth," "Christmas Cha Cha," "My
River Home," "I Dream All Night of You," and "Did You Mean What You
Said Last Night?"

SOURCES
Dahl, Linda. *Stormy Weather.*
Kinkle, Roger. *Complete Encyclopedia of Popular Music and Jazz.*
Lynn Farnol Group. *ASCAP Biographical Dictionary.*
New York Times Film Reviews.
Spaeth, Sigmund. *History of Popular Music in America.*
Wilder, Alex. *American Popular Song.*

PREVIN, DORY *See* Motion Pictures.

RAITT, BONNIE (1949–   )   **"Nick of Time"**

She was born Bonnie Lynn Raitt in Burbank, California, on November 8, 1949, the daughter of Broadway and motion picture singer John Raitt. Her family moved to New York when she was a child, and she grew up there. Coming from a musical family, she learned to play both the piano and guitar as a child, and her Quaker background gave her a commitment to social activism. She attended Radcliffe College in 1967 but left after two years to begin playing in blues clubs and touring.

Bonnie Raitt's repertory consists of a mixture of rhythm and blues, rock, folk, and blues. Her first album was *Bonnie Raitt* (1971), which included three blues songs by **Sippie Wallace.** It was well received. In the years that followed, she continued to release about one album a year. In some of the later albums she added jazz, rock, and calypso numbers to appeal to a pop audience. Through the 1970s she toured continually and played at blues and folk festivals.

On television she made guest appearances on shows such as "Midnight Special," "Soundstage," and "Saturday Night Live." She also co-starred in "The Bonnie Raitt and Paul Butterfield Show" in 1974.

After achieving success, Bonnie Raitt went through a difficult time in the late 1980s with both her professional and personal life. First her record company dropped her contract. Then a long-term relationship she had, ended. It was during this difficult time that she developed problems with alcohol. She was eventually able to seek help and to recover.

In 1989, at the age of 40, Bonnie Raitt made a resounding comeback with her tenth album, *Nick of Time,* issued by her new record company. It sold more than 2 million copies. That year she won four Grammys: Best Female Pop Vocalist, Best Female Rock Vocalist, Best Album of the Year, and Best Traditional Blues. The latter she shared with blues singer John Lee Hooker.

In 1991 she was on the top 20 charts again with two songs, "Something to Talk About" and "I Can't Make You Love Me."

Now Bonnie Raitt has a new record contract with Capitol Records, as well as a new husband. April 30, 1991, she married actor Michael O'Keefe.

Among the songs that Bonnie Raitt has written are "Give It Up or Let Me Go," "Have a Heart," "The Road's My Middle Name," "Nothing Seems to Matter," "Standin' by the Same Old Love," and "Thank You."

SOURCES
Dahl, Linda. *Stormy Weather*.
Harris, Sheldon. *Blues Who's Who*, 1989.
Hitchcock, H. Wiley. *New Grove Dictionary of American Music*.
Moritz, Charles. *Current Biography*, 1990.
Who's Who of American Women, 1989–90.

SAGER, CAROLE BAYER   *See* Motion Pictures.

SIMON, CARLY (1945–   )
"That's the Way I Always Heard It Should Be"

Carly Simon was born in New York City on June 25, 1945, the daughter of Richard Simon, of the Simon & Schuster publishing company. Carly Simon's family was musical: Her father was a fine pianist; her older sister became an opera singer; and her second sister became a composer (however, her brother became a photographer). At the private elementary school Carly attended, folk singer Pete Seeger was her music teacher. She admired the folk singer Odetta, and to be a performer like her she taught herself to play guitar and piano.

After high school she attended Sarah Lawrence College. She and her sister, Lucy, formed the Simon Sisters and sang in Greenwich Village clubs. Lucy Simon broke up the duo by getting married, but years later she composed the score for the Broadway musical *The Secret Garden* (1991). When her sister got married, Carly joined the rock group Elephant's Memory, but her fear of flying and her anxiety about performing kept her from touring. So she turned her energies to songwriting and began writing with a friend she had known from childhood, Jacob Brackman.

In 1970 she signed a contract with Elektra Records. Her first solo album, *Carly Simon*, included the hit song "That's the Way I Always Heard It Should Be," which she and Jacob Brackman had written. The album sold 400,000 copies, and in 1971 Carly Simon won a Grammy for Best New Artist. In her second album two more of the songs she co-authored became hits, "Anticipation" and "Legend in Your Own Time." This album sold 600,000 copies. Her popularity was growing. Three years later her album *Hotcakes* (1974) sold half a million copies in one week. Since then Carly Simon has recorded many more albums that have become gold records.

As a songwriter, Carly Simon works in various ways, sometimes at the piano and sometimes at the guitar. Sometimes she writes the melody first and the lyrics later, and other times she'll start with a verse and set it to music at the piano. Generally she finds it easier to write the melody than the lyrics. She has written a number of gold record hits, among them "Mockingbird," "You're So Vain," and "Nobody Does It Better." Among her other songs are "That's the Way I've Always Heard It Should Be," "Anticipation," "Hotcakes," "Haven't Got Time for the Pain," "One More Time," and "Attitude Dancing," the latter written with Jacob Brackman.

In recent years she has been writing songs for motion pictures. She wrote "Coming around Again," the theme song for Mike Nichols' film *Heartburn* (1986). For the motion picture *Working Girl,* she wrote "Let the River Run," which won a Grammy in 1990.

Carly Simon's personal life has not always run smoothly. The stress of a divorce and the illness of her son caused her to have panic attacks on stage. "Coming around Again" was her first hit in seven years. With that success and a new record contract, she began to find her confidence again. She has decided not to tour anymore but instead to concentrate on writing songs and recording, although she did perform on HBO television in 1990 in "Carly in Concert: My Romance." In 1990 she also completed two albums, *Have You Seen Me Lately?* and *Happy Birthday.*

Carly Simon married singer James Taylor in 1972 and had two children. They divorced, and she later married novelist James Hart, with whom she now lives in Boston. Carly and her husband also have a home in Manhattan.

She has appeared in two films, *Taking Off* (1971) and *No Nukes* (1980), and has written an autobiography, *Carly Simon Complete* (1975).

SOURCES

Davis, Sheila. *Craft of Lyric Writing.*
Hitchcock, H. Wiley. *New Grove Dictionary of American Music.*
Jacques Cattel. *ASCAP Biographical Dictionary.*
Moritz, Charles. *Current Biography,* 1976.
Plaskin, Glenn. "*Carly Simon Fights Fear.*" *SF Chronicle,* August 29, 1990, p. B5.
Stambler, Irwin. *Encyclopedia of Pop, Rock and Soul.*
Who's Who of American Women, 1989–90.

STREISAND, BARBRA   *See* Motion Pictures.

SUESSE, DANA (1911–1987)   **"My Silent Love"**

Composer-lyricist Dana Nadine Suesse was born on December 3, 1911, in Shreveport, Louisiana. A child prodigy, she played the piano at the age of five and composed her first song at eight. When she was a year older, she gave her first concert playing a Rachmaninoff prelude and three of her own compositions. That same year at the age of nine she won a prize from the National Federation of Music for a musical composition. She moved to New York at the age of 16 to study piano and composition. At 18 she wrote her first hit song, "Syncopated Love Song." Her second hit was "Ho Hum," a song she had written in 15 minutes.

In New York she played piano with Paul Whiteman's orchestra. Whiteman presented her at a 1933 concert at Carnegie Hall, in which she played her own composition, "Valses for Piano and Orchestra." She could write music very quickly even without a piano, and she frequently wrote sitting up in bed. In just three weeks she finished *Jazz Concerto in Three Rhythms*, which Whiteman introduced at Carnegie Hall along with her *Symphonic Waltzes* and her suite *Young Man with a Harp*. She also wrote *Eight Valses* for Paul Whiteman in 1934. Her tone poem *Two Irish Fairy Tales* was introduced at a Town Hall concert by the New Chamber Orchestra. Symphony orchestras in Boston, Philadelphia, and New York also played her works.

In 1935 she performed as pianist on a radio program of symphonic music. Later she became a staff writer for two music publishers, writing popular music from 1939 to 1949. For Billy Rose she composed music for a night-club revue, *The Casa Mañana Show*, and his aquacade at the World's Fair. She also composed the score of the movies *Young Man with a Horn* and *Sweet Surrender*.

Later she went to Paris and studied with Nadia Boulanger. After that she devoted herself to composing. Among her other works are "Afternoon of a Black Faun," "Evening in Harlem," "Danza á Medianoche," and "Jazz Nocturne."

Besides classical music, Dana Suesse composed some very beautiful popular songs. Her "My Silent Love" and "You Oughta Be in Pictures" had lyrics by Ed Heyman. She wrote "Whistling in the Dark" with the lyrics of Allen Boretz and "The Night Is Young and You're So Beautiful" with the lyrics of Billy Rose and Irving Kahal. Other songs composed by Dana Suesse include "Another Mile," "Have You Forgotten?" and "Yours for a Song." She also worked with Leo Robin, Nathaniel Shilkret, and E. Y. Harburg.

Dana Suesse died in New York City on October 16, 1987.

SOURCES

Block, Maxine. *Current Biography*, 1940.
Dahl, Linda. *Stormy Weather*.

THOMPSON, KAY (1902/1913–   )   "You Gotta Love Everybody"

Kay Thompson is a singer, pianist, actress, author, and songwriter. She was born in St. Louis, Missouri, on November 9, 1902 or 1913.

As a youngster she studied classical music and when only 16 was a piano soloist with the St. Louis Symphony. Then she turned to popular music and became a singer on radio, on television, and in night clubs. For a time she was a vocalist and arranger for Fred Waring's choir and orchestra.

In 1937 Kay Thompson and her radio choir appeared in the film *Manhattan Merry-Go-Round*. After this she began to work in motion pictures as an MGM choreographer, vocal coach, lyricist, and music arranger. She wrote songs for Red Skelton's movie *I Dood It* (1943) and for *Ziegfeld Follies* (1946), collaborating with Roger Edens.

In 1957 she had a singing and acting role in the film *Funny Face*, starring Audrey Hepburn and Fred Astaire.

Kay Thompson is also the author of the charming children's book *Eloise* and a song, "Eloise."

Among the songs Kay Thompson has written are "Promise Me Love," "You Gotta Love Everybody," "Just a Moment Ago," "Love on a Greyhound Bus," "What More Can I Give You?" "Isn't It Wonderful?" "Vive l'Amour," and "This Is the Time."

SOURCES

Dahl, Linda. *Stormy Weather.*
Lynn Farnol Group. *ASCAP Biographical Dictionary.*
New York Times Film Reviews.
Zailian, Marian. " 'Funny Face' Fabulous Feet." *San Francisco Examiner-Chronicle*, December 24, 1989, p. 20.

TWOMEY, KATHLEEN (1914–   )   "Serenade of the Bells"

Kathleen Twomey wrote the lyrics to many popular songs.

Born in Boston, Massachusetts, on April 27, 1914, she attended the New England Conservatory of Music and studied voice privately. After that she had a variety of jobs—from fashion model, jewelry designer, and copywriter for advertising agencies to talent manager.

For a time she wrote songs for a music publisher and collaborated with many composers. She, Al Goodhart, and Al Urbano wrote "Serenade of the Bells" and "Johnny Doughboy Found a Rose in Ireland." With Ben Weisman and Fred Wise she wrote "Never Let Her Go." With Sammy Cahn and Bee Walker she wrote "Hey, Jealous Lover." With Dick Manning she wrote "Johnny Jingo." For the film *G. I. Blues* (1961) she wrote the song "Wooden Heart" with Berthold Kaempfert, Ben Weisman, and Fred Wise.

Some of her other songs include "The Robe of Calvary," "Heartbreak Hill," and "Why Pretend?"

SOURCES

Lynn Farnol Group. *ASCAP Biographical Dictionary.*
Mattfeld, Julius. *Variety Music Cavalcade.*
Spaeth, Sigmund. *History of Popular Music in America.*

VEGA, SUZANNE (1960–   )   "Luka"

Suzanne Vega was born in Santa Monica, California, on July 11, 1960, but grew up in Spanish Harlem in New York City. Her mother, a computer analyst, and her stepfather, a Puerto Rican novelist and teacher, often played the guitar and sang to Suzanne and her three siblings. As a youngster Suzanne learned to play the guitar, and she began writing songs at the age of 14.

For ten years she studied ballet and modern dance, and she majored in dance at the High School for Performing Arts. But at Barnard College she decided to major in English literature. After college she found a job as a receptionist to earn a living. But at night she pursued her main interest, music, by singing in folk music clubs.

By 1985 she had an album contract and made her debut album, *Suzanne Vega.* The album was well received by the critics and was particularly popular on college radio stations. It sold 250,000 copies—an impressive beginning.

Solitude Standing (1987), her second album, was more rock than folk music, with the rock sound produced by a synthesizer and a backup band. The album included "Calypso," which Suzanne Vega wrote at college when she was 18, "Tom's Diner," and "Luka," which became enormously popular. The album sold over a half million copies in the first three months and became the number two song in England. That year Suzanne Vega was nominated for three Grammys.

After her second album came out, Suzanne Vega began touring throughout Europe, the Far East, Canada, and the United States. In England she had the unnerving experience of receiving death threats just before a performance at a huge outdoor concert. However, she didn't cancel. Instead she put on a bulletproof vest and sang her songs to the gathering of 60,000 people, never knowing if one of them was going to carry out the threat. Later the whole incident turned out to be a prank.

Suzanne Vega's third album, *Days of Open Hand* (1990), included such songs as "Institution Green," "Tired of Sleeping," "Men in War," and "Predictions."

Although Suzanne Vega has said in interviews that she has been influenced by Woody Guthrie, Pete Seeger, Canadian poet-songwriter Leonard Cohen, and rocker Lou Reed, her songs are like no others. They are carefully crafted poems set to rock music. Some are concerned with serious issues like child abuse, as in "Luka," for example. But the lyrics are spare and unemotional, and Vega presents the song in a dispassionate voice nearly in a whisper. Nevertheless, the effect is very powerful. Certainly Suzanne Vega is one of the more gifted singer-songwriters at work today and one worth watching.

One of Suzanne Vega's future projects is to complete a musical about the life of novelist Carson McCullers, a subject Vega became interested in in college. She also hopes to do a Broadway show with playwright Harvey Fierstein, of *Torch Song Trilogy*, the brother of her manager, Ron Fierstein.

Meanwhile she lives in Greenwich Village and has been a practicing Buddhist for more than ten years.

Among the songs she has written are "Tom's Diner," "Wooden Horse (Caspar Hauser's Song)," "Calypso," "Undertow," "Straight Lines," "Some Journey," "Knight Moves," "Neighborhood Girls," "Marlene on the Wall," "Cracking," "Room off the Street," "Big Space," "Those Whole Girls (Run in Grace)," and "Tired of Sleeping." She has also written lyrics for composer Philip Glass for his album *Songs from Liquid Days*. She wrote the song "Left of Center" for the film *Pretty in Pink*.

> I think it's because I'm clumsy
> I try not to talk too loud
> Maybe it's because I'm crazy
> I try not to act too proud
> They only hit until you cry
> After that you don't ask why
> You just don't argue anymore.

—"Luka" lyrics by Suzanne Vega

SOURCES
Fried, Stephen. "Bulletproof Waif." *Gentlemen's Quarterly*, May 1990, pp. 91ff.
Gareffa, Peter. *Newsmakers*, 1988.
Givens, Ron. "Suzanne Vega's Vision." *Stereo Review*, July 1990, p. 79.
Hitchcock, H. Wiley. *New Grove Dictionary of American Music*.
Hubbard, Kim. "When Suzanne Vega Peeled Away." *People*, June 8, 1987, p. 71.
McGuigan, Cathleen. "Suzanne Vega, Ethereal Girl," *Newsweek*, Aug. 3, 1987, p. 69.

WASHINGTON, DINAH   *See* Jazz.

WEIL, CYNTHIA (n.d.)   "I Just Can't Help Believin' "

Cynthia Weil and her husband, Barry Mann, have been a successful songwriting team for many years.

They began working together in the 1960s at Aldon Music Publishers, where a group of talented songwriters worked, among them **Carole King,** Gerry Goffin, Neil Sedaka, and Howard Greenfield. The songwriters plugged away writing songs day after day each in a tiny cubicle with a piano. They could often hear their neighbors at work next door.

Some of the songs Cynthia Weil and Barry Mann have written include "It's Getting Better," "Conscience," "Uptown," "Blame It on the Bossa Nova," "Make Your Own Kind of Music," "Just Once," "Here You Come Again," "He's Sure the Boy I Love," "We Gotta Get Out of This Place," "Holding Out for Love," "My Dad," "Somewhere down the Road," "I'm Gonna Be Strong," "Hungry," "Kicks," "Saturday Night at the Movies," "You're My Soul and Inspiration," and "I Just Can't Help Believin'."

Sometimes they work with other collaborators, and they find bringing in someone new helps revitalize their work. With Phil Spector, Cynthia Weil wrote "You've Lost That Lovin' Feelin' " and "Walking in the Rain." Together with Jerry Leiber and Mike Stoller she wrote the hit "On Broadway." Cynthia has also worked with songwriters James Ingram, Leon Ware, and Tom Snow, among others.

Cynthia Weil prefers to start with the music, then add the words to it. She and Barry Mann write in a variety of styles—pop, rock, country, and rhythm and blues—and have been able to keep up with the trends in music for more than two decades. For their song "Somewhere out There," written with James Horner, they won a Grammy in 1987.

SOURCES

Davis, Sheila. *Craft of Lyric Writing.*
Davis, Tracy. "Close-up of Cynthia Weil and Barry Mann." *Song Writer's Market,* 1983, p. 199.
80 Years of American Song Hits.
New York Times Film Reviews, 1960.

WHITNEY, JOAN (1914–   )   "Candy"

Joan Whitney wrote the lyrics for a number of hit songs in the 1940s and 1950s. She was born Zoe Parenteau in Pittsburgh, Pennsylvania, on June

26, 1914, the daughter of composer Zoel Parenteau. Educated at Carnegie Tech. and Finch College, she began her career as a singer with dance bands.

In 1934 she had a small part in the Broadway musical *The Great Waltz*. After this she sang in clubs, made recordings, and performed on her own radio show. In 1940 she became a staff writer for a music-publishing company.

She married composer Alex Charles Kramer, and together they formed a successful songwriting team. In the 1940s they wrote "High on a Windy Hill," "That's the Beginning of the End," "Weep No More, My Lady," and "Curiosity." For the film *Stars on Parade* (1944) they wrote "It's Love, Love, Love" with Mack David. They also collaborated with Bruno Coquatrix, Pierre Dudan, and Hy Zaret. In 1946 they opened their own Kramer-Whitney Publishing Company.

Joan Whitney and Alex Kramer wrote many top songs together, among them "Candy" with Mack David, "Ain't Nobody Here but Us Chickens," "I Only Saw Him Once," "Far Away Places," "Comme-ci, Comme-ça," "Love Somebody," "Unchained Melody," and "It All Comes Back to Me Now," the last two written with Hy Zaret. They also wrote "So Long for Awhile," the theme of the television show "Your Hit Parade."

SOURCES

Dahl, Linda. *Stormy Weather*.
Davis, Sheila. *Craft of Lyric Writing*.
Kinkle, Roger. *Complete Encyclopedia of Popular Music and Jazz*.
Lynn Farnol Group. *ASCAP Biographical Dictionary*.
Spaeth, Sigmund. *History of Popular Music in America*.

II

MOTION PICTURES

INTRODUCTION

When silent movies were shown in the early days of motion pictures, they were usually accompanied by music. A pianist sitting in the darkened theater was employed to play music appropriate to the action on the screen. In 1927 the first sound movie, *The Jazz Singer,* changed all of that. Up on the big screen Al Jolson sang "My Mammy," and everyone heard him.

Sound brought new opportunities for songwriters. After *The Jazz Singer* Hollywood went wild producing movie musicals. Seventy were made in 1929. Many songwriters who had worked on Broadway moved to Hollywood to write songs for the movies.

Women, also, were among those pioneer motion picture songwriters. The year after the first sound movie Mabel Wayne composed the title song for the motion picture *Ramona* (1928), and it became one of the hit songs of that era. Elsie Janis, who had starred in vaudeville and silent movies, wrote for the movie *The Trespasser* (1930) the lyrics to another hit song, "Love, Your Magic Spell Is Everywhere." Dorothy Fields came from Broadway in the mid-1930s to write lyrics for motion picture musicals. She became the first woman songwriter to win an Academy Award for a motion picture song. In the 1930s Ann Ronell and Alberta Nichols, also, were writing songs for movies.

Although some Broadway songwriters like Betty Comden of Comden & Green came to Hollywood for periods of time to write film musicals, more women came to live in Hollywood and work in the film industry. In those days there were huge studios, like Metro Goldwyn Mayer (MGM), that had their own stable of stars and production people under exclusive contract. Some women, like Doris Fisher and Inez James, were songwriters under contract to a studio. Other women songwriters worked primarily in other aspects of the motion picture business—in screenwriting, like Helen Deutsch, or in music arranging, like Kay Thompson—but occasionally they also wrote songs for films. After the studio system ended in the 1960s, many women songwriters had considerably less access to the motion picture industry.

After that, women were more likely to write only the occasional theme song for a film. A few like Marilyn Bergman, who writes lyrics with her husband, Alan Bergman, became successful songwriters for motion pictures after beginning in television; they are multiple Oscar winners. Carole Bayer Sager, who came from Broadway, has also written theme songs for motion pictures, as have singers Peggy Lee, Carly Simon, and Barbra Streisand. Sager and Streisand are both Oscar winners for their songs.

This chapter profiles those women whose songwriting was primarily for motion pictures.

BERGMAN, MARILYN (1929–   )   "The Way We Were"

Marilyn Bergman and her husband, Alan, form one of the most successful lyric-writing teams in Hollywood. They have won many awards for their work, including three Oscars.

Marilyn Bergman was born Marilyn Keith in Brooklyn, New York, on November 10, 1929, and was educated at New York University. Her early songwriting was for revues, night clubs, and television specials, including the theme songs for *Oh, Susannah!, Jacques and Jill,* and "The Nat King Cole Show."

In 1958 she married Alan Bergman and began a long and successful partnership.

The Bergmans' first hit song was "Yellow Bird" (1957), with Norman Luboff's music. Following this success they had many offers to write songs for motion pictures, which has since become their primary focus.

Among their best songs are "The Windmills of Your Mind" (1968), music by Michel Legrand, and "The Way We Were" (1973), music by Marvin Hamlisch, both of which won Academy Awards. They also won an Oscar for their contribution to the score of the film *Yentl* (1984).

Other songs that they've authored include "What Are You Doing the Rest of Your Life?" "The Summer Knows," "Little Boy Lost," all with music by Michel Legrand. "In the Heat of the Night" had lyrics by the Bergmans and music by Quincy Jones. "Make Me Rainbows" was set to music by composer John Williams. The Bergmans wrote "I Believe in Love," with music by Kenny Loggins. With Neil Diamond's music they wrote "Don't Bring Me Flowers," and with Lew Spence's music they supplied the lyrics for "Sleep Warm" and "Nice and Easy."

The Bergmans also wrote lyrics for Broadway shows: *Something More* (1964), with music by Sammy Fain, *Ice Capades* (1957), and *Ballroom* (1978), with music by Billy Goldenburg.

Although Marilyn and Alan Bergman centered their efforts on writing songs for motion pictures, they also wrote for television. They wrote the themes for many shows: "Maude," "Good Times," and "The Sandy Duncan Show," all with music by David Grusin, as well as "The World Goes On," with music by Quincy Jones. They also received Emmys for their lyrics for the television movies *Queen of the Stardust Ball* and *Sybil*.

Their procedure for working on a song is to have the music first and then to set words to it. If the song is for a film, they watch the whole movie first to be sure that their words are in keeping with the whole story. Then they concentrate on the section of the motion picture where their song will be featured. They work together, each adding words and ideas, so that when they finish neither is sure who wrote which part.

> Mem'ries light the corners of my mind,
> Misty water color mem'ries of the way we were.
> Scattered pictures of the smiles we left behind,
> Smiles we gave to one another for the way we were.
>
> Can it be that it was all so simple then,
> Or has time rewritten ev'ry line?
> If we had the chance to do it all again,
> Tell me would we? Could we?
>
> Mem'ries may be beautiful and yet,
> What's too painful to remember
> We simply choose to forget.
> So it's the laughter we will remember,
>
> Whenever we remember the way we were.
> The way we were.
> —"The Way We Were" by Alan Bergman, Marilyn Bergman,
> and Marvin Hamlisch

Marilyn and Alan Bergman have a daughter and live in Los Angeles.

SOURCES
Ewen, David. *American Songwriters.*
Gertner, Richard. *International Motion Picture Almanac.*
Jacques Cattel Press. *ASCAP Biographical Dictionary.*
Who's Who of American Women, 1990.

CALDWELL, ANNE   *See* Musicals.

COMDEN, BETTY   *See* Musicals.

DEUTSCH, HELEN (1906–   )   "Hi-Lili, Hi-lo"

Born on March 21, 1906, in New York City, Helen Deutsch was a screenwriter and a lyricist.

She was educated at Barnard College, graduating Phi Beta Kappa. After college she worked in the press department of the Theater Guild, in time becoming the manager of the department. In 1931 she and Stella Hanau wrote a book, *The Provincetown*, about the Provincetown Theater.

Moving to Hollywood in the 1940s, Helen Deutsch worked as a screenwriter for more than 20 years. Among her many screenplays were *Seventh Cross, Loves of Carmen, Plymouth Adventure, It's a Big Country, Golden Earrings, The Glass Slipper, Forever Darling, I'll Cry Tomorrow, National Velvet, Unsinkable Molly Brown,* and *Valley of the Dolls*. She also wrote the screenplays of a number of adventure stories, including *Robinson Crusoe, King Solomon's Mines,* and *Kim*. MGM often assigned adventure films to Helen Deutsch because she included in her screenplays so many details regarding the flora and fauna that her stories had great authenticity. However, as she explained in an interview, her knowledge came from the library. She had not traveled widely.

Helen Deutsch's most memorable song was written for the motion picture *Lili*, for which she also wrote the screenplay. To Bronislaw Kaper's music she wrote the lyrics of the charming "Hi-Lili, Hi-lo," which Leslie Caron sang in the film.

Besides writing for motion pictures Helen Deutsch also wrote the book for a Broadway musical, *Carnival* (1961). For television she wrote the score for "Jack and the Beanstalk," and occasionally she wrote short stories for magazines like *Redbook, McCalls,* and *Cosmopolitan*.

Among Helen Deutsch's songs are "Twelve Feet Tall," "Looka Me," "I'll Go Along with You," "Sweet World," "The Ballad of Jack and the Beanstalk," "He Never Looks My Way," and "Take My Love," the latter with music by Bronislaw Kaper.

SOURCES
Baxter, Ian. *Who's Who in Theatre.*
Gertner, Richard. *International Motion Picture Almanac.*

Lynn Farnol Group, *ASCAP Biographical Dictionary*.
Mattfeld, Julius. *Variety Music Cavalcade*.
New York Times Film Reviews.
Who's Who of American Women, 1958.

DONNELLY, DOROTHY   *See* Musicals.

DUNHAM, KATHERINE   *See* Pop Rock.

FIELDS, DOROTHY   *See* Musicals.

FINE, SYLVIA (1913–1991)   "Anatole of Paris"

Sylvia Fine was the wife of comedian Danny Kaye. She was also an author of comic material and zany songs, many of which were written for Danny Kaye's Broadway and motion picture performances. In her later years she was a film and television producer.

She was born in 1913, raised in New York City, and educated at Brooklyn College. One of her first opportunities as a songwriter was writing two songs with James Shelton for *The Straw Hat Revue* in 1939. The show featured Imogene Coca and Danny Kaye, who sang Sylvia Fine's song "Anatole of Paris." The following year Sylvia Fine and Danny Kaye were married.

In 1941 Danny Kaye appeared with Eve Arden in the Cole Porter musical *Let's Face It*. For this show Sylvia Fine and Max Liebman wrote Kaye's song "Melody in Four F."

Then Hollywood offered Danny Kaye a motion picture contract and the family moved to the West Coast. Danny appeared in the movie *Up in Arms* (1944) with Dinah Shore and again sang "Melody in Four F." The next year Kaye starred in the film *Wonder Man* with Virginia Mayo, and in it he sang Sylvia Fine's "Bali Boogie." In 1946 he and Virginia Mayo did *Kid from Brooklyn*. His song "Pavlova" was by Sylvia Fine.

In 1956 Sylvia Fine wrote the film score for Danny Kaye's hilarious comedy *The Court Jester*. In it Kaye sang one of the clever tongue-twisters for which he was famous, Sylvia Fine's "Stanislavsky Vonschtickfitz Monahan."

Other films for which she wrote material include *The Secret Life of Walter Mitty* and *The Inspector General*.

Two of Sylvia Fine's songs were nominated for Academy Awards, "The Moon Is Blue," with music by Herschel Burke Gilbert, and "The Five Pennies," with words as well as music by Sylvia Fine. Among her other songs are "The Man with a Golden Arm," "Lobby Number," "Knock on Wood," and "Happy Times."

For Public Television she wrote, produced, and hosted a three-part series called "Musical Comedy Tonight," which won a Peabody Award. She also won an Emmy in 1976 for a children's special on television.

She and Danny Kaye had a daughter and lived in Beverly Hills for many years. Sylvia Fine died of emphysema in New York City on October 28, 1991, at the age of 78.

SOURCES

Burton, Jack. *Blue Book of Hollywood Musicals.*
Kinkle, Roger. *Complete Encyclopedia of Popular Music and Jazz.*
Krafsur, Richard. *American Film Institute,* 1961–70.
Lewine, Rich. *Songs of American Theater.*
Lynn Farnol Group. *ASCAP Biographical Dictionary.*
New York Times Film Reviews.
New York Times. Obituaries, October 29, 1991, p. B5.

FISHER, DORIS (1915–)   "You Always Hurt the One You Love"

Composer Doris Fisher grew up in a family of songwriters and music publishers, including her father, Fred Fisher, and her two brothers, Dan and Marvin. So it wasn't surprising when Doris Fisher also became a song-writer.

She was born in New York City on May 2, 1915, and studied music at the Juilliard School of Music. She began her career as a vocalist singing in night clubs and on the radio. By 1943 she was a vocalist with the Eddie Duchin Orchestra. With her own group, Penny Wise and Her Wise Guys, she made many recordings.

Doris Fisher's first songwriting hit, "Whispering Grass," was a song she wrote with her father in 1940. Then Columbia Pictures hired her to compose film scores for motion pictures, and in 1944 she had a song in the film *A Small World.*

By 1946 Doris Fisher and her collaborator, Allan Roberts, were turning out their best songs. That year they wrote the scores for three movies: *Gilda, Dead Reckoning,* and *Thrill of Brazil.* For *Gilda* they wrote "Amado Mio" and the sizzling "Put the Blame on Mame," which Rita Hayworth immortalized. The Humphrey Bogart film *Dead Reckoning* featured another of their hit songs, "Either It's Love or It Isn't."

The next year for the Rita Hayworth–Larry Parks musical *Down to Earth* (1947), Doris Fisher and Allan Roberts wrote "They Can't Convince Me" and "Let's Stay Young Forever"; and for *Variety Girl* (1947), the song "Tired." The following year they wrote "Please Don't Kiss Me" for Rita Hayworth in the Orson Welles film *Lady from Shanghai.*

Some of Doris Fisher's other hit songs include "Tutti Frutti," written with Slim Gaillard, "Tampico," and "Into Each Life Some Rain Must Fall." With Allan Roberts she wrote "You Always Hurt the One You Love," "Gee, It's Good to Hold You," "That Ole Devil Called Love," "Angelina," "Good, Good, Good," "You Can't See the Sun When You're Crying," "I Wish," and "Invitation to the Blues," the latter with Allan Roberts and Arthur Gershwin.

Doris Fisher is married and has two children.

SOURCES

Anderson, E. Ruth. *Contemporary American Composers.*
Dahl, Linda. *Stormy Weather.*
Hanson, Patricia. *American Film Institute, 1920–30.*
Kinkle, Roger. *Complete Encyclopedia of Popular Music and Jazz.*
Lynn Farnol Group, *ASCAP Biographical Dictionary.*
New York Times Film Reviews.
Who's Who of American Women, 1970.

HAMILTON, NANCY   *See* Musicals.

JAMES, INEZ (1919–   )   "Vaya Con Díos"

Inez Eleanor James was a composer of popular songs and film scores.

She was born in New York City on November 15, 1919, and studied music at the Hollywood Conservatory before she began writing for films in 1942.

During the 1940s she was a songwriter for Universal Pictures. She composed songs for several Donald O'Connor films—*Top Man* (1943), *Mr. Big* (1943), *This Is the Life* (1944), *Patrick the Great* (1945), and *Are You with It?* (1948)—collaborating with Sidney Miller and Buddy Pepper.

In the years that followed she and Buddy Pepper wrote the title songs to the movies *Pillow Talk* (1952), a Doris Day–Rock Hudson comedy, and *Portrait in Black* (1960), a Lana Turner film.

Among the songs that she wrote with Sidney Miller were "Come to Baby, Do," "Sing a Jingle," "I Can See It Your Way," "Ok'l, Baby, Dok'l," and "Walk It Off." Songs she wrote with Buddy Pepper include "What Good

Would It Do?" "I'm Sorry but I'm Glad," "Now You've Gone and Hurt My Southern Pride," "That's the Way He Does It," and "It's Christmas."

Inez James's biggest hit was "Vaya Con Díos," which she wrote with Buddy Pepper and Larry Russell.

SOURCES
Dahl, Linda. *Stormy Weather.*
Lynn Farnol Group, *ASCAP Biographical Dictionary.*
Mattfeld, Julius. *Variety Music Cavalcade.*
New York Times Film Reviews.

JANIS, ELSIE   *See* Musicals.

LINCOLN, ABBEY   *See* Jazz.

MADONNA   *See* Pop Rock.

McDANIELS, HATTIE   *See* Blues.

MIDLER, BETTE   *See* Pop Rock.

PREVIN, DORY (1925–   )   **"Come Saturday Morning"**

Dory Langdon was born October 22, 1925, in Rahway, New Jersey. Her father had always wanted to be a musician and made Dory take singing and dancing lessons. By the age of 11 she was performing at the local night spots.

After high school she attended the American Academy of Dramatic Art for a year. She found a job as a chorus girl, worked in summer stock, and then did television commercials. When she was hired for the road company of *Top Banana*, she thought her career was taking off, but she was fired in Chicago and returned home broke. After this disappointment, she looked for a new career and started writing short stories and song lyrics. She sent some songs to a New York producer, and he hired her as a junior writer.

Working on songs for the movie *Subterraneans* (1960), she met and married Andre Previn. With Previn she wrote theme songs and title songs for films, including *One, Two, Three* (1960), *Irma La Douce* (1963), and *Good-bye Charlie* (1964). For *Inside Daisy Clover* (1966), she wrote "You're Gonna Hear from Me." The movie *The Sterile Cuckoo* (1969) featured a song she wrote with Fred Karlin, "Come Saturday Morning." Three times her songs were nominated for an Academy Award.

Other writing she has done for motion pictures includes some Gerald McBoing-Boing cartoons and the screenplay for the musical *Coco*. She has also written for television.

Dory Previn has had some problems with her health. For therapy she went back to writing songs. The first album on which she performed her songs sold 25,000 copies; the second album sold twice as many, which opened up a new career for her as a performer. She finally conquered her fear of traveling and in 1973 went to New York to give a concert at Carnegie Hall.

Some of the songs for which Dory Previn had written lyrics are "You're Gonna Hear from Me," "The Bad and the Beautiful," "Goodbye Charlie," and "Come Saturday Morning." She has collaborated with David Raksin, Harold Arlen, Johnny Green, Andre Previn, Jimmy Van Heusen, Fred Astaire, and John Williams.

SOURCES
May, Hal. *Contemporary Authors*, vol. 3, 1984.
Moritz, Charles. *Current Biography*, 1975.
Shapiro, Nat. *Popular Music*.
Who's Who in America, 1982.

RONELL, ANN (c. 1903–)   "Willow Weep for Me"

Ann Ronell's most famous song is "Who's Afraid of the Big Bad Wolf?" although undoubtedly it is not the way she would wish to be remembered. She was a composer of classical music, including operas, but she made her living writing songs and conducting background music for motion pictures.

Ann Ronell was born in Omaha, Nebraska, on Christmas Day c. 1903. She was educated at Radcliffe and afterward taught music, played rehearsal piano for Broadway musicals, and coached singers.

In 1929 she wrote the music and lyrics to *Down by the River* for a show at Radio City Music Hall. She had one song, "Let's Go out in the Open Air," in the Broadway revue *Shoot the Works* (1931).

In 1932 she wrote the words and music for two of her best songs, "Rain on the Roof" and "Willow Weep for Me." The latter song was revived a decade later with great success by vocalist June Christie and the Stan Kenton Band.

The following year the Disney studio hired Ann Ronell to write songs for the cartoon *Three Little Pigs* (1933). One of the songs she and Frank Churchill wrote became a children's classic, "Who's Afraid of the Big Bad Wolf?"

She married film producer Lester Cowan and settled in Hollywood.

In the 1930s she was employed to write songs for a number of movies, among them *Down to Their Last Yacht* (1935), *The Big Broadcast* (1936), *Champagne Waltz* (1937), *The River Is So Blue* (1938), *Blockade* (1938), *Algiers* (1938), *You Can't Beat an Honest Man* (1939), and *Magic in Music* (1940).

Ann Ronell had always been drawn to opera. In 1935 she wrote both the music and lyrics of an opera, *The Magic Spring*, which was performed in Los Angeles. She was co-lyricist of an English adaptation of the *Magic Flute* and of *La Serva Padrona*. The Metropolitan Opera commissioned her to write the libretto for *The Gypsy Baron*, and she also was co-librettist for the opera *Martha*. She also composed the folk opera *Oh! Susanna* and a ballet, *Ship South*.

In 1942 Ann Ronell composed the score for the Broadway musical *Count Me In*. The book was written by Walter Kerr, Leo Grady, and **Nancy Hamilton,** with lyrics by Will Irwin. Some of the songs were "You've Got It All," "Someone in the Know," and "On Leave for Love."

After this Ann Ronell was music production assistant at a film studio and then music director on such films as *The Story of GI Joe* (1945), *One Touch of Venus* (1948), *Love Happy* (1949), *Main Street to Broadway* (1953), and *The Crucible* (1953). She was the first woman to conduct music for the soundtrack of a motion picture.

Ann Ronell received a nomination for an Academy Award in 1945 for the song, "Linda," and also for the best musical score for *The Story of GI Joe*.

Some of the other songs Ann Ronell wrote include "Beach Boy," "Andy Panda," "Baby's Birthday Party," "On a Merry-Go Round," "In a Silly Symphony," "C'est la Vie," "Take Me, Take Me to the Moon," "Don't Look Now but My Heart Is Showing," "Mickey Mouse," "Love Happy," "Beloved," "The River," "You're Lovely," "Hondo," and "Dark Moon."

SOURCES
Burton, Jack. *Blue Book of Broadway Musicals.*
Dahl, Linda. *Stormy Weather.*
Kinkle, Roger. *Complete Encyclopedia of Popular Music and Jazz.*
Krafsur, Richard. *American Film Institute, 1961–70.*
Lewine, Richard. *Songs of American Theater.*
Lynn Farnol Group. *ASCAP Biographical Dictionary.*
New York Times Film Reviews.
Rigdon, Walter. *Biographical Encyclopedia of American Theatre.*
Rigdon, Walter. *Notable Names in American Theatre.*

Who's Who of American Women, 1966.
Wilder, Alex. *American Popular Song*.

SAGER, CAROLE BAYER (1947–)
"That's What Friends Are For"

Carole Bayer Sager is a singer, songwriter, and novelist.

Born Carole Bayer in New York City on March 8, 1947, she began writing songs in high school when she was 15. Her first hit, "A Groovy Kind of Love," was written with Toni Wine when Carole was a teenager. A teacher helped her get a songwriting contract with a music publisher, but she also continued her education and graduated from New York University. She married Andrew Sager in 1970 but later divorced.

She was the youngest lyricist of a Broadway musical, *Georgy* (1970), which ran only five days. However, her next Broadway show was an enormous success. She and Marvin Hamlisch did the score and Neil Simon the book for *They're Playing Our Song* (1979). The show, which starred Lucie Arnaz and Robert Klein, had a long run of 1,082 performances.

In addition to writing songs for Broadway shows, Carol Bayer Sager has written songs for motion pictures, including *Ice Castles*, "*10,*" *Starting Over*, *All That Jazz*, and *Three Men and a Baby*. In 1977 she and Marvin Hamlisch wrote "Nobody Does It Better," for the James Bond film *The Spy Who Loved Me*. Then in 1981 she won an Oscar together with Peter Allen, Christopher Cross, and Burt Bacharach for the theme song of the film *Arthur*.

The following year she married her songwriting partner, Burt Bacharach. They had a son, but the marriage ended after nine years.

Carole Sager has collaborated with a number of composers, among them Peter Allen, Marvin Hamlisch, Neil Diamond, Michael Masser, Toni Wine, Albert Hammond, Bette Midler, Bruce Roberts, and Melissa Manchester. Her songs include "On My Own," "Ah My Sister," "They're Playing Our Song," "When I Need You," "It's My Turn," "Stronger than Before," "You're Moving Out Today," "Don't Cry Out Loud," "Come in from the Rain," and "Midnight Blue." In 1985 she and Burt Bacharach wrote the hit song "That's What Friends Are For" for an AIDS benefit. It subsequently won a Grammy. She has also made recordings of songs that she wrote with Burt Bacharach.

Besides songwriting, Carole Sager has also written a novel, *Extravagant Gestures* (1987).

SOURCES

Clarke, Donald. *Penguin Encyclopedia of Popular Music*.
La Blanc, Michael. *Contemporary Musicians*, vol. 5.
"Songwriters Sager, Bacharach to Be Divorced," *San Francisco Chronicle*, July 13,
      1991, p. C8.
Who's Who in America, 1989.

STREISAND, BARBRA (1942–   )   "Evergreen"

Singer and film star Barbra Joan Streisand was born on April 24, 1942, in Brooklyn, New York. Her father died when she was a year old, and she and her brother and sister were raised by their mother. The family was very poor. After graduating from high school, where she was a top student, Barbra Streisand decided to become an actress. For a time she attended Yeshiva University.

Then she won a talent contest at a club in Greenwich Village, which started her on a singing career. She began singing in night spots in the village and making television guest appearances.

In 1961 she made her theater debut in *Another Evening with Harry Stoones,* but her big break came when she was signed for the show *I Can Get It for You Wholesale* (1962). She had good reviews, and after that many offers came in. She sang at the White House for President John Kennedy and appeared on television on the shows of Bob Hope, Jack Paar, and Ed Sullivan. The next year she sang at the Coconut Grove in Hollywood.

Her album *Barbra Streisand* became the top-selling album by a female vocalist in 1963. Two more top-selling albums followed.

In 1963 she married Elliot Gould, who had been her leading man in *I Can Get It for You Wholesale.* They had a son and have since divorced.

Her role as Fanny Brice in *Funny Girl* on Broadway in 1964 gave Barbra Streisand a chance to show her ability as a comedienne. Then, performing on television in 1965 in "My Name Is Barbra," she won an Emmy.

After her success on Broadway she went to Hollywood and became one of the top box office performers in the movies. Her first film there, a remake of the Broadway show *Funny Girl*, won her an Oscar. Since then she has made many more musicals, among them *Hello, Dolly!, On a Clear Day You Can See Forever, The Owl and the Pussycat,* and *Funny Lady.* Although she began as a singer, she has moved into acting roles and comedy parts. Among her straight dramatic films are *What's Up Doc?, The Way We Were, Up the Sandbox, For Pete's Sake, A Star Is Born, Main Event, All Night Long,* and *Nuts.*

After years of starring in films, Barbra Streisand began to work as a film producer and director. Probably her most ambitious film was *Yentl* (1983), in which she was the co-author, producer, director, and star. In 1992 she directed and co-starred in the film *Prince of Tides,* which was nominated for several Oscars.

Barbra Streisand has won numerous awards, including two Academy Awards, a Tony, an Emmy, and many Grammys for Best Female Vocalist.

As a songwriter, her most successful effort was "Evergreen," which she wrote with Paul Williams. It won an Academy Award for Best Song in 1976. She has also co-authored "Answer Me" and "Lost Inside of You," the latter with Leon Russell.

SOURCES

Hitchcock, H. Wiley. *New Grove Dictionary of American Music.*
Moritz, Charles. *Current Biography,* 1964.
Who's Who of American Women, 1990.

THOMPSON, KAY   *See* Pop Rock.

WATERS, ETHEL   *See* Blues.

WAYNE, MABEL (1898/1904–1978)   "It Happened in Monterrey"

Composer Mabel Wayne was among the first to write songs for motion pictures in the new era of sound movies.

Born in Brooklyn, New York, on July 16, 1898 or 1904, she studied music at the New York School of Music and studied privately in Switzerland. At the age of 16 she began a career in vaudeville as a pianist, singer, and dancer. In the 1920s she turned to songwriting.

She composed her first hit song, "In a Little Spanish Town," in 1926. It had lyrics by Sam M. Lewis and Joe Young.

In 1928, a year after the first sound motion picture, she and L. Wolfe Gilbert wrote the song "When the Right One Comes Along" for the movie *Marriage by Contract.* But their big hit that year was for the movie *Ramona* (1928), which starred Dolores Del Rio. Mabel Wayne's title song, with lyrics by L. Wolfe Gilbert, became the biggest-selling song of its day, selling nearly 2 million records.

For the film *King of Jazz* (1930), Mabel Wayne composed "It Happened in Monterrey," with lyrics by Billy Rose. In 1936 she wrote songs with Buddy Rogers for the movie *Dance Band.*

Among Mabel Wayne's hit songs were "Little Man You've Had a Busy Day," written with Al Hoffman and Maurice Sigler, and "As Long as You're Not in Love with Anyone Else," with lyrics by Al Lewis. Among the other songs she wrote with L. Wolfe Gilbert were "Chiquita," "Indian Cradle," and "Don't Wake Me Up, Let Me Dream." The latter was written by Wayne, Gilbert, and Abel Baer.

In the 1940s Mabel Wayne wrote the poignant "I Understand" and "A Dreamer's Holiday," both with lyrics by Kim Gannon. Other songs she composed in the 1940s include "A Cabana in Havana," "Be Fair," and "It Happened in Hawaii." She also collaborated on songs with Mitchell Parish.

Mabel Wayne died in 1978.

SOURCES

Burton, Jack. *Blue Book of Hollywood Musicals.*
Claghorn, Charles E. *Biographical Dictionary of American Music.*
Dahl, Linda. *Stormy Weather.*
Ewen, David. *Life and Death of Tin Pan Alley.*
Kinkle, Roger. *Complete Encyclopedia of Popular Music and Jazz.*
Lynn Farnol Group. *ASCAP Biographical Dictionary.*
Mattfeld, Julius. *Variety Music Cavalcade.*
Munden, Kenneth. *American Film Institute*, 1920–30.
New York Times Film Reviews.
Spaeth, Sigmund. *History of Popular Music in America.*

III

MUSICALS

INTRODUCTION

During the early years of the twentieth century the most popular musical shows were operettas. They had romantic, sentimental stories in European settings. The shows had extensive music, large orchestras, and large casts of singers with classically trained voices. The leading operetta composers Victor Herbert, Sigmund Romberg, and Rudolf Friml frequently worked with women lyricists. Rida Johnson Young, Dorothy Donnelly, Anne Caldwell, and Clare Kummer worked with one or more of these composers. The women usually wrote both the book and lyrics, and they created many successful operettas, among them *Naughty Marietta, Blossom Time, The Student Prince,* and *Maytime*. They also wrote many memorable songs such as "Ah! Sweet Mystery of Life," "Deep in My Heart Dear," "Will You Remember?," "Golden Days," and "Your Land Is My Land."

Besides operettas, many women wrote songs for vaudeville and revues. Even stars like Nora Bayes and Elsie Janis wrote their own material, including songs. Nora Bayes co-authored "Shine On Harvest Moon" for her performance in the *Ziegfeld Follies* of 1908. The multitalented Elsie Janis in addition to performing wrote many revues, books, and screenplays, as well as songs.

Even while the operetta was still popular, some composers had grown tired of it and were trying to create a more indigenous type of musical. Jerome Kern in 1915 began developing small, intimate situational comedies with catchy songs and clever lyrics. His collaborators for these shows were

British writers Guy Bolton and P. G. Wodehouse, but Kern also worked with several women. Anne Caldwell wrote eight musicals with him and Elsie Janis, Clare Kummer, and Rida Johnson Young each wrote one with Kern. "Some Sort of Somebody" was the best Janis-Kern song, and "Once in a Blue Moon" was a hit Caldwell-Kern song.

By the end of the 1920s another woman was beginning her long career on Broadway, Dorothy Fields. She wrote the lyrics to her first hit, "I Can't Give You Anything but Love," in 1928 with music by Jimmy McHugh.

By the mid-1930s three of the great early lyricists had died: Rida Johnson Young, Dorothy Donnelly, and Anne Caldwell. Clare Kummer wrote her last musical in 1937. It was the end of that generation of great women librettists and lyricists.

Throughout the 1940s and 1950s, however, new women composers and lyricists came on the scene. Kay Swift composed the musical *Fine and Dandy* with its hit title song. Nancy Hamilton wrote the lyrics to several musicals. *Two for the Show* contained her hit "How High the Moon." Betty Comden also began her career during this period. She has written songs and appeared in shows on Broadway for nearly 50 years. Two of her hit show tunes for which she co-authored lyrics are "Make Someone Happy" and "The Party's Over."

In the 1960s and 1970s Carolyn Leigh was one of the top lyricists. She wrote lyrics for a number of musicals and for these tunes: "Hey, Look Me Over" and "I've Got Your Number." The team of Gretchen Cryer and Nancy Ford wrote several musicals during this period, including a rock musical, *The Last Sweet Days of Isaac*, and a feminist musical, *I'm Getting My Act Together and Taking It on the Road*.

Today women are still involved in writing songs for Broadway musicals. Cryer and Ford continue writing provocative, experimental musicals, as they have done since the 1960s. Elizabeth Swados continues as a composer-lyricist of distinctive and highly original works. Betty Comden co-authored lyrics for *The Will Rogers Follies* in 1991, and the same year two new talents emerged with the musical *The Secret Garden* (1991), composer Lucy Simon and librettist-lyricist Marsha Norman.

BAYES, NORA (1880–1928)   "Shine on Harvest Moon"

Nora Bayes was a famous performer in vaudeville and on Broadway in the early 1900s. She was one of the top stars along with **Elsie Janis** and Eva Tanguay. Billed as "The Greatest Single Woman Singing Comedienne in the World," she was a small woman with sparkling eyes and a deep voice. She lived a flamboyant life, married five times, and adopted three children.

She was born Dora Goldberg in 1880 in Joliet, Illinois. In her teens she worked as a chorus girl in vaudeville at the Chicago Opera House and made her first Broadway appearance in *Rogers Brothers in Washington* (1901). In subsequent years she appeared in the *Ziegfeld Follies* and in numerious musicals and revues.

She and her second husband, Jack Norworth, wrote songs for several of the stage shows in which they appeared. Their most famous song was "Shine on Harvest Moon." Her husband wrote the words, and together they wrote the music. They introduced it in the *Ziegfeld Follies of 1908*, and it became a huge success. Some of their other songs were "Fancy You Fancying Me," "Way Down in Cuba," "My Mandy," "I'm Sorry," "Come Along," and "Young America." Other songs that Nora Bayes wrote or co-authored include "Back to My Old Home Town," "Falling Star," "Prohibition Blues," "Without You," and "When Jack Comes Sailing Home Again." She and Seymour Simons wrote the song "Just like a Gypsy" for the 1918 show *Ladies First* in which Nora Bayes appeared. Her last appearance was in *Queen o' Hearts* in 1922.

Although Nora Bayes, reportedly, had earned as much as $100,000 a year, she died insolvent on March 19, 1928, in Brooklyn, New York.

The 1944 movie *Shine on Harvest Moon*, starring Dennis Morgan and Ann Sheridan, was based on the life of Jack Norworth and Nora Bayes.

SOURCES

Bloom, Ken. *American Song.*
James, Edward. *Notable American Women.*
Kinkle, Roger. *Complete Encyclopedia of Popular Music and Jazz.*
Mattfeld, Julius. *Variety Music Cavalcade.*
Slide, Anthony. *Vaudevillians.*
Spaeth, Sigmund. *History of Popular Music in America.*

CALDWELL, ANNE (1867–1936)   "Once in a Blue Moon"

For more than 20 years Anne Caldwell was a Broadway librettist and lyricist. Between 1907 and 1928 she wrote the book for more than 25 successful musicals and the lyrics for many more, collaborating with composers such as Jerome Kern, Vincent Youmans, Victor Herbert, and Jean Schwartz.

She was born in Boston, Massachusetts, on August 30, 1867. As a child she was encouraged by her mother to write music and plays. She attended a school in Fairhaven, Massachusetts, and the Friends Academy in New

Bedford, where she wrote the school play. But it was as a singer with the Juvenile Opera Company that she began her career. Then for a few years she was an actress; but she turned to writing plays and songs with James O'Dea, who became her husband.

By 1906 she and O'Dea had a song interpolated into a Broadway show, *The Social Whirl*. The following year she and Manuel Klein wrote the music, and James O'Dea the lyrics, for the musical *Top o' the World*.

By 1910 two of Anne Caldwell's plays were being performed, *A Model Girl* and *The Nest Egg*. With her husband she wrote *Uncle Sam*, which was produced the following year.

In 1912 Anne Caldwell began working with Victor Herbert. She and Lawrence McCarty wrote the libretto, and James O'Dea the lyrics, for Victor Herbert's musical Cinderella story, *The Lady of the Slipper*. It had a fine cast including Fred Stone, **Elsie Janis,** David Montgomery, dancer Vernon Castle, and Peggy Wood. It ran for two seasons in New York and also played Chicago and Boston.

Next came *When Claudia Smiles* (1914), for which she wrote the book and lyrics to the music of Jean Schwartz. Two of the songs were "I've Got Everything I Want but You" and "You're My Boy."

The following year she and R. H. Burnside co-authored the book of an exotic extravaganza called *Chin Chin* (1914). The music was by Ivan Caryll, with lyrics by Anne Caldwell and James O'Dea. This modern Aladdin story ran a successful 295 performances.

This was James O'Dea's last work. In April 1914 he died. Thus at the age of 47 Anne Caldwell was a widow. Fortunately their two children were grown, but Anne had lost both her husband and her main songwriting partner. For solace she turned to her work.

By 1916 she had written two more shows, the book for *Go to It*, and the book and lyrics for *Pom-Pom*, with Hugo Felix's music. The latter starred Gertrude Vanderbilt.

Jack O'Lantern (1917) followed, with music by Ivan Caryll and lyrics by Anne Caldwell. The show featured the Caldwell-Caryll hit "Wait Till the Cows Come Home."

The following year she co-authored with P. G. Wodehouse the lyrics for the musical *The Canary* (1918). Two of her songs were "The Hunting Song," with music by Ivan Caryll, and "Oh, Doctor," with music by Harry Tierney.

For *She's a Good Fellow* (1919), she joined Jerome Kern to write both the libretto and the lyrics. The cast included the **Duncan** sisters, **Rosetta** and **Vivian.** The show ran 120 performances and featured the song "The

First Rose of Summer." The critics found the libretto "gossamer," "fresh and sparkling," and "dangerously clever" (Bordman, *Oxford,* p. 120).

The same year Anne Caldwell wrote the lyrics and book for *The Lady in Red,* with music by Robert Winterberg, but it was not a success.

The next year, 1920, was a very productive year for Anne Caldwell. She did four shows. With Jerome Kern she did the musical *Hitchy Koo,* co-authoring the book with Glen MacDonough. A young Grace Moore was in the cast, but the show ran only seven performances. However, the other Kern-Caldwell show that year was a hit, *The Night Boat* (1920), for which she wrote the book as well as the lyrics. The top songs from the show were "Left All Alone Again Blues," and "Whose Baby Are You?" The same year she did the book and lyrics for both *The Sweetheart Shop* (1920), with music by Hugo Felix, and *Tip Top* (1920), with music by Ivan Caryll. She also had one of her songs, "The Lorelei," interpolated into Jerome Kern's musical *Sally.*

The next year she had another hit with Jerome Kern, *Good Morning Dearie* (1921), for which she authored the book and lyrics. Her hit song from this show was "Ka-lu-a." The show starred Ina Claire.

The Caldwell-Kern *Bunch and Judy* (1922) show featured Adele and Fred Astaire. Anne Caldwell wrote the lyrics and co-authored the book with Hugh Ford. The featured songs were "How Do You Do, Katinka?" and "Lovely Lassie." Also in 1922 she wrote the story for a silent motion picture, *The Top o' the Morning.*

The following year she and Jerome Kern wrote *Stepping Stones* (1923). It starred Fred Stone and Allene Crater (Mrs. Stone), and introduced daughter Dorothy Stone in a modern version of the Red Riding Hood tale. The show featured one of Kern and Caldwell's loveliest songs, "Once in a Blue Moon," in addition to "Raggedy Ann" and "In Love with Love." Anne Caldwell wrote the lyrics and co-authored the book with R. H. Burnside.

In 1924 she wrote the lyrics to Hugo Felix's music in *Peg o' My Dreams,* as well as the book and lyrics for *The Magnolia Lady,* with music by Harold Levey.

In 1925 Anne Caldwell, James Montgomery, and Jerome Kern wrote *The City Chap.* The cast included Richard "Skeet" Gallagher, Irene Dunne, Betty Compton, and George Raft, but the musical had a short run. The same year Anne Caldwell wrote another movie. She adapted her play *The Nest Egg* for the movie *Marry Me,* which starred Florence Vidor and Edward Everett Horton.

The Broadway musical *Oh, Please!* (1926) had music by Vincent Youmans and lyrics by Anne Caldwell and Otto Harbach. It starred Beatrice Lillie and Charles Winninger. The featured song was Caldwell-Youmans's "I Know That You Know." The same year Anne Caldwell and Otto Harbach wrote the book and lyrics for *Criss-Cross* (1926), with Jerome Kern's music. The show starred Fred Stone and daughter Dorothy in a comic musical with such songs as "Hydrophobia Blues" and "Indignation Meeting." It had a successful run.

At the age of 60 Anne Caldwell was still turning out one or two shows a year for Broadway. In 1927 she co-authored the book for *Take the Air* and wrote lyrics for *Yours Truly*. Her last Broadway show was *Three Cheers* (1928), for which she wrote the lyrics and co-authored the book.

Then in 1930 she moved to Hollywood to write for the movies. That year she collaborated with Harry Tierney on the story and songs for *Dixiana* and on the songs for the film *Half Shot at Sunrise*. She may also have worked on the films *Flying Down to Rio* (1933) and *Babes in Toyland* (1934).

Of the songs that Anne Caldwell wrote, most had significance only in the context of the musical. However, a few did achieve success on their own, such as "I Know That You Know" and "Once in a Blue Moon." Some of her other songs include "Whose Baby Are You?," "Raggedy Ann," "Left All Alone Again Blues," "Ka-lu-a," "Wait Till the Cows Come Home," "Come and Have a Swing with Me," "In Araby with You," "You Will, Won't You?," "Look at the World and Smile," "Somebody Else," and "In Love with Love."

Anne Caldwell spent the remaining years of her life in California, where her two children, Molly and Kenneth O'Dea, lived. She wrote for the movies until her death on October 22, 1936, in Beverly Hills at the age of 69.

Anne Caldwell was one of the few women elected to the Songwriters' Hall of Fame.

SOURCES
Bloom, Ken. *American Song.*
Bordman, Gerald. *Jerome Kern.*
Bordman, Gerald. *Oxford Companion to American Theatre.*
Dahl, Linda. *Stormy Weather.*
Davis, Sheila. *Craft of Lyric Writing.*
Ewen, David. *Complete Book of American Musical Theater.*
Ewen, David. *New Complete Book of American Musical Theater.*
Green, Stanley. *World of Musical Comedy.*
Kinkle, Roger. *Complete Encyclopedia of Popular Music and Jazz.*
Lewine, Richard. *Songs of American Theater.*
Munden, Kenneth. *American Film Institute, 1921–30.*
New York Times Film Reviews.
New York Times Theater Reviews.
New York Times. Obituaries, October 24, 1936, p. 17.
Spaeth, Sigmund. *History of Popular Music in America.*
Who Was Who in the Theatre.

CARROLL, JUNE (n.d.)   "Love Is a Simple Thing"

June Carroll has been a singer, actress, screenwriter, and songwriter. She worked in Broadway musical revues for more than 30 years.

Born June Betty Sillman on June 22 in Detroit, Michigan, she made her stage debut at the age of five singing in a local theater. Her family moved to Los Angeles, where she went to school and studied voice privately. There she performed in several local shows before moving to New York for a try at Broadway.

New Faces of 1934 gave her a chance as an understudy and as one of the lyricists. After this she wrote lyrics for several other shows: *Fools Rush In* (1935), *New Faces of 1936*, and *Who's Who* (1938), in which she also appeared. She wrote both the lyrics and music for *All in Fun* (1940).

In the 1940s June Carroll worked in Hollywood as a screenwriter for Republic Pictures and also appeared in the film *An Angel Comes to Brooklyn* (1943). She also worked for the Broadway stage, in 1943 writing sketches and lyrics for *New Faces of 1943*, with music by Lee Wainer and Will Irwin. She then collaborated with David Raksin on the show *If the Shoe Fits* (1946), which had only a short run.

For *New Faces of 1952*, in which she also appeared, she wrote songs with Arthur Siegel—"Love Is a Simple Thing," "He Takes Me off His Income Tax," "Penny Candy," and the song that introduced Eartha Kitt, "Monotonous." Two years later a film, titled simply *New Faces*, was made of this show; this movie version featured June Carroll, Eartha Kitt, Alice Ghostley, Paul Lynde, Ronny Graham, and Robert Clary.

Arthur Siegel and June Carroll continued to collaborate. The following year they worked together on *Shoestring Revue* (1955) for off-Broadway. The next year they did *New Faces of 1956*, writing the songs "Tell Her," "A Doll's House," "Don't Wait Till It's Too Late to See Paris," and "Boy Most Likely to Succeed." The show ran a successful season.

In 1957 June Carroll wrote both lyrics and music for *Mask and Gown*, which toured the country. The story was conceived and staged by her brother, Leonard Sillman, who also co-authored the show with Ronny Graham and June's husband, Sidney Carroll. Music and lyrics were by Ronny Graham, June Carroll, Arthur Siegel, and Dorothea Freitag.

Hi, Paisano! (1961), for which June Carroll wrote the lyrics to Robert Holton's music, was not successful and closed after three performances.

The following year she and Arthur Siegel again collaborated, doing the songs for *New Faces of 1962*, among them "I Want You to Be the First to

Know," "The Other One," and "Love Is Good." For *New Faces of 1968* they wrote "Where Is Me," among other songs.

In 1973 she wrote the lyrics to "Open Your Eyes and Dream" for the television special "Miracle on 34th Street."

As a singer and actress, June Carroll has also performed in many night clubs and theaters, on radio and television, and in summer stock.

She was first married to Leonard Reich and had a son. In 1940 she married writer Sidney Carroll. They had three children. She is the sister of Leonard Sillman, author, performer, and producer of many of the *New Faces* revues.

SOURCES

Lewine, Richard. *Songs of American Theater.*
Lynn Farnol Group. *ASCAP Biographical Dictionary.*
Rigdon, Walter. *Notable Names in American Theatre.*
Salem, James. *Guide to Critical Reviews.*
Who's Who of American Women, 1964.

COMDEN, BETTY (1915/1919–   )   "Make Someone Happy"

Betty Comden is probably best known as half of the team of Comden and Green, performers and also writers of lyrics, musicals, comic sketches, and screenplays. She has had a long career on Broadway and in motion pictures.

Born Betty Cohen in New York City on May 3, 1915/1919, she was educated at New York University. While she was a student, she performed with the Washington Square Players. In her early twenties she joined Adolph Green and Judy Holliday in a night club act called The Revuers, which did satirical songs and sketches. Leonard Bernstein, a friend of Green's, sometimes accompanied them at the piano. Later they moved uptown and performed in clubs and theaters. Then they took their act to Hollywood. While there, they had a small role in the film *Greenwich Village* (1944).

In the meantime Leonard Bernstein wrote a ballet, *Fancy Free,* which became a hit, and plans were made to turn it into a Broadway musical. Bernstein suggested hiring Comden and Green to write the book and lyrics. The musical, called *On the Town* (1944), was an exuberant, funny, poignant story of three sailors on a 24-hour leave in search of girls. Both Comden and Green had parts in the show. It opened in December 1944 during the dark days of World War II, and its sprightly story lifted audiences' spirits. It became a hit, running 463 performances.

With this first effort, which proved so successful, Comden and Green began their more than 40 years of writing books and lyrics for Broadway.

They wrote with top composers. In addition to Leonard Bernstein, they worked with Morton Gould, Jule Styne, and Andre Previn.

In 1945 they did the lyrics to Morton Gould's music for *Billion Dollar Baby*, which ran seven months. Then Metro Goldwyn Mayer (MGM) hired them to write the screenplay for the film *Good News* (1947) and the lyrics to the song "The French Lesson."

This was followed by *The Barkleys of Broadway* (1949), a Fred Astaire–Ginger Rogers musical for which Comden and Green wrote the witty screenplay. They also wrote the scenario for the film *On the Town* (1949), with Gene Kelly and Frank Sinatra. They added a new song, "Prehistoric Man," with music by Roger Edens, to the film version. Also that year they wrote the scenario for *Take Me Out to the Ball Game*, again with Sinatra and Kelly.

Back on Broadway, they wrote sketches and lyrics for the revue *Two on the Aisle* (1951), with music by Jule Styne. The cast included Bert Lahr, Dolores Gray, Colette Marchand, and Elliott Reid. Their songs included "Hold Me, Hold Me, Hold Me" and "Give a Little, Get a Little Love."

In 1952 they wrote the original story and screenplay for a film that became a Gene Kelly classic, *Singin' in the Rain*.

The motion picture *The Band Wagon* (1953) also had a Comden and Green screenplay.

In 1953 they were given a real challenge. The original lyricist and composer of a show had suddenly quit, and it was only five weeks before the show was to begin rehearsals. Together with Leonard Bernstein, they agreed to write a musical in five weeks. The show they wrote was *Wonderful Town*, which became a hit. It was based on a play by Joseph Fields (**Dorothy Fields's** brother) and Jerome Chodorov called *My Sister Eileen*, which itself was based on the novel by Ruth McKenney. The story was about two sisters from Ohio who go to New York City to find success and fame, one as a writer, the other as an actress. The show, which starred Rosalind Russell and Edith Adams, included such songs as "Ohio" and "A Little Bit in Love." Comden and Green received both a Tony and a Donaldson award for their lyrics.

In 1954 they contributed songs to a new version of the perennial favorite, *Peter Pan*. Several songwriting teams worked on the show. A little more than half the songs were written by **Carolyn Leigh** and Mark Charlap, but Comden, Green, and Jule Styne contributed many of the songs, among them the lovely "Never-Never Land," "Wendy," "Ugg-a-Wugg," "Pow-Wow Polka," and "Captain Hook's Waltz." This revival starred Mary Martin as Peter Pan and Cyril Ritchard as the wicked Captain Hook. Jerome Robbins staged the production. Although this revival did not run on Broadway as long as Leonard Bernstein's *Peter Pan* had, the television production and reruns have made it the version most people remember.

In 1955 Comden and Green wrote the screenplay and lyrics for another Gene Kelly musical, *It's Always Fair Weather*. For this they won their second Screenwriter's Award.

A Party with Betty Comden and Adolph Green, which they wrote, brought Comden and Green back to the stage as performers. In this show they sang their hit songs. They had a successful off-Broadway run and then toured. The show was revived in 1975 and televised in 1977. For this show they won an Obie.

In 1958 they wrote the screenplay for *Auntie Mame*. The same year they wrote the lyrics for *Say, Darling,* with music by Jule Styne. The show starred David Wayne, Vivian Blaine, and Johnny Desmond.

Another screenplay followed, *Bells Are Ringing* (1960), which starred their old friend from the Revuers, Judy Holliday, who had since become a successful movie star. *Do Re Mi* (1960) had music by Jule Styne and lyrics by Betty Comden and Adolph Green with book by Garson Kanin. Phil Silvers, Nancy Walker, and John Reardon starred in the show, which ran only 40 performances. However, the show contained a hit song that became very popular, "Make Someone Happy."

The following year Comden and Green wrote the book and lyrics for *Subways Are for Sleeping* (1961), another collaboration with Jule Styne. The featured songs were the title song and "Comes Once in a Lifetime." In the cast were Sydney Chaplin, Carol Lawrence, Orson Bean, and Phyllis Newman.

They followed this with book and lyrics to *Fade Out–Fade In* (1964), a screenplay for *What a Way to Go* (1964), and lyrics for *Hallelujah, Baby!* (1967). Then in 1970 they wrote the libretto for the musical *Applause,* which starred Lauren Bacall.

The 1974 musical *Lorelei,* starring Carol Channing, had songs by Comden and Green, Leo Robin and Jule Styne. The main Comden and Green songs were "I Won't Let You Get Away" and the title song, "Lorelei." The show was a success, running 320 performances.

Other songs from the collaboration of Betty Comden, Adolph Green, and Jule Styne are "Just in Time," "The Party's Over," "Comes Once in a Lifetime," "Make Someone Happy," and "Long before I Knew You." With Leonard Bernstein Comden and Green wrote "New York, New York," "Lonely Town," "Lucky to Be Me," "It's Love," and "Ya Got Me."

In 1981 Comden and Green were inducted into the New York drama critics' Theater Hall of Fame. A few years later, in 1984, Betty Comden appeared in the show *Isn't It Romantic?*

The lifelong collaboration of Betty Comden and Adolph Green has continued into the 1990s. In 1991 they wrote the lyrics for the show that reopened the historic Palace Theater in New York City, *The Will Rogers Follies*. The music was by Cy Coleman, the book by Peter Stone, and the direction and choreography by Tommy Tune. Keith Carradine starred in the title role. For their work Betty Comden, Adolph Green, and Cy Coleman won a Tony for the best original musical score.

Betty Comden is married to designer Steven Kyle and has two children. Adolph Green is married to actress Phyllis Newman and also has two children.

SOURCES

Baxter, Ian. *Who's Who in Theatre.*
Davis, Sheila. *Craft of Lyric Writing.*
Ewen, David. *American Songwriters.*
Ewen, David. *Complete Book of American Musical Theater.*
Ewen, David. *New Complete Book of American Musical Theater.*
Green, Stanley. *World of Musical Comedy.*
Lewine, Richard. *Songs of American Theater.*
Lynn Farnol Group. *ASCAP Biographical Dictionary.*
New York Times Film Reviews.
"Renovated NY Palace to Reopen." *San Francisco Chronicle*, April 1, 1991, p. E4.
Rothe, Anna. *Current Biography.*
Salem, James. *Guide to Critical Reviews.*

CRYER, GRETCHEN (1935–   )   "Strong Woman Number"

Actress, composer, librettist, and lyricist Gretchen Cryer was born Gretchen Kiger in Dunreith, Indiana on October 17, 1935. She attended DePauw University. In 1958 she married actor David Cryer. They had two children and are now divorced.

Gretchen Cryer began writing musicals with her long-time collaborator **Nancy Ford** when they were in college together. Cryer wrote the libretto and lyrics, and Ford the music. After college, Gretchen Cryer worked as a secretary, putting her husband through school. Then she became an actress and appeared in many of her own musicals.

In 1967 Cryer and Ford wrote *Now Is the Time for All Good Men*, which dealt with the Vietnam War issues. Some of their songs were "All Alone," "On My Own," and "Rain Your Love on Me." The musical ran 112 performances. They continued their collaboration and in 1970 wrote the rock musical *The Last Sweet Days of Isaac*, which received critical acclaim and an Obie Award for best musical. It ran 485 performances off-Broadway.

Some of the songs were "Love You Came to Me," "A Transparent Crystal Moment," and "My Most Important Moments Go By."

Then in 1971 Gretchen Cryer worked with Doug Dyer and Peter Link to write the libretto for *The Wedding of Iphigenia,* which was adapted from Euripides' play. Peter Link also wrote the music. The off-Broadway production ran several months.

Cryer and Ford's first on-Broadway musical, *Shelter* (1973), ran 31 performances. It had book and lyrics by Gretchen Cryer and music by Nancy Ford. Some of the songs from *Shelter* included "Don't Tell Me It's Forever," "She's My Girl," and "Changing."

Their *I'm Getting My Act Together and Taking It on the Road* (1978) explored feminist issues. The public liked the show even though it received mostly unfavorable reviews from the critics. Nevertheless, it had a long run, including performances in Chicago and Los Angeles. Some of the songs were "Dear Tom," "Feel the Love," "Natural High," "Strong Woman Number," and "Lonely Lady," the latter with both words and music by Gretchen Cryer.

In the 1980s she authored the musicals *Booth Is Back in Town* (1981) and *Eleanor* (1984), as well as a musical revue with Nancy Ford, *Hang On to the Good Times* (1985). Gretchen Cryer also wrote the play *The House That Goes On Forever* (1988).

SOURCES

Lewine, Richard. *Songs of American Theater.*
Lyons, H. "Gretchen Cryer: Friends and Lovers." *Ms,* December 1978, p. 49.
May, Hal. *Contemporary Authors.*
Salem, James. *Guide to Critical Reviews.*
Who's Who in America, 1990.

CUSHING, CATHERINE (1874–1952)

"L'Amour, Toujours, L'Amour"

Catherine Cushing was primarily a playwright, but she also wrote the book and lyrics for several musicals.

She was born Catherine Chisholm in Mt. Perry, Ohio on April 15, 1874, and was educated at the Pennsylvania College for Women in Pittsburgh. Before turning to playwriting, she was an editor for *Harper's Bazaar.* She was married to Henry Howard Cushing.

Among the plays she wrote were *Miss Ananias* (1911), *The Real Thing* (1911), *Kitty McKay* (1913), *Widow-by-Proxy* (1913), *Jerry* (1914), and *Pollyanna* (1916).

In 1918 she began working on musicals. She wrote the book and lyrics to *Glorianna*, with Rudolf Friml's music. The cast included Eleanor Painter and Alexander Clark, and the show ran 96 performances.

Catherine Cushing also wrote the book and lyrics for *Lassie* (1920) and the book for *Marjolaine* (1922), both with music by Hugo Felix.

The following year she collaborated with the **Duncan** sisters and wrote the book for *Topsy and Eva*. The Duncan sisters wrote the lyrics and music. The show was developed from a vaudeville routine the Duncans had performed for years and was based on the book *Uncle Tom's Cabin*. It became the Duncans' most successful vehicle.

In 1925 Catherine Cushing wrote *Edgar Allan Poe*, a play about the famous poet and short story writer. That same year she also adapted *Masters of the Inn*.

Of the songs Catherine Cushing wrote the most successful was "L'Amour, Toujours, L'Amour," with music by Rudolf Friml. It was written in 1922 and years later was sung by Susanna Foster in a film, *This Is the Life* (1944). Other songs by Catherine Cushing include "Chianti," "Dilly-Dally-O," "Read between the Lines," "John and Priscilla," and "When Brown Eyes Looked in Eyes of Blue."

Catherine Cushing died in New York after a long illness on October 19, 1952, at the age of 78.

SOURCES

Bloom, Ken. *American Song*.
Bordman, Gerald. *Oxford Companion to American Theatre*.
Lynn Farnol Group. *ASCAP Biographical Dictionary*.
Mantle, Burns. *Contemporary American Playwrights*.
Mattfeld, Julius. *Variety Music Cavalcade*.
New York Times. Obituaries, October 21, 1952, p. 29.
Salem, James. *Guide to Critical Reviews*.
Spaeth, Sigmund. *History of Popular Music in America*.
Who Was Who in Theatre.

DONNELLY, DOROTHY (1880–1928)

"Deep in My Heart Dear"

Dorothy Agnes Donnelly was born into a theater family. Her father managed the Grand Opera House of New York, her mother was an actress, and her brother became director of a theater stock company; so it was not surprising that Dorothy Donnelly chose to make her career in the theater.

She was born on January 28, 1880, in New York City and educated at the Convent of Sacred Heart before beginning her stage career in her brother's stock company. In 1903 she was the actress who introduced the

role of Shaw's *Candida* to America, but her most celebrated role was starring in *Madame X* (1910).

From 1914 to 1916 she starred in three silent films, including the film
version of *Madame X*.

After ten years as an actress, Dorothy Donnelly gave up acting and began writing librettos for musicals. Her early work as a co-librettist of *Flora
Bella* (1916) and also of *Fancy Free* (1918) was so successful that she decided to leave acting for writing, but World War I intervened. During the
war years, she gave up her work and went overseas to entertain the troops.

When the war was over, she returned to Broadway and started working
on a musical with Sigmund Romberg. It was the beginning of a very successful collaboration that produced some of America's most beloved light
opera ballads. Their first musical was *Blossom Time* (1921), based on a Viennese operetta about Franz Schubert's life and music. Sigmund Romberg
adapted Schubert's music, and Dorothy Donnelly wrote the book and lyrics. The show was an enormous success and ran for almost two years. Many
road companies took it across the United States, and it was often revived
in subsequent years. It featured the songs "Serenade," "Ave Maria," and
"Song of Love."

Two years later Dorothy Donnelly wrote the book and lyrics for the mu-
sical *Poppy* (1923), with composers Stephen Jones and Arthur Samuels.
The show, which starred W. C. Fields, included the songs "Stepping
Around," "The Girl I've Never Met," "Choose a Partner Please," and "Poppy
Dear."

The following year Dorothy Donnelly rejoined Sigmund Romberg to cre-
ate what became their most successful musical, *The Student Prince* (1924),
for which she wrote both the book and the lyrics. Like *Blossom Time*, *The
Student Prince* was based on a drama that had been successful in Europe.
It was the story of a thwarted romance between a prince and a commoner.
When his father dies, the prince must choose between his love for a girl
and his duty to his country. The sentimental story together with Sigmund
Romberg's fine score made this an enduring favorite. It ran 608 perfor-
mances on Broadway and had numerous tours and revivals. In addition,
two motion pictures were made of it—the first in 1927 with Ramon No-
varro and Norma Shearer, the second in 1954 with Ann Blyth and Edmund
Purdom singing with the dubbed-in voice of Mario Lanza. Memorable
Donnelly-Romberg songs from this show were "Golden Days," "Deep in
My Heart, Dear," "Serenade," and "Drinking Song."

Hello, Lola! (1926) had a book and lyrics by Dorothy Donnelly and music
by William Kernell, but it ran only a month.

Donnelly and Romberg wrote two more shows in 1927. She wrote the book and lyrics for both *My Maryland,* which was successful, and *My Princess,* which was not. The best-known songs from *My Maryland* were "Your Land and My Land" and "Silver Moon."

Before *My Princess* went into rehearsals, Dorothy Donnelly had fallen ill and was unable to help with the revisions that might have enabled the show to succeed. However, her illness was serious. For five years she had suffered from a kidney disease and yet continued to work. On January 3, 1928, just two months after she was taken ill, she died of pneumonia at home in New York City. She was 47.

SOURCES

Bloom, Ken. *American Song.*
Bordman, Gerald. *Oxford Companion to American Theatre.*
Ewen, David. *Complete Book of American Musical Theater.*
Ewen, David. *New Complete Book of American Musical Theater.*
Green, Stanley. *World of Musical Comedy.*
Hanson, Patricia. *American Film Institute, 1911–20.*
Kinkle, Roger. *Complete Encyclopedia of Popular Music and Jazz.*
Lewine, Richard. *Songs of American Theater.*
Lynn Farnol Group. *ASCAP Biographical Dictionary.*
New York Times Film Reviews.
New York Times. Obituaries, January 4, 1928, p. 25.
Spaeth, Sigmund. *History of Popular Music in America.*
Who Was Who in Theatre.

DUNCAN, ROSETTA (1900–1959)
DUNCAN, VIVIAN (1902–   )   "Rememb'ring"

The Duncan sisters, Rosetta and Vivian, were well-known performers in vaudeville and in Broadway musicals in the 1920s and 1930s. Both sisters were born in Los Angeles, Rosetta on November 23, 1900, and Vivian on June 17, 1902.

As youngsters the Duncan sisters developed a Topsy and Eva routine based on *Uncle Tom's Cabin.* Rosetta, in blackface, played Topsy, and Vivian played the blonde Eva. After performing their Topsy song-and-dance routine in San Francisco, they decided to take it to New York. They arrived in that city with only $4 between them, but fortunately they were given a chance to perform and New York loved them.

On Broadway they were featured in many musicals, such as *She's a Good Fellow, Tip Top,* and *Doing Our Bit.* In 1923 they expanded their Topsy routine into a musical, *Topsy and Eva.* **Catherine Cushing** wrote the book for the show, and the Duncans wrote the music and lyrics. The musical was so successful that the Duncan sisters played in it for four years, touring throughout the United States, England, Europe, and South America. *Topsy and Eva* was one of the most profitable musicals of the decade, and with it the Duncans made their fortune. They even made a silent film of it called *Topsy*.

In 1927 the Duncans appeared in *Two Flaming Youths* on Broadway. In Hollywood, they wrote an early sound movie, *It's a Great Life* (1930), and they opened a music-publishing company.

Although it is believed that the Duncan sisters made more than a million dollars from their work, they lost it all in the Depression and declared bankruptcy in 1931. But like the old troupers that they were, they just started over again. In 1936 they were featured in the revue *New Faces of 1936*. In the 1940s during World War II they entertained the troops.

On December 4, 1959, Rosetta was involved in an auto accident in Chicago and died. Vivian worked solo for a time, but then retired with her husband, Frank Herman, in the San Francisco Bay area.

Some of the songs the Duncan sisters wrote were "Rememb'ring," "I Never Had a Mammy," "Do Re Mi," "The Moon Am Shinin'," "Someday Soon," "Los Angeles," "Hollywood Belongs to the World," and "United We Stand."

SOURCES
Bordman, Gerald. *Oxford Companion to American Theatre.*
Lynn Farnol Group. *ASCAP Biographical Dictionary.*
Mattfeld, Julius. *Variety Music Cavalcade.*
New York Times. Obituaries, December 5, 1959, p. 23.
Slide, Anthony. *Vaudevillians.*
Spaeth, Sigmund. *History of Popular Music in America.*

DUNHAM, KATHERINE   *See* Pop Rock.

FIELDS, DOROTHY (1905–1974)   "The Way You Look Tonight"

Undoubtedly the most successful woman lyricist of stage and screen was Dorothy Fields. During her career of nearly 50 years she worked with the top composers of Broadway and Hollywood. She was the first woman to receive an Academy Award for Best Song.

Dorothy Fields was born into a theater family. Her father, Lew Fields (Lewis Maurice Schoenfeld), had performed in vaudeville for years as part of the comedy team of Weber and Fields before becoming a producer. Three of his four children followed in his footsteps. Joseph became a playwright; Herbert, a librettist; and Dorothy, the youngest, a lyricist. Frances didn't choose to work in the theater.

Born in Allenhurst, New Jersey on July 15, 1905, Dorothy Fields played piano and wrote poetry from early childhood. She was raised in New York City and educated at the Benjamin School for Girls and Benjamin Franklin High School.

She grew up surrounded by theater people and theater activities. When Dorothy was 14, Richard Rodgers came to her home to play one of his songs in hopes of selling it to Lew Fields. The family listened as Richard Rodgers played "Any Old Place with You." Lew Fields liked it and bought it for one of his shows. It was Rodgers's first song on Broadway. Dorothy's brothers were friends of Richard Rodgers, and both of them worked with him in later years. In the 1920s Herbert Fields wrote the libretto for most of the Rodgers and Hart shows, and Joseph Fields worked with Rodgers and Oscar Hammerstein on *The Flower Drum Song* (1958). Dorothy sang in two of Richard Rodgers's early shows. They were for a benefit and ran only one night each. For the first show when she was 15, Dorothy Fields sang the role of Mary Queen of Scots. For the second show she appeared as Francois Villon in *If I Were King* (1922).

Dorothy Fields, however, was not so interested in performing as in writing. She began to write lyrics, for Jimmy McHugh, who paid her $50 for writing the lyrics to his song "Our American Girl." In 1926 she and McHugh began writing songs for the Cotton Club revues in Harlem, where black performers entertained a white audience.

Producer Lew Leslie was impressed with the Fields-McHugh work and hired them to write *Blackbirds of 1928*. The show was slow to catch on, and in order to keep it running, Fields and McHugh gave up their royalty payments. In time the show attracted an audience and became the biggest hit of the season. Their song "I Can't Give You Anything but Love" sold 3 million copies of sheet music.

Hello, Daddy (1929) followed, with libretto by Herbert Fields and songs by Dorothy Fields and Jimmy McHugh. That year Fields and McHugh also sold a song to the movies, "Collegiana," for the film *The Time, the Place and the Girl* (1929).

They had two hit songs in the *International Revue* (1930), which starred Gertrude Lawrence and Harry Richman, "On the Sunny Side of the Street" and "Exactly like You." They also wrote songs for the film *Love in the Rough* (1930), but their show *The Vanderbilt Revue* (1930) ran only 13 performances. It was a year of mixed results.

The following year, 1931, was more productive. They wrote three stage shows: *Rhapsody in Black, Shoot the Works,* and *Singin' the Blues,* as well as two films: *Flying High* and *The Cuban Love Song.* In 1932 they did songs for *Meet the Baron.*

Fields and McHugh had a hit song, "Don't Blame Me," in *Dancing Lady* (1933), the film in which Fred Astaire made his movie debut dancing with Joan Crawford. After this Fields and McHugh wrote songs for *The Prize-fighter and the Lady* (1933) and *Fugitive Lovers* (1934).

For the next few years Dorothy Fields worked only in films. In 1935 she wrote songs for seven motion pictures, including *Alice Adams, The Nitwits, In Person,* and *Hooray for Love. Roberta* (1935) was a film based on the Broadway musical of the same name by Jerome Kern and Otto Harbach. It had two classics, "Lovely to Look At," by Jerome Kern, Dorothy Fields, and Jimmy McHugh, and "I Won't Dance," by Kern, McHugh, Fields, Oscar Hammerstein, and Otto Harbach. This motion picture was one of the great dance films of Fred Astaire and Ginger Rogers. For the film *Every Night at Eight,* she and Jimmy McHugh wrote "I'm in the Mood for Love" and "I Feel a Song Comin' On." For *I Dream Too Much* (1935), Fields and Kern wrote the title song and "Jockey on the Carousel." It was an extraordinarily productive year.

The next year Dorothy Fields collaborated with Jerome Kern on the film *Swing Time,* another Ginger Rogers–Fred Astaire film. For their song "The Way You Look Tonight," Jerome Kern and Dorothy Fields won an Academy Award for the Best Song of 1936. The film had other fine songs by Fields and Kern as well: "Pick Yourself Up," "Bojangles of Harlem," "The Waltz in Swingtime," and "A Fine Romance."

> A fine romance! With no kisses!
> A fine romance, my friend, this is!
> We should be like a couple of hot tomatoes,
> But you're as cold as yesterday's mashed potatoes.
>
> A fine romance! You won't nestle,
> A fine romance! You won't wrestle!
> I might as well play bridge with my old maid aunts!
> I haven't got a chance. This is a fine romance!
>
> A fine romance! My good fellow!
> You take romance, I'll take Jello!
> You're calmer than seals in the Arctic Ocean,
> At least they flap their fins to express emotion,
> A fine romance! With no quarrels,
> With no insults, and all morals!

Jerome Kern, Dorothy Fields, and George Gershwin, Hollywood, 1936. (Frank Driggs Coll.)

> I've never mussed the crease in your blue serge pants,
> I never get the chance. This is a fine romance!
> —"A Fine Romance" by Dorothy Fields and Jerome Kern*

Dorothy and her brother, Herbert Fields, wrote the screenplay for the Carole Lombard film *Love before Breakfast* (1936) and the screenplay for *Riviera* (1936). Dorothy also wrote the lyrics for several songs in the Grace Moore film *The King Steps Out* (1936), among them the lovely "Stars in My Eyes," with music by Fritz Kreisler.

More films followed: *When You're in Love* (1937) and *Joy of Living* (1938). She and Herbert Fields wrote the screenplay for another Carole Lombard movie, *Fools for Scandal* (1938), from an original story by **Nancy Hamilton.**

Dorothy Fields also managed to find time to get married to Eli D. Lahm, a clothing manufacturer in New York. Following her marriage, she reduced her work schedule somewhat, working on fewer shows per year.

However, in 1939 she went back to work on Broadway with a new col-

*Copyright © 1936 PolyGram International Publishing, Inc. Copyright renewed.

laborator, Arthur Schwartz. The show was *Stars in Your Eyes*, with Jimmy Durante and Ethel Merman. The following year Dorothy Fields rejoined Jerome Kern for the film *One Night in the Tropics* (1940).

In 1941 Dorothy Fields and Eli Lahm had their first child, a son, and three years later, a daughter.

During the early 1940s Dorothy again collaborated on several projects with her brother, Herbert. They wrote a musical for the movie *The Father Takes a Wife* (1941). Then they wrote the book for three Cole Porter musicals, *Let's Face It* (1943), *Something for the Boys* (1944), and *Mexican Hayride* (1944). All three of these were very successful and ran more than 400 performances each.

Next Dorothy and Herbert Fields wrote a charming musical set in the early days of New York City. Sigmund Romberg wrote the music with Dorothy Fields's lyrics. The show, *Up in Central Park* (1945), ran 504 performances and was so popular that it was revived again in the 1952 season. The hit song was the lovely "Close as Pages in a Book."

After this success the Fields team wrote the book for another show that turned out to be an even greater success, *Annie Get Your Gun* (1946). They had planned to do the musical with Jerome Kern, but his untimely death left them without a composer. They turned to Irving Berlin, who wrote both the music and the lyrics for the show. *Annie* was a huge success and ran 1,147 performances.

Later, in 1950, Dorothy Fields collaborated with Morton Gould on *Arms and the Girl*, but it was unsuccessful. The same year she and her brother Herbert wrote the screenplay for the movie of *Annie Get Your Gun*. Then the following year she wrote song lyrics for three other films: *Mr. Imperium*, with Lana Turner and Ezio Pinza, *Excuse My Dust*, and *Texas Carnival*. The latter was an Esther Williams film that featured the song "Young Folks Should Get Married." Also, the Broadway show she did that year, *A Tree Grows in Brooklyn*, with music by Arthur Schwartz, produced two memorable songs, "Make the Man Love Me" and "I'll Buy You a Star." It had been a busy year for Dorothy Fields. During 1951 she had written 62 sets of lyrics.

Back in Hollywood, MGM planned to remake the 1935 movie *Roberta*. It would star Kathryn Grayson and Howard Keel. They hired Dorothy Fields and Jerome Kern to write some new songs to be added to the original score. The film was called *Lovely to Look At* (1952). Fields and Kern wrote three songs, but none as successful as the Fields-McHugh title song written for the 1935 film.

The following year Dorothy wrote songs for the film *The Farmer Takes a Wife* (1953). After this she went back to Broadway.

Collaborating once again, Dorothy Fields and Herbert Fields wrote the book and she wrote the lyrics for *By the Beautiful Sea* (1954). Arthur Schwartz wrote the music. The show featured "Alone Too Long" and "More Love than Your Love." Unfortunately the show was not a financial success.

In 1957 Dorothy supplied the lyrics for a television musical, *Junior Miss*, which was written by her other brother, Joseph Fields.

Then in 1958 her husband, Eli Lahm, died. The same year her brother, Herbert Fields, died. Up until his death Fields had been collaborating with her on the book for *Redhead*. Despite these heavy losses, Dorothy completed her work on the show.

Redhead opened in 1959. Very successful, it won a Tony for the best musical and also several Grammy Awards. Dorothy and Herbert Fields, Sidney Sheldon, and David Shaw won a Tony for the book. Dorothy and Albert Hague wrote the songs, but since there was no Tony given for lyrics in 1959, only Hague won a Tony for composing the musical score. Gwen Verdon and Richard Kiley starred in *Redhead*, and Bob Fosse directed and choreographed the show. Featured songs were "Merely Marvelous" and "Look Who's in Love."

For *Sweet Charity* (1965), Dorothy worked with composer Cy Coleman. The book was by Neil Simon. Bob Fosse choreographed and directed the show, which starred Gwen Verdon. Coleman and Fields created several memorable songs: "Where Am I Going," "If My Friends Could See Me Now," and "Hey, Big Spender." The show was a hit, running 608 performances. Following its Broadway run, *Sweet Charity* was made into a 1969 movie starring Shirley MacLaine. Dorothy Fields and Cy Coleman were called upon to add two new songs to the score, coming up with "My Personal Property" and "It's a Nice Face."

Dorothy Fields's last show was the hit *See-Saw* (1973), with Cy Coleman's music. The show starred Michele Lee and Ken Howard and featured a brief appearance by then-mayor of New York City John Lindsay.

Dorothy was hard at work writing lyrics for a new show when she died of a heart attack on March 28, 1974, at the age of 68.

She left an impressive legacy of musical theater and motion picture songs. Many of her songs have become American pop classics: "I Can't Give You Anything but Love," "On the Sunny Side of the Street," "Exactly like You," "Don't Blame Me," "Lovely to Look At," "I Feel a Song Comin' On," "I'm in the Mood for Love," "I Won't Dance," "The Way You Look Tonight," "A Fine Romance," "Stars in My Eyes," "Close as Pages in a Book," and "Where Am I Going."

In his book *American Popular Song*, songwriter Alec Wilder wrote, "McHugh was a very fortunate man to have such a talented lyricist as Dorothy Fields to work with. Her lyrics often swung and their deceptive ease gave a special luster to McHugh's music" (Wilder, p. 407).

Dorothy Fields was the first woman elected to the Songwriters' Hall of Fame.

SOURCES

Candee, Marjorie. *Current Biography.* 1958.
Craig, Warren. *Great Songwriters of Hollywood.*
Ewen, David. *New Complete Book of American Musical Theater.*
Ewen, David. *Richard Rodgers.*
Furia, Philip. *Poets of Tin Pan Alley.*
Green, Stanley. *Encyclopedia of Musical Film.*
Green, Stanley. *World of Musical Comedy.*
Kanter, Kenneth. *Jews on Tin Pan Alley.*
Kinkle, Roger. *Complete Encyclopedia of Popular Music and Jazz.*
Krafsur, Richard. *American Film Institute,* 1961–70.
Lewine, Richard. *Songs of American Theater.*
Lynn Farnol Group. *ASCAP Biographical Dictionary.*
New York Times Film Reviews.
New York Times. Obituaries, March 29, 1974, p. 38.
Rodgers, Richard. *Musical Stages.*
Shapiro, Nat. *Hear Me Talkin' to Ya.*
Spaeth, Sigmund. *History of Popular Music in America.*

FORD, NANCY (1935–   )   "Natural High"

Composer Nancy Louise Ford was born in Kalamazoo, Michigan, on October 1, 1935. She is the daughter of Henry Ford III. While attending DePauw University, she and another student, **Gretchen Cryer,** began writing songs together.

Since their college days Cryer and Ford have written a number of musicals, among them *Now Is the Time for All Good Men, The Last Sweet Days of Isaac, I'm Getting My Act Together and Taking It on the Road,* and *Shelter.* Their work is notable for its focus on social issues like the Vietnam War and feminism, as well as Ford's use of rock music for some of the scores.

In addition to composing musicals, Nancy Ford has also written popular daytime soap operas for television. Through the 1970s and the early part of the 1980s, she wrote for such shows as *Love of Life, Search for Tomorrow,* and *As the World Turns.* She also has performed on stage and in television and has won two Emmys. She has an honorary doctorate of arts from Eastern Michigan University.

Among her songs are "Love You Came to Me," "A Transparent Crystal

Moment," "My Most Important Moments Go By," "Don't Tell Me It's Forever," "Dear Tom," "Feel the Love," "Natural High," "She's My Girl," and "Changing," all with lyrics by Gretchen Cryer.

Nancy Ford is married to Keith W. Charles.

SOURCES

Lewine, Richard. *Songs of American Theater.*

Lyons, H. "Gretchen Cryer: Friends and Lovers." *Ms*, December 1978, p. 49.

Who's Who in America, 1990.

HAMILTON, NANCY (1908–)   "How High the Moon"

Although she had a long career as a singer, actress, and author, Nancy Hamilton also wrote lyrics for many popular songs.

Born in Sewickley, Pennsylvania on July 27, 1908, she was educated at Smith College and the Sorbonne in Paris.

Her acting career began when she was understudy for Katharine Hepburn in *The Warrior's Husband* (1931). She also appeared in *Pride and Prejudice* and *The Barretts of Wimpole Street.*

Besides performing in *New Faces of 1934*, she wrote some of the sketches and also wrote lyrics for several songs. She wrote "He Loves Me" with Cliff Allen, "People of Taste" with Martha Caples, and "Something You Lack" with Warburton Guilbert's music. The following year she wrote scripts for comedienne Beatrice Lillie's radio show.

After this Nancy Hamilton teamed up with composer Morgan Lewis on a series of shows. She wrote the book, sketches, and lyrics while Lewis wrote the music for *One for the Money* (1939), *Two for the Show* (1940), and *Three to Make Ready* (1946). She also appeared in *One for the Money*. Between the last two shows, she co-authored with Walter Kerr and Leo Grady the book for another musical, *Count Me In* (1942).

However, her best-known song, "How High the Moon," was written with Morgan Lewis for *Two for the Show*. Alfred Drake and Frances Comstock introduced it in the original show, and it has become a classic.

Some of the other songs Nancy Hamilton wrote with Morgan Lewis include "The Old Soft Shoe," "Lazy Kind of Day," "I Only Know," "Teeter Totter Tesse." She also wrote "Barnaby Beach," "If It's Love," and "My Day." For an episode of radio's "Duffy's Tavern," in which she appeared, she wrote "I Hate Spring."

Nancy Hamilton also wrote for the movies. She wrote the original story for the film *Fools for Scandal* (1938) and co-authored the screenplay. In 1943 she adapted *DuBarry Was a Lady* for the movies. This lively romp starred Red Skelton, Lucille Ball, and Gene Kelly.

During the war years she wrote for the USO hospital shows and for the Office of War Information.

In 1954 Nancy Hamilton won an Academy Award for a documentary film she co-authored and produced, *The Unconquered: Helen Keller in Her Story*.

SOURCES

Kinkle, Roger. *Complete Encyclopedia of Popular Music and Jazz.*
Lewine, Richard. *Songs of American Theater.*
Lynn Farnol Group. *ASCAP Biographical Dictionary.*
New York Times Film Reviews.
Rigdon, Walter. *Notable Names in American Theatre.*
Spaeth, Sigmund. *History of Popular Music in America.*
Who's Who of American Women, 1961.

HAMMERSTEIN, ALICE (1921–   )   "I've Never Been Away"

Daughter of librettist Oscar Hammerstein II, Alice Hammerstein was born on May 17, 1921, in New York City.

She attended the University of Chicago and Columbia University. After that she wrote songs for a children's television show, "Bobo the Hobo and His Traveling Troupe." She wrote the lyrics to songs by George Lessner.

She also wrote an English libretto for Richard Strauss's *Intermezzo*.

Some of Alice Hammerstein's songs include "What I Say Goes," "Give Me Rome," "Ramblin'," "Creole Song," "I've Never Been Away," and "Results Are Just the Same."

SOURCES

Lynn Farnol Group. *ASCAP Biographical Dictionary.*
Woolery, George. *Children's Television.*

JANIS, ELSIE (1889–1956)
"Love Your Magic Spell Is Everywhere"

Born Elsie Bierbower in Columbus, Ohio, on March 16, 1889, Elsie Janis was one of the great stars of vaudeville and the Broadway stage. As a performer she was a slender, energetic singer and mimic. She was also a librettist, author, producer, and songwriter.

Elsie Janis made her theater debut at the age of five. She was known as Little Elsie in the vaudeville circuit from 1898 to 1903. By the age of 16 she had a part in a Broadway show, *When We Were Forty-One* (1905), in which she did imitations of popular personalities and stole the show. From that point on she was the toast of Broadway.

The next year she appeared in *The Vanderbilt Cup* (1906), followed by *The Hoyden* (1907). She starred with Arthur Stamford in *The Fair Co-ed* in 1909, then in *The Slim Princess* (1911) and *The Lady of the Slipper* (1912). Two years later she went to London and made her debut there in *The Passing Show* (1914).

Returning to New York the following year she wrote the lyrics to Jerome Kern's music for *Miss Information* (1915) and also starred in the show. The featured songs were "Some Sort of Somebody" and "A Little Love (but Not for Me)." The show ran about a month. After it closed some of its songs, including her "Some Sort of Somebody," were moved to Jerome Kern's *Very Good Eddie* (1915), which opened later the same year. That year Elsie Janis also went to Hollywood, where she wrote and starred in four silent movies: *Betty in Search of a Thrill, The Caprices of Kitty, Nearly a Lady,* and *'Twas Ever Thus.*

During 1918, when World War I was raging, Elsie Janis traveled to Europe to entertain the troops, as did many other entertainers. She sang and did impersonations, including one of the great actress Sarah Bernhardt singing "Yes, We Have No Bananas." After she returned to the United States, she wrote about her six months with the American Expeditionary Forces in her book *The Big Show* (1919).

When the war was over, she wrote, produced, and starred in a revue, *Elsie Janis and Her Gang* (1919). She also starred in two David Selznick silent films, *A Regular Girl* and *The Imp*. The latter she wrote with Edmund Goulding.

The following year she returned to London to star in a show she had written and for which she had composed some of the music, *It's All Wrong* (1920). Then she made her Paris music hall debut with great success in *La Revue de Elsie Janis* (1921).

Returning to Broadway, she acted in *Puzzles of 1925*, which she also wrote and directed. The show included her songs "The Undecided Blues" and "You've Got to Dance," as well as one she wrote with Vincent Scotto, "Tra-la-la-la."

Again Elsie Janis went back to Hollywood, this time to star in the movie *Vitaphone* (1926). She wrote a movie adaptation, *Oh, Kay!* (1928), and co-authored with Gene Markey another musical, *Close Harmony* (1929), which starred Buddy Rogers, Nancy Carroll, and Jack Oakie.

Perhaps her most lasting contribution was writing the lyrics to the song "Love, Your Magic Spell Is Everywhere," with music by Edmund Goulding. It was written for the motion picture *The Trespasser* (1929).

She continued in movies writing dialogue and lyrics for Cecil B. de Mille's musical *Madam Satan* (1930). That year she also supervised the musical revue *Paramount on Parade* (1930). The film director was Dorothy Arzner. Elsie Janis and Jack King wrote several of the movie's songs, including "Any Time's the Time to Fall in Love."

Then, in 1931, Elsie Janis married Gilbert Wilson. She continued her work in the movies and theater, staging the revue *New Faces of 1934*. She and Jack King had one song, "You Still Belong to Me," in the film *Slightly Scarlet* in 1935.

The next year, at the age of 47, Elsie Janis decided to retire. However, she tried a comeback in a 1939 musical but was unsuccessful. Her final motion picture appearance was made in 1940 in *Women in War*.

In addition to performing, Elsie Janis wrote many articles and short stories for magazines. Her 1932 autobiography, *So Far, So Good*, was followed with two other books, *Love Letters of an Actress* and *You Know What I Mean*.

As a songwriter, Elsie Janis composed over 50 songs, among them "Your Eyes," "I'm True to the Navy Now," "Molly-O-Mine," and "From the Valley." She wrote the lyrics to "Oh, Give Me Time for Tenderness," with music by Edmund Goulding.

In 1936 she moved to Beverly Hills, California, where she lived until her death on February 26, 1956. When Elsie Janis died, her friend Mary Pickford said, "This ends the vaudeville era."

SOURCES

Bloom, Ken. *American Song.*
Dahl, Linda. *Stormy Weather.*
Green, Stanley. *World of Musical Comedy.*
Hanson, Patricia. *American Film Institute*, 1911–20.
Janis, Elsie. *So Far, So Good.*
Janis, Elsie. *The Big Show.*
Lewine, Richard. *Songs of American Theater.*
Lynn Farnol Group. *ASCAP Biographical Dictionary.*
Munden, Kenneth. *American Film Institute*, 1921–30.
New York Times Film Reviews.
New York Times. Obituaries, February 28, 1956, p. 1.
Salem, James. *Guide to Critical Reviews.*
Slide, Anthony. *Vaudevillians.*
Spaeth, Sigmund. *History of Popular Music in America.*
Truitt, Evelyn. *Who Was Who on Screen.*
Who Was Who in Theatre.

KERR, JEAN (1923–   )   "This Had Better Be Love"

Jean Kerr, wife of drama critic Walter Kerr, is a well-known author of humorous plays, books, and lyrics.

Born Jean Collins in Scranton, Pennsylvania, on July 10, 1923, she graduated from Marywood College and earned a master's degree at the Catholic University of America. Before becoming a writer, she was a teacher. She married Walter Kerr in 1943, and they had five sons and one daughter.

Jean Kerr's plays include *Jenny Kissed Me* (1948), *King of Hearts*, written with Eleanor Brooke (1954), *Mary, Mary* (1961), *Poor Richard* (1964), *Finishing Touches* (1973), and *Lunch Hour* (1980). The only fault the critics found with her long-running hit *Mary, Mary* was that the play had almost too many jokes.

She wrote lyrics and sketches for the revue *Thank You, Just Looking*, which was first called *Touch and Go* (1949). She also wrote sketches for *John Murray Anderson's Almanac* (1953). In 1958 she and Walter Kerr wrote the book and lyrics for the musical *Goldilocks*, which had music by Leroy Anderson. Joan Ford also contributed to the lyrics and Agnes de Mille did the choreography. The show ran 161 performances.

Her book *Please Don't Eat the Daisies* (1954) was a bestseller. It was made into a motion picture in 1963 and later became a television series. Other books she has written include *The Snake Has All the Lines* (1960), *Penny Candy* (1970), and *How I Got to Be Perfect* (1978).

Some of the songs Jean Kerr has written include "This Had Better Be Love," "I Never Know When to Say When," "Be a Mess," "Save a Kiss," and "The Pussy Foot." She has collaborated on songs with Leroy Anderson, Jay Gorney, Walter Kerr, and Joan Ford.

SOURCES
Green, Stanley. *World of Musical Comedy.*
Lewine, Richard. *Songs of American Theater.*
Lynn Farnol Group. *ASCAP Biographical Dictionary.*
Salem, James. *Guide to Critical Reviews.*

KUMMER, CLARE (1873–1958)   "Dearie"

For more than 30 years Clare Kummer was a successful playwright on Broadway. In addition to writing plays, she wrote librettos and lyrics for musicals and occasionally wrote the music as well.

Born Clare Rodman Beecher, on January 9, 1873, in Brooklyn, New York, she was related to Henry Ward Beecher and Harriet Beecher Stowe. The actor William Gillette was her cousin. She was educated at the Packer Institute and also studied music privately.

In 1895 she married businessman Frederic Arnold Kummer. Clare wrote songs and plays while Frederic worked as assistant editor of the *Railroad*

Gazette and later as general manager of Eastern Paving Brick Company. Clare Kummer's first success was as a songwriter with three hit songs; "The Night We Did Not Care" (1901), "Egypt" (1903), and "Dearie" (1906). The marriage, however, was not successful and by 1907 had ended. Frederic Kummer later left the business world and, like his ex-wife, became a playwright and author.

Clare went on with her work. She had been writing plays as well as songs, but it wasn't until 1912 that one of her shows, *The Opera Ball*, opened on Broadway. She and Sydney Rosenfeld co-authored the book and lyrics, and Richard Heuberger composed the music.

After this success she was hired to work with Jerome Kern on the musical *Ninety in the Shade* (1915). She co-authored the book with Guy Bolton and also wrote the lyrics to several interpolations, namely "Rich Man, Poor Man," "Jolly Good Fellow," "My Mindanao Chocolate Soldier," all with music by Richard Heuberger. She wrote both the words and music of the song "Lonely in Town." Kern's lyricist was Harry B. Smith.

The next year Clare Kummer had a hit with her play *Good Gracious, Annabelle!* (1916), a farce in three acts. It also had one of her songs in it, "Other Eyes." In the cast were Roland Young and Lola Fisher.

After this success she decided to put all her efforts into play writing. In 1917 three of her works were playing simultaneously at different theaters in New York City: *Good Gracious, Annabelle!*, *A Successful Calamity*, and *The Rescuing Angel*. The cast of *A Successful Calamity* (1917) featured her cousin, actor William Gillette. She followed these successes with *Be Calm, Camilla* (1918), *Rollo's Wild Oats* (1920), *Bridges* (1921), *Banco* (1922), *Pomeroy's Past* (1926), *Her Master's Voice* (1933), and others. More than 20 of her plays were produced on Broadway during her 30-year career.

She adapted the book and lyrics for the musical comedy *One Kiss* (1923), with music by Maurice Yvain. Two of the songs were "Don't Ever Be a Poor Relation" and "A Little Love."

In 1924 she adapted *Good Gracious, Annabelle!* as a musical and called it *Annie Dear*. She collaborated with Sigmund Romberg on the music and with Clifford Grey on the lyrics. Billie Burke starred in the show, which ran 103 performances. Some of her songs were "Annie," "Etiquette," and "In Love Again."

For *Madame Pompadour* (1924) she wrote the book and lyrics with music by Leo Fall. One of the Kummer-Fall songs was "Magic Moments."

In 1925 she did the film adaptation of a play for the silent motion picture *Lost—a Wife*.

For *The Three Waltzes* (1937) she and Roland Leigh adapted the book and wrote the lyrics to the music of the Strausses: Oscar, Johann Senior, and Junior. One of the songs was "Springtime Is in the Air." In the cast was Kitty Carlisle.

Clare Kummer's second marriage was to Arthur Henry. Her daughter married actor Roland Young, who starred in some of Clare Kummer's plays.

After writing her last play in 1944, *Many Happy Returns,* she retired to Carmel, California. There she lived until her death on April 22, 1958, at the age of 85.

Some of the other songs Clare Kummer wrote were "Lover of Mine," "Blushing June Roses," "Somebody's Eyes," "Only with You," "Thro' All the World," "Garden of Dreams," "Today," "The Road to Yesterday," "The Bluebird," and "Sunset."

SOURCES
Bloom, Ken. *American Song.*
Burke, W. J. *American Authors and Books.*
Green, Stanley. *World of Musical Comedy.*
Lewine, Richard. *Songs of American Theater.*
Lynn Farnol Group. *ASCAP Biographical Dictionary.*
Mattfeld, Julius. *Variety Music Cavalcade.*
Millett, Fred. *Contemporary American Authors.*
"A New 'Comedy Gift.' " *Literary Digest,* October 27, 1917, p. 27.
New York Times Film Reviews.
Salem, James. *Guide to Critical Reviews.*
Spaeth, Sigmund. *History of Popular Music in America.*
Who Was Who in Theatre.

LEIGH, CAROLYN (1926–1983)   "Young at Heart"

Carolyn Leigh wrote lyrics for popular songs and for Broadway musicals. Born Carolyn Rosenthal in New York City on August 21, 1926, she was educated at Queens College and New York University. After college she worked as a copywriter for an advertising agency and for a radio station.

In 1951 a music publisher encouraged her to write lyrics for songs. She wrote, "I'm Waiting Just for You," and then with Johnny Richards's music, "Young at Heart," which became a major hit in 1954.

That same year Carolyn Leigh was hired to write lyrics to Mark Charlap's music for a new production of *Peter Pan.* Leonard Bernstein had composed a very successful *Peter Pan* in 1950, but this was to be an entirely new version starring Mary Martin and Cyril Ritchard. The majority of the songs were written by Carolyn Leigh and Mark Charlap, but nearly half were written by the songwriting team of **Betty Comden,** Adolph Green, and Jule Styne. Leigh and Charlap wrote the charming "I've Gotta Crow,"

"I'm Flying," and "I Won't Grow Up," and the hilarious "Captain Hook's Tango," among others. Although this 1954 version of *Peter Pan* had a shorter run than Leonard Bernstein's 1950 version, it nevertheless became the most familiar *Peter Pan* because it was telecast and because of the many reruns of that telecast, as recently as 1989.

Carolyn Leigh and composer Philip Springer had one song in *The Shoestring Revue* (1956), "Always One Day More," and two more songs, "Salesmanship" and "The Lover in Me," in the *Ziegfeld Follies of 1957*.

After this Carolyn Leigh began working with composer Cy Coleman on *Wildcat* (1960), starring Lucille Ball. The main songs were "Hey, Look Me Over," "One Day We Dance," "Give a Little Whistle," and "Tall Hope."

Two years later Cy Coleman and Carolyn Leigh had another musical on the boards, *Little Me* (1962), based on a novel by Patrick Dennis. The main songs were "Real Live Girl," "Here's to Us," and "I've Got Your Number." Carolyn Leigh's lyrics for this show were nominated for a Grammy and a Tony Award.

Carolyn Leigh also wrote songs for a few motion pictures: "Stay with Me" was written for *The Cardinal* (1963), with music by Jerome Moross; and "Pass Me By," with music by Cy Coleman, for *Father Goose* (1964). In addition she wrote songs for the television special *Heidi*.

In 1967 she wrote the lyrics to Elmer Bernstein's music for *How Now, Dow Jones*, which ran 220 performances and earned Carolyn Leigh another Tony nomination for best lyrics. Some of the songs were "Live a Little," "Walk Away," "One of Those Moments," and "That's Good Enough for Me."

For the U.S. Bicentennial in 1976, she wrote lyrics for *Something to Do*, a musical about the American worker that was sponsored by the U.S. Department of Labor.

Other songs by Carolyn Leigh include "The Rules of the Road" and "How Little We Know." Among the songs she wrote with composer Cy Coleman were "Witchcraft," "The Best Is Yet to Come," "I Walked a Little Faster," "A Doodlin' Song," "Firefly," "You Fascinate Me So," and "It Amazes Me."

Carolyn Leigh was modest about her accomplishments. She described herself as a typist, copywriter, and secretary who couldn't take dictation. She said that she hadn't been specifically educated to write lyrics and didn't think a person could be.

Carolyn Leigh was first married to Julius Levine, and in 1959 to David W. Cunningham, Jr., an attorney, whom she later divorced.

Carolyn Leigh died of a heart attack on November 19, 1983, at the age of 57.

In the *New York Times* obituary (November 21, 1983, p. D20) Cy Coleman recalled, "She was a poet, and she had a great feeling for music." She was "always fastidious." At the time of her death she was working on a musical with Marvin Hamlisch, who said that he had "always wanted to work with her because she was not only a good craftsman, but also was one of the few people who had genuine wit in her lyrics." He said, "She also had a lot of heart. She was very human and also very funny."

SOURCES

Bloom, Ken. *American Song.*
Davis, Sheila. *Craft of Lyric Writing.*
Green, Stanley. *World of Musical Comedy.*
Lewine, Richard. *Songs of American Theater.*
Lynn Farnol Group. *ASCAP Biographical Dictionary.*
Mattfeld, Julius. *Variety Music Cavalcade.*
New York Times. Obituaries, November 21, 1983, p. D20.
Rigdon, Walter. *Biographical Encyclopedia of American Theatre.*
Rigdon, Walter. *Notable Names in American Theatre.*
Shapiro, Nat. *Popular Music.*
Who Was Who in Theatre.
Who's Who of American Women, 1983.

MORGAN, AGNES (n.d.)   "Aurory Bory Alice"

Agnes Morgan was a playwright, producer, director, and lyricist for a number of off-Broadway shows in the 1920s. She was primarily associated with the perennial revue *The Grand Street Follies.*

Born in Le Roy, New York, Agnes Morgan graduated from Radcliffe College in 1901.

She wrote the play *When We Two Write History* and in 1910 staged it in Chicago. With Paul Potter she co-authored the book for *The Man with Three Wives* (1913). With Henry Benrimo she adapted *Taking Chances* in 1915. The same year she became director of the Neighborhood Playhouse in New York.

Later, in 1922, she wrote the book and lyrics and directed the first edition of the *The Grand Street Follies,* with music by Lily Hyland. The show was popular, and many editions followed. From 1924 through 1929 she wrote the book and lyrics, directed, and often performed in each new edition of *The Grand Street Follies,* working with many different composers, including Randall Thompson, Lily Hyland, Arthur Schwartz, Max Ewing, and Serge Walters. Among her songs were "Fixed for Life," "The Boosters' Song of the Far North," "Taxi Drivers' Lament," "Beatrice Lillie Ballad,"

"My Icy Floe," "Aurory Bory Alice," "Little Igloo for Two," "Three Little Maids," "The Naughty Nineties," "Hey, Nonny, Ney," "Someone to Adore," "The Amoeba's Lament," "The Double Standard," and "The Vineyards of Manhattan." The *Follies* was a workshop for many talented writers, performers, and musicians who later went on to greater acclaim, among them actor James Cagney and composer Arthur Schwartz.

Agnes Morgan also produced many of her own plays at the Neighborhood Playhouse. One was *The Little Legend of the Dance* (1923).

In 1937 she and Lehman Engel wrote *A Hero Is Born*. She wrote the play *If Love Were All* under the pseudonym Cutler Hatch and also directed it. In 1938 her play *Grandpa* was produced at the Casino Theater in Newport, Rhode Island.

In 1940 Agnes Morgan became the co-producer and director of the year-round theater stock company the Paper Mill Playhouse in Millburn, New Jersey.

SOURCES

Ewen, David. *Complete Book of American Musical Theater*.
Green, Stanley. *World of Musical Comedy*.
Lewine, Richard. *Songs of American Theater*.
Rigdon, Walter. *Notable Names in American Theatre*.
Who's Who of American Women, 1968.

RODGERS, MARY (1931–   )   "Shy"

Daughter of composer Richard Rodgers, Mary Rodgers was born on January 11, 1931, in New York City. She was educated at Wellesley College and later studied at the David Mannes College of Music. Like her father she became a composer of Broadway musicals.

She began by writing music for night clubs, television, and revues, often collaborating with her sister, Linda Rodgers Melnick. An early score she wrote with her sister was *Three to Make Music* (1957).

In 1959 Mary Rodgers wrote the score for Mary Martin's children's special on NBC television. She also wrote the music and lyrics for a marionette production of *Davy Jones' Locker*. From 1957 to 1970 she was an assistant to the producer of Leonard Bernstein's "Young People's Concerts" on CBS television.

Mary Rodgers composed her first Broadway musical, *Once upon a Mattress*, in 1959. It was based on the fairy tale "The Princess and the Pea." The show was very successful and established Mary Rodgers as a Broadway composer in her own right. The critics found the score inventive and full of cheerful melodies. Marshall Barer wrote the lyrics and Carol Burnett starred as the zany heroine, Princess Winnifred. Featured songs were "Shy," "In a Little While," "Happily Ever After," and "Yesterday I Loved You."

The following year, for the revue *From A to Z*, she and Marshall Barer wrote two songs, "Hire a Guy" and "Countermelody," the music composed with Jay Thompson.

In 1963 Mary Rodgers and Martin Charnin wrote the score for *The Hot Spot*. The featured songs were "Don't Laugh," "Smiles," and "I Think the World of You." The show had a run of 41 performances.

Mary Rodgers's greatest success was *The Mad Show* (1966), which was based on *Mad Magazine*. The show was so popular that it ran a little more than two years, with 871 performances. Several different lyricists wrote the lyrics to Mary Rodgers's music, among them Stephen Sondheim, Stephen Vinaver, and Marshall Barer.

In 1974 she did the score for *Pinocchio* for Bill Baird's Marionettes. She composed the music for *Working* (1978), with lyrics by Susan Birkenhead.

Some of the other songs Mary Rodgers has composed include "In a Little While," "Counter Melody," "Very Soft Shoes," "Happily Ever After," "Many Moons Ago," and "Normandy." She has also written albums of children's songs.

In addition to composing music, Mary Rodgers has written several books: *The Rotten Book, Freaky Friday, A Word to the Wives, A Billion for Boris.* From 1971 to 1978 she and her mother wrote a monthly column, "Of Two Minds," for *McCalls* magazine.

Mary Rodgers is married to Henry Guettel and has five children.

SOURCES
Bloom, Ken. *American Song.*
Green, Stanley. *Encyclopaedia of Musical Theatre.*
Green, Stanley. *World of Musical Comedy.*
Lewine, Richard. *Songs of American Theater.*
Lynn Farnol Group. *ASCAP Biographical Dictionary*
Who's Who in America, 1980.

SANDERS, ALMA (1882–1956)
"That Tumble-down Shack in Athlone"

Alma Sanders and her husband, Monte Carlo, were a well-known song-writing team who wrote a number of musicals and popular songs.

Born in Chicago on March 13, 1882, Alma Sanders won a scholarship to the Chicago Musical College and studied to become a concert singer. After college she got a job writing songs for a music publisher, and she married songwriter Monte Carlo.

In 1918 Alma Sanders, Monte Carlo, and R. W. Pasco had one of their songs interpolated into *The Voice of McConnell*. Their song, "That Tumble Down Shack in Athlone," became the hit of the show.

After this they tried their hand at writing musicals. In 1921 Alma Sanders and Monte Carlo wrote the music for *Tangerine*, with lyrics by Howard Johnstone. Among their songs were "She Was Very Dear to Me" and "Give Me Your Love."

Sanders and Carlo had several songs in the Noble Sissle–Eubie Blake musical *Elsie* (1923), including, "One Day in May" and "Clouds of Love."

The next year they wrote the score for *The Chiffron Girl*, which featured the songs "Just One Rose" and "The Kind of a Girl for Me." The same year they wrote the music for *Princess April* and *Bye, Bye Barbara*, the latter with lyrics by Sidney Toler and Alonzo Price.

Sanders and Carlo's *Oh! Oh! Nurse* (1925) ran only a month. However, their next effort, *The Houseboat on the Styx* (1928), ran 103 performances. It featured the songs "Cleopatra, We're Fond of You," "The Fountain of Youth," and "Someone Like You."

Mystery Moon, which they wrote in 1930, closed after opening night. Their last show, *Louisiana Lady* (1947), had a short run. Alma Sanders later wrote the musical score for the film *Ireland Today*.

Other songs by Alma Sanders and Monte Carlo include "Little Town in the Ould Country Down," with lyrics by Richard W. Pascoe, "Two Blue Eyes," "The Hills of Connemara," "Hong Kong," "Dreaming of Louise," "No One to Care," "My Home in County Mayo," and "Ten Baby Fingers."

Alma Sanders died in New York City on December 15, 1956, at the age of 74.

SOURCES
Bloom, Ken. *American Song.*
Green, Stanley. *World of Musical Comedy.*
Lewine, Richard. *Songs of American Theater.*
Lynn Farnol Group. *ASCAP Biographical Dictionary.*
New York Times. Obituaries, December 16, 1956, p. 83.
Salem, James. *Guide to Critical Reviews.*
Spaeth, Sigmund. *History of Popular Music in America.*

SUNSHINE, MARION (1894–1963)   "The Peanut Vendor"

Actress-composer Marion Sunshine was born Mary Tunstall Ijames on May 15, 1894, in Louisville, Kentucky. Her family moved to Mount Vernon, New York, when she was young.

She began her stage career at the age of five in vaudeville touring in the melodrama *Two Little Waifs*. In 1907 she appeared in the *Ziegfeld Follies* and from then on appeared in many musicals and revues, among them *Broadway to Paris, The Beauty Shop, Stop! Look! Listen!, Going Up, Nothing but Love, The Girl from Home, The Blue Kitten, Daffy Dill*, and *Captain Jinks*.

In 1930 she married E. S. Azplazu, whose professional name was Mario Antobal. Marion Sunshine introduced Latin-American music to the United States with the Latin-flavored songs she wrote for her vaudeville acts. In addition to creating her own material for vaudeville, she wrote special material for other performers such as Fanny Ward and Hildegarde.

Some of her songs include "My Cuban Sombrero," "Playtime in Brazil," "Here Comes the Conga," "I've Got Everything I Want but You," "I Got a Guy," "Have You Seen My Love?" "Mama, I Wanna Mambo," "One Side of Me," "The Cuban in Me," and "Bossa Nova Stomp." "The Peanut Vendor" was written with L. Wolfe Gilbert and Moises Simons.

Marion Sunshine died on January 25, 1963.

SOURCES
Lynn Farnol Group. *ASCAP Biographical Dictionary*.
New York Times Film Reviews.
Truitt, Evelyn. *Who Was Who on Screen*.
Who's Who of American Women, 1958.

SWADOS, ELIZABETH (1951–)   "The Ballad of the Sad Cafe"

Among the women songwriters working on Broadway today is Elizabeth Swados. She was born in Buffalo, New York on February 5, 1951, into a family of actors, writers, and musicians. Her father studied to be an actor before becoming a lawyer. Her mother was an actress, poet, and journalist. Her grandparents had been musicians in Russia. As a child she was creative and independent, writing stories and music. She played the piano at the age of five and learned the guitar later. At the age of 12 she began performing as a folk singer. At Bennington College she studied creative writing and music and began composing musicals. Then she left college to work with the La Mama Experimental Theater Company in New York City.

Her first show off-Broadway was at the La Mama Experimental Theater Company during the early 1970s. There she and Andrei Serban wrote a musical adaptation of *Medea*, which was performed in both Greek and Latin. Elizabeth Swados won an Obie Award from the *Village Voice* for her score. While touring with the show in England, she joined Peter Brook's International Theater Group as musical director and composer and toured Africa with the group. The following year she worked with various ethnic theater groups within the United States.

Returning to La Mama she wrote the music for *The Trojan Women*, which was performed with *Electra* and *Medea* under the title *Fragments of a Trilogy*. The music she composed revealed the wide range of her musical interests. It incorporated themes based on Oriental, African, Middle Eastern, and Native American music.

In 1975 she and Andrei Serban wrote an adaptation of Bertold Brecht's *The Good Woman of Setzuan*.

In 1977 Elizabeth Swados began working on her own. She wrote the revue *Nightclub Cantata*. Besides writing the book, words, and music, she also directed and performed in the show, which consisted of a collection of poems and narratives by a variety of authors. The literary pieces were set to music that varied from calypso to ragtime. A success, the show ran 145 performances off-Broadway. Some of the songs she wrote were "The Ballad of the Sad Cafe," "Indecision," and "Things I Didn't Know I Loved." For *Nightclub Cantata* she won her second Obie. The show played Boston and Washington; it also toured Europe.

In that same year Andrei Serban asked her to compose music for his adaptation of *The Cherry Orchard*, for which she chose to write waltzes and mazurkas. She and Serban then produced a new version of *Agamemnon*. For this she wrote music that conveyed the spirit of ancient Greek music.

In 1978 Elizabeth Swados had her greatest success. She wrote the book, music, and lyrics for *Runaways*, a revue she also choreographed and directed for the New York Shakespeare Festival. About adolescent alienation, the show consisted of a collection of songs and monologues portraying adolescents estranged from their families. The material for the show was developed from interviews she did with youngsters. Actors were recruited from the different ethnic areas of the city, and the show was set on a playground where the youngsters sang and spoke about their lives on the streets as prostitutes and victims of child abuse. Some of the songs were "Every Now and Then," "Find Me a Hero," and "We Are Not Strangers." The revue ran a successful season off-Broadway and received five Tony Award nominations. The show also received much critical acclaim and was recorded by Columbia Records.

Wonderland in Concert (1978) was an off-Broadway show for the New York Shakespeare Festival. The book, words, and music were all by Elizabeth Swados, and she also directed the show.

Her "rock-war musical" *Dispatches* (1979) was based on Michael Herr's

book about the Vietnam War and was also written for the New York Shakespeare Festival. She wrote both the music and lyrics. The show received
mixed reviews. Some of the songs were "Take Glamour Out of War," "This
War Gets Old," "I See a Road," "Crazy," and "Thou Shalt Not Be Afraid."

For the New York Shakespeare Festival in 1980 she wrote *Alice in Concert,* a reworking of her own *Wonderland in Concert* of 1978, which was
based on *Alice in Wonderland.* Some of the songs included "Beautiful Soup,"
"Jabberwocky," "If You Knew Time," "Cheshire Puss," and "Lobster
Quadrille." The cast included Meryl Streep and Amanda Plummer. The
show ran 32 performances off-Broadway.

Also in 1980 she wrote *The Haggadah* for the New York Shakespeare
Festival, writing the book, music, and lyrics and also directing the show.
Some of the songs were "Burning Bush," "A Blessing," "Death of Moses,"
and "Crossing the Red Sea."

In 1982, again for the New York Shakespeare Festival, she wrote the
book, music, and lyrics for *Lullaby and Goodnight.* Songs in this production included "I'm Sick of Love," "Keep Working," "You Gave Me Love,"
and "You're My Favorite Lullaby."

The following year she composed the music for the musical *Doonesbury,*
based on the popular cartoon strip by Garry Trudeau. Trudeau wrote the
book and lyrics. Some of the songs were "Another Memorable Meal," "It's
All Right to Be Rich," "Complicated Man," and "I Can Have It All."

Swing (1987) had both words and music by Elizabeth Swados. Two of
the songs were "Don't Come inside My Head" and "Twelve Rough Years."

Besides her theater work, Elizabeth Swados has written a children's book,
composed a song cycle based on Sylvia Plath's poetry, and written music
for several television shows.

She has also taught at several colleges and universities. A documentary
film, *The Girl with the Incredible Feeling,* is about her.

Elizabeth Swados has been described as a small, slender woman with
large eyes, long brown hair, and high energy who works all the time.

SOURCES
Bloom, Ken. *American Song.*
Hitchcock, H. Wiley. *New Grove Dictionary of American Music.*
Moritz, Charles. *Current Biography.*
Who's Who of American Women, 1989.

SWIFT, KAY (1905–)   "Fine and Dandy"

Composer Kay Swift was born in New York City on April 19, 1905. As a
youngster she was talented in music and won a scholarship to the Juilliard

School of Music. She also studied at the New England Conservatory of Music. After this, she became an accompanist for touring artists. At the age of 22 she worked as a rehearsal pianist for the Broadway show *A Connecticut Yankee* (1927). For two years during the Depression she was a staff composer at Radio City Music Hall and for a time wrote radio scripts.

In the late 1920s she married a banker, James P. Warburg, who wrote lyrics under the name Paul James. In 1929 Swift and James had one of their songs accepted for the Howard Dietz–Arthur Schwartz revue *The Little Show*. The song—"Can't We Be Friends?"—became a hit.

The following year Kay Swift composed the music and Paul James wrote the lyrics for *Fine and Dandy* (1930), with a book by Donald Ogden Stewart. The songs included "Can This Be Love?" and the title song, "Fine and Dandy," which became a hit. The same year their *9:15 Revue* featured the songs, "Up among the Chimney Pots" and "How Would a City Girl Know?" For *The Garrick Gaieties* (1930) they contributed the song "Johnny Wanamaker."

The New York World's Fair of 1939 proved to be a turning point in Kay Swift's personal life. Her marriage to James Warburg had ended, and she had taken the job of chairman of music for the fair. At a rodeo at the fair she met a rancher whom she decided to marry. Leaving New York, she married Hunter Galloway and went to live on his ranch in the West. There they raised three daughters.

In 1947 she adapted George Gershwin's music for *The Shocking Miss Pilgrim*, a musical starring Betty Grable and Dick Haymes.

Having been raised in New York City, Kay Swift found her adjustment to life on a ranch amusing, and she thought it might make a good movie. A studio bought her story and made it into the film *Never a Dull Moment* (1950). She also wrote the songs for the film.

Then in 1952 Kay Swift returned to Broadway. She composed the music and wrote the lyrics for *Paris Ninety*, a one-woman show starring Cornelia Otis Skinner. The featured songs were "The Waltz I Heard in a Dream," "Calliope," and "The House Where I Was Born."

After that she did a variety of jobs. In 1960 for the Campfire Girls' Fiftieth Anniversary Show she wrote *One Little Girl*, and for the Seattle World's Fair in 1962 she wrote *Century 21*. She was also commissioned by George Balanchine to compose a ballet, *Alma Mater*.

Some of Kay Swift's other songs include "A Moonlight Memory," "Forever and a Day," "Calliope," "Once You Find Your Guy," "In-Between-Age," and "I Gotta Take Off My Hat to You." In addition to songs, she has also composed many piano pieces.

SOURCES
Anderson, E. Ruth. *Contemporary American Composers.*
Dahl, Linda. *Stormy Weather.*
Ewen, David. *Complete Book of American Musical Theater.*
Kinkle, Roger. *Complete Encyclopedia of Popular Music and Jazz.*
Lewine, Richard. *Songs of American Theater.*
Lynn Farnol Group. *ASCAP Biographical Dictionary.*
New York Times Film Reviews.
Spaeth, Sigmund. *History of Popular Music in America.*
Wilder, Alex. *American Popular Song.*
Who's Who of American Women, 1958.

YOUNG, RIDA JOHNSON (1869–1926)
"Ah, Sweet Mystery of Life"

One of the most successful and prolific women dramatists of the early twentieth century was Rida Johnson Young. She was also a top lyricist. She wrote 34 plays and musical comedies, three novels, and approximately 500 songs. She collaborated with some of the leading operetta composers of the day, including Victor Herbert, Sigmund Romberg, Rudolf Friml, and Emmerick Kalman, and she wrote the lyrics to a number of memorable songs, including "Ah, Sweet Mystery of Life," "I'm Falling in Love with Someone," and "Mother Machree."

Born on February 28, 1869, in Baltimore, Maryland, she attended Wilson College in Chambersburg, Pennsylvania. As a child she wrote poems and articles, some of which were published in local newspapers. By the age of 18 she had written her first play, an enormous unwieldy spectacle about Omar Khayyam that had almost 100 characters and would have taken at least eight hours to perform. Somehow she persuaded her parents to let her go to New York to become a playwright.

Unsuccessful in trying to find a publisher for her play, she mailed it to one of the leading stage actors, E. H. Sothern, whom she thought might be interested in the leading role. He was unable to help her with her play, but he did offer her a small acting part that enabled her to support herself. For two years she continued as an actress, although writing was what she really wanted to do.

In time she found a job writing songs in the New York music-publishing firm of Isadore Witmark. Witmark was the publisher of many well-known composers, and at her job she met many of the operetta composers with whom she later collaborated. At Witmark she worked turning out songs at a bewildering rate. When a song was needed to fit a particular play or actor, someone wrote the music and Rida would fit words to it, or she wrote the words first and the music was composed later. She wrote continuously for two years, which was a valuable experience. One of her successful songs from this period was "The Fife and Drum" (1903), with music by Paul Rubens. After two years with the publishing house she had a chance for a good part in a play, and so she left Witmark.

Then in 1904 she married James Young, an actor and writer who later became a motion picture director. However, the marriage didn't last and they were later divorced.

Rida Young continued to write plays. Her next effort had a small cast and few scenery changes, to make it less costly to produce. It was about Lord Byron and was actually produced, but with little success. Nevertheless, Rida Young kept at it.

She enjoyed writing plays, but the process of rehearsing and rewriting the play was not a pleasant experience for her. She had many quarrels with the director, whom she thought was "murdering her child." Later she realized that the changes had improved the play, and she made a mental note that you should "never be quite sure you are right" (American Magazine, December 1920, p. 184).

In 1906 Rida Young wrote Brown of Harvard, which was her first big hit. The play contained a song she had written, "When Love Is Young in Springtime," which also became a hit.

Rida Young discovered that play writing could be a profitable business. In the 1920s a successful play could net the producer a $140,000 to $160,000 profit. The playwright was paid a percentage of the gross house receipts each week, 3 percent for musical comedy and 5 to 10 percent for a comedy. A musical paid less because the composer also received a share of the profits. At that time few plays paid the playwright less than $300 a week for every company producing the play, and in larger cities a successful play might pay double that amount. There might also be movie rights, which varied from $25,000 to over $100,000 a play. There would be book rights when the play was published, and song rights both for sheet music and records. A single successful play might net a playwright anywhere from 50 thousand to several hundred thousand dollars.

After Brown of Harvard Rida Young wrote The Boys of Company B (1907), which starred John Barrymore. She followed it with The Lancers (1907), Glorious Betsy (1908), and The Lottery Man (1909).

In 1910 she was hired to write the book and the lyrics to Victor Herbert's music for the operetta Naughty Marietta. After the writing was finished, she found that the out-of-town tryouts were even more arduous than writing. The lyricist and the composer often had to work nearly 24-hour days revising or creating new material at night so that it could be rehearsed the next day. Often when they were most fatigued, they had to produce new material in order to meet the morning deadline for rehearsals. The rewriting continued for two or three weeks before the show arrived in New York. Then they would find out if their efforts had been worthwhile or not.

Naughty Marietta could not have been more beautifully mounted. It was sung by two stars of the Manhattan Opera Company, Emma Trentini and Orville Harrold, and supported by the opera chorus and orchestra. The songs that Rida Young and Victor Herbert wrote for this show were among their best, including "Ah! Sweet Mystery of Life," "I'm Falling in Love with Someone," "Italian Street Song," "Tramp! Tramp! Tramp!" and " 'Neath the Southern Moon." The operetta was very successful and ran more than 500 performances, after which it went on tour. Over the years there have been many stage revivals. The film of *Naughty Marietta* in 1935 became the first of many Nelson Eddy and Jeanette MacDonald motion picture musicals.

Besides *Naughty Marietta*, Rida Young had two other shows on stage in 1910, her play *Ragged Robin* and the musical *Barry of Ballymore*. She wrote the book for *Barry of Ballymore*, as well as the lyrics to a song in the show, "Mother Machree," with music by Chauncey Olcott and Ernest R. Ball. This song was enormously successful. It sold more than a million copies of sheet music and an even larger number of phonograph records.

> Sure I love the dear silver that shines in your hair,
> And the brow that's all furrowed, and wrinkled with care.
> I kiss the dear fingers, so toil-worn for me,
> Oh, God bless you and keep you, Mother Machree!
> —"Mother Machree" by Rida Johnson Young,
> Chauncey Olcott and Ernest R. Ball

The following year she wrote the play *Next* and adapted it in 1912 as a musical, *The Red Petticoat*. It was the first musical comedy–western. The story concerned a lady barber in the mythical mining town of Lost River, Nevada. The music was by Jerome Kern and the lyrics by Paul West.

After this Rida Young wrote the plays *Isle of Dreams* (1912); *The Girl and the Pennant*, written with Christy Mathewson (1913); *Shameen Dhu* (1913); and *Lady Luxury* (1914), written with William Schroeder.

In 1916 she had two projects, the play *Captain Kidd Jr.* and a musical, *Her Soldier Boy*, with music by Sigmund Romberg and Emmerich Kalman. For the latter Rida Young wrote the book and lyrics. One of the songs was "I'd Be Happy Anywhere with You."

The following year Rida Young and Sigmund Romberg had a tremendous hit with *Maytime* (1917). She wrote the lyrics and adapted the libretto from a sentimental Viennese operetta about lovers who are separated by fate, but whose grandchildren become lovers and find happiness. The show starred Peggy Wood and Charles Purcell, who sang the hit duet "Will You Remember?" The show was so popular that it ran in two theaters on Broadway simultaneously. Twenty years later *Maytime* became another successful motion picture musical for Jeanette MacDonald and Nelson Eddy.

In addition to *Maytime*, Rida Young had another musical on stage the same year, *His Little Widows* (1917).

In 1918 she was busy writing the book and lyrics for two more shows, Rudolf Friml's musical *Sometime* and Augustus Barratt's *Little Simplicity*.

Taking a new direction, she began writing for motion pictures in 1919, beginning with two silent films: *The Little Boss* and *The Lottery Man*. In later years she adapted several of her plays to film, including *Brown of Harvard*, *Glorious Betsy*, and *Hearts Divided*. She also wrote original stories for the movies *Hell Harbor* and *Mother Machree*, the latter directed by John Ford.

Back on Broadway she had two new plays, *Little Old New York* (1920) and *Macushla* (1920), followed by *The Front Seat* (1921).

Then Rida Young rejoined Victor Herbert in 1924 for *The Dream Girl*. She and Harold Atteridge wrote the book and lyrics. The show starred Fay Bainter and Walter Woolf and featured the song "My Dream Girl." Unfortunately, Victor Herbert died shortly before the musical opened. Nevertheless, the show went on successfully.

Some of Rida Young's other plays include *The Rabbit's Foot*, *Cock o' the Roost*, *One of the Boys*, *The Yellow Streak*, *Look Who's Here*, *Fair Play*, *Lot 79*, and *Miss I-Don't-Know*, the latter written with Augustus Barratt.

Besides plays and operettas, she wrote three novels in the 1920s: *The Girl That Came Out of the Night*, *Virginal*, and *Red Owl*.

In an interview Rida Johnson Young described how her work habits had developed. "When I began writing plays I used to work at night when I had something that felt like an inspiration. But I've found that for me at least, it is 'dogged as does it.' I can do better work and keep myself in better health by doing my regular half-day stint" (*New York Times*, May 9, 1926, p. 9).

Every day she went to her desk at a certain hour and would stay there for four hours whether or not she was able to write. "Even if nothing comes to me for a long time, I sit there." When the four hours were up, she would reward herself by doing something enjoyable like swimming or playing tennis. "My writing is labor! It takes me from four to six months to write a play after this fashion." Yet by working just four hours a day, day after day, she had produced a large body of work.

Although she was very successful, Rida Young remained modest about her accomplishments. "One must make it a business. That is the real reason I have succeeded. I have never undertaken anything really big. I have contented myself with writing plays that are popular and within my ability" (*American Magazine*, December 1920, p. 185).

Rida Johnson Young died in her fifties at her home in Southfield Point near Stamford, Connecticut, on May 8, 1926.

SOURCES

Bennett, Helen. "Woman Who Wrote," *American Magazine*, December 1920, pp. 34–185.

Bordman, Gerald. *Jerome Kern.*

Bordman, Gerald. *Oxford Companion to American Theatre.*

Claghorn, Charles. *Biographical Dictionary of American Music.*

Ewen, David. *Complete Book of American Musical Theater.*

Ewen, David. *New Complete Book of American Musical Theater.*

Green, Stanley. *World of Musical Comedy.*

Hanson, Patricia. *American Film Institute Catalog.*

Harker, David. *One for the Money.*

Kinkle, Roger. *Complete Encyclopedia of Popular Music and Jazz.*

Logan, Mary. *Part Taken by Women in American History.*

Lynn Farnol Group. *ASCAP Biographical Dictionary.*

Mainiero, Lina. *American Women Writers.*

Mattfeld, Julius. *Variety Music Cavalcade.*

New York Times Film Reviews.

New York Times. Obituaries, May 9, 1926, p. 9.

Spaeth, Sigmund. *History of Popular Music in America.*

Waters, Edward. *Victor Herbert.*

Witmark, Isidore. *Story of House of Witmark.*

IV | BLUES

257571

INTRODUCTION

Classical blues singers like Ma Rainey and Bessie Smith are thought of primarily as performers. Yet in addition to singing, dancing, and entertaining on stage, most of the blues women also wrote many of the songs they sang. A few, like Victoria Spivey, were prolific songwriters.

The blues, like jazz, gospel, and other African-American music, were influenced by the experiences of a people brought to this country in slavery, as well as by their African musical traditions. As LeRoi Jones has written, "Blues could not exist if the African captives had not become American captives." The "blue notes" of jazz and blues may be explained as the attempt to adjust the African pentatonic (five-note) scale to the European diatonic (seven-note) scale, thereby causing the "bluing" or flatting of notes; but the emotional content of the blues is a reflection of the sorrow and suffering people endured under oppression.

Africans brought with them a tradition of work songs to set the tempo for repetitious work like chopping wood and hoeing. Plantation overseers encouraged this kind of music, for they felt it increased productivity. Giles Oakley in his book *The Devil's Music* quotes James Hungerford's account of his visit to a plantation in 1859. Hungerford describes a woman slave who was particularly valued for her ability to improvise work songs. Clotilda "can make you rhymes all day long, and is a great help to the cornbank singers, furnishing them with any number of jingling lines for the corn-husking season, and with tunes for them too for she can make melodies as well as rhymes" (Oakley, pp. 17–18).

Although some instruments, such as drums, were prohibited, music was permitted for work songs, for entertainment when work was done, and for church music. African music, which had been closely associated with all the activities and rituals of African daily life, was transplanted to America, but the experience of captivity in America gave those songs a sorrowful sound.

By the 1920s when the blues were beginning to find a mass audience through recordings, they had absorbed not only the influences of the African work songs, field hollers, and spirituals but also the influences of ragtime, marches, funeral dirges, and minstrel songs. Blues were characterized by the use of harsh vocal sounds—growls and moans—and by seemingly off-key notes, the "blue notes." Blues generally featured the call-and-response pattern of work songs in which the leader sang a line and the group repeated it. In this pattern, the leader improvising the song would sing a line and then repeat the line, which gave him or her time to think of a new third line to rhyme with the first. The group would echo the lines the leader sang. Blues often used this same pattern.

> Going to the Louisiana bottom to get me a hoodoo hand,
> Going to the Louisiana bottom to get me a hoodoo hand,
> Gotta stop these women from taking my man.
> —"Louisiana Hoodoo Blues" by Ma Rainey

The blues encouraged improvisation and spontaneity. Singers and instrumentalists were free to reshape the old songs as they performed them, changing phrases, adding lines, borrowing images, and providing new words for old melodies and new tunes to the old phrases, recreating the song. Consequently, in the blues as in other kinds of folk music there may be many versions of the same song. Frequently the original authorship is impossible to determine.

Although she was known as the Mother of the Blues and was the first to sing the blues professionally, Ma Rainey was not the first to record the blues. That distinction went to Mamie Smith, a Harlem cabaret singer. Her 1920 rendition of "Crazy Blues" was a tremendous hit, selling 75,000 copies in the first month and making Mamie Smith a star. After this, companies began recording every black woman singer they could find who might possibly repeat Mamie Smith's success. Many of the women they recorded were vaudeville and musical revue singers who brought a polish and sophistication to their interpretation of the blues. It was Ma Rainey, and others who maintained a close connection with the rural South, who produced the rough and gritty traditional blues in their singing and songwriting.

ARMSTRONG, LILLIAN HARDIN (1898/1902–1971)
"Perdito Street Blues"

Lillian Hardin may have been best known as Mrs. Louis Armstrong, but in her own right she was a pianist, arranger, composer, and working musician all her life.

Born in Memphis, Tennessee, on February 3, 1898/1902, she studied music at Fisk University, Chicago College of Music, and the New York College of Music, where she earned a postgraduate degree in 1929.

Her first job was as a song demonstrator playing sheet music in a music store. Then she was pianist for several different groups before forming her own band about 1920. She worked as pianist and arranger with King Oliver's Creole Jazz Band in the early 1920s and there met Louis Armstrong, whom she married in 1924. He played in her Lil Armstrong's Dreamland Syncopators before starting his own band in 1927. She appeared on Broadway in *Hot Chocolates* (1929) and *Shuffle Along* (1933). She also performed on the radio and toured Europe as a soloist.

Because she knew how to arrange music, her husband often relied on her to transcribe his songs, and sometimes they wrote songs together. In Shapiro and Hentoff's *Hear Me Talkin' to Ya*, Preston Jackson recalled, "Most of the tunes Louis composed, Lil wrote the music to. Louis would play the melody and Lil would write it down as fast as Louis played." "Struttin' with Some Barbecue" and "Perdito Street Blues" are songs she wrote with Louis Armstrong. Among the 150 pieces that she wrote are the songs "Brown Gal" and "Just for a Thrill," the latter written with Don Raye.

In 1938 she and Louis Armstrong divorced. Subsequently, she went to work as staff pianist for Decca recording studios.

Lil Armstrong lived into her eighties and was still playing right up to the end. She died in August 1971 in Chicago while performing in a memorial concert for Louis Armstrong, who had died a month earlier.

SOURCES
Chilton, John. *Who's Who of Jazz.*
Dahl, Linda. *Stormy Weather.*
Lynn Farnol Group. *ASCAP Biographical Dictionary.*
Shapiro, Nat. *Hear Me Talkin' to Ya.*

Southern, Eileen. *Biographical Dictionary of Afro-Americans and African Musicians.*
Southern, Eileen. *Music of Black Americans.*

AUSTIN, LOVIE (1887–1972)   "Jealous Hearted Blues"

A working musician all her life, Lovie Austin was a pianist, arranger, composer, and accompanist for many of the great blues singers. With her group, the Blues Serenaders, she accompanied such notables as **Ida Cox, Ma Rainey, Ethel Waters,** and **Alberta Hunter.**

She worked as a pianist and arranger for Paramount and Vocalion record companies and for more than 20 years was the musical director and house pianist at The Monogram Theater in Chicago.

Lovie Austin was born Cora Calhoun in Chattanooga, Tennessee, on September 19, 1887. She studied music at Roger Williams College in Nashville and Knoxville College.

In her early years she was an accompanist for her husband and his partner in their vaudeville act, Austin and Delaney. She toured on the TOBA (Theater Owners' Booking Association) circuit in a musical revue and played in a New York Club before settling in Chicago and beginning her long residence at the Monogram Theater.

When jazz pianist **Mary Lou Williams** was a young, aspiring musician, she saw Lovie Austin in performance. Down in the orchestra pit sat Austin with a cigarette in her mouth, accompanying the show with her left hand while with her right hand writing music for an act later in the program. Very impressed with Lovie Austin, Mary Lou said to herself, "Mary, you'll do that one day" (Shapiro and Hentoff, *Hear,* p. 248). And, of course, Mary Lou Williams did follow in Lovie Austin's footsteps.

Alberta Hunter also knew Lovie Austin, for she was the person who had copied down on paper Alberta Hunter's "Down Hearted Blues," a song Hunter had written as a child. "Austin was a good, honest woman because somebody else might have stolen the whole thing from me," Alberta Hunter recalled (Oakley, *Devil's,* p. 39).

Lovie Austin also wrote songs. Among them are "Bleeding Hearted Blues," "Any Woman Blues," "Chicago Bound Blues," "Bad Luck Blues," "Barrel House Blues," "Jealous Hearted Blues," and "Ya-Da-Do." With **Ma Rainey** she wrote "Walking Blues," and with Katie Winters she wrote "Lucky Rock Blues."

It was not always easy for Lovie Austin to make a living as a musician. Although many of her recordings were reissued over the years, she didn't receive any royalties from them, even on her own compositions. During World War II she found work in the defense industry. In her later years she worked as a pianist for a dance school.

In 1961 Lovie Austin appeared in the film *The Great Blues Singers,* the same year that she made her last recording. She died in Chicago in 1972.

SOURCES

Brooks, Edward. *Bessie Smith Companion.*
Chilton, John. *Who's Who of Jazz.*
Dahl, Linda. *Stormy Weather.*
Jones, Hettie. *Big Star Fallin' Mama.*
Lieb, Sandra. *Mother of the Blues.*
Moore, Carman. *Somebody's Angel Child.*
Oakley, Giles. *Devil's Music.*
Shapiro, Nat. *Hear Me Talkin' to Ya.*
Southern, Eileen. *Music of Black Americans.*
Stewart-Baxter, Derrick. *Ma Rainey and the Classic Blues Singers.*

BIGEOU, ESTHER (c. 1895–c. 1936)   "West Indies Blues"

Esther Bigeou was a blues singer born about 1895 in New Orleans. She toured in revues throughout the South and played Baltimore, Philadelphia, Washington, and Chicago on the TOBA circuit, which booked black entertainment.

In the 1920s she began recording with OKeh Records. She recorded her own "West Indies Blues" with J. Piron's Orchestra in 1923. Other songs Esther Bigeou wrote include "Panama Limited Blues," "Tee Pee Valley Blues," and "You Ain't Treatin' Me Right."

She was married to Irvin C. Miller.

With the Depression, Esther Bigeou retired, reportedly to New Orleans. It is thought that she died about 1936 in Los Angeles.

SOURCES

Harris, Sheldon. *Blues Who's Who.*
Oliver, Paul. *Story of the Blues.*

COX, IDA (1896–1967)   "Wild Women Don't Have the Blues"

Ida Cox was another of the classic blues singers who wrote many of her own songs. She was born Ida Prather in Toccoa, Georgia, on February 25, 1896. She sang in church as a child, but ran away from home and joined a minstrel group. Like **Ma Rainey** and **Bessie Smith,** Ida Cox got her early

training working with the Rabbit Foot Minstrels. She began at the age of
fourteen and for a time appeared as Topsy.

From 1910 on she toured extensively in vaudeville and revues. She recorded from 1923 to 1929, working with many of the top jazzmen, including King Oliver and Tommy Ladnier. From 1929 to 1930 she toured in her
own revue *Raisin' Cain.* She played theaters, did a revue with Bessie Smith
in New York, and sang on the radio. She was one of the few classic blues
singers to work right through the Depression. In 1939 and 1940 she sang
at Carnegie Hall. She was still touring in the 1950s.

Little is known about her private life except that she was married to
Jesse Crump, her accompanist for many years, and they had a child.

The songs she wrote were about death, rejection, superstition, abandon-
ment, and misery—the traditional topics of blues. Some of the songs she
wrote are "Blues Ain't Nothin' Else But," "Blues for Rampart Street,"
"Graveyard Dream Blues," "Hard Time Blues," "Lovin' Is the Thing I'm
Wild About," "Mean Papa Turn Your Key," "Misery Blues," "Mistreatin'
Daddy Blues," "Moaning Groaning Blues," and "Wild Women Don't Have
the Blues."

She made her last recording a few years before her death on November
10, 1967, at the age of 70 in Knoxville, Tennessee.

SOURCES
Albertson, Chris. *Bessie.*
Bogle, Donald. *Brown Sugar.*
Cook, Bruce. *Listening to Blues.*
Harris, Sheldon. *Blues Who's Who.*
Jones, Hettie. *Big Star Fallin' Mama.*
Oakley, Giles. *Devil's Music.*
Stewart-Baxter, Derrick. *Ma Rainey and the Classic Blues Singers.*
Oliver, Paul. *Story of the Blues.*

EDWARDS, SUSIE (1896–1963)   "I Got Your Bath Water On"

Susie Edwards was born in Pensacola, Florida, in 1896. She came up
through the tent shows and the TOBA circuit. She toured as a cakewalk
dancer in Tolliver's Circus from 1910 to 1916. Later she formed a comedy
song-and-dance team with her husband, Jody Edwards, and together they
worked the vaudeville circuits. She also appeared in revues. In 1940 she
was in the Broadway hit *Cabin in the Sky* with Ethel Waters.

Among the songs that Susie Edwards wrote were "I Got Your Bath Water
On" and "When My Man Shimmies."

She continued working in theaters until a heart attack ended her life in Chicago on December 5, 1963.

SOURCE
Harris, Sheldon. *Blues Who's Who.*

GRANT, LEOLA "COOT" (1893–)   "Gimme a Pigfoot"

Born Leola Pettigrew on June 17, 1893, in Birmingham, Alabama, Leola "Coot" Grant grew up in a family of 15 children. She danced in local vaudeville shows, eventually joining a touring company. Leola Grant appeared in musical comedies and revues, and she also recorded with Paramount, Columbia, and Decca.

About 1912 she married Wesley Wilson, with whom she had a son. Together Leola Grant and Wesley "Socks" Wilson performed in vaudeville for more than 20 years; they wrote more than 400 songs, most of them for their act.

In 1933 Leola Grant appeared in the Paul Robeson film *The Emperor Jones.*

Several of the songs Leola Grant and Wesley Wilson wrote were recorded by Bessie Smith; these included "Gimme a Pigfoot, "Do Your Duty," "I'm Down in the Dumps," and "Take Me for a Buggy Ride." Among the other songs they wrote were "Boodle Boo," "Blue Monday Up on Sugar Hill," "Come On, Coot, Do That Thing," "Crying Won't Make Him Stay," "Deceiving Man Blues," "Dish Rag Blues," "I Ain't Going to Sell You None," "Stevedore Man," "When Your Man Is Going to Put You Down," and "Your Kitchen Floor Is Plenty Good for Me."

SOURCES
Albertson, Chris. *Bessie.*
Feinstein, Elaine. *Bessie Smith.*
Harris, Sheldon. *Blues Who's Who.*
Oliver, Paul. *New Grove Gospel, Blues and Jazz.*
Oliver, Paul. *Story of the Blues.*

GREEN, LILLIAN (1919–1954)   "Why Don't You Do Right?"

Lillian Green was born in Mississippi on December 22, 1919, into a family of ten children. When her parents died, she left Mississippi for Chicago, where she found a job as a singing waitress. Then she began singing in clubs in Detroit and also in the South. Later she went to New York and sang at Cafe Society and at the Apollo Theater. She recorded with Victor, Bluebird, and Atlantic Records.

Of the songs she wrote, the best known became a hit for **Peggy Lee:** "Why Don't You Do Right?" Some of her other songs were "Mr. Jackson from Jacksonville," "Now What Do You Think," "Blow Top Blues," "Knockin' Myself Out," and "Romance in the Dark."

She became ill in Chicago and succumbed to pneumonia there on April 14, 1954, at the age of 34.

SOURCES
Dahl, Linda. *Stormy Weather.*
Harris, Sheldon. *Blues Who's Who.*
Shirley, Kay. *Book of the Blues.*
Stambler, Irwin. *Encyclopedia of Pop, Rock and Soul.*
Stewart-Baxter, Derrick. *Ma Rainey and the Classic Blues Singers.*

HEGAMIN, LUCILLE (1894–1970)   "Mississippi Blues"

Another of the early jazz and blues singers was Lucille Hegamin. She was born Lucille Nelson in Macon, Georgia, on November 29, 1894, the same year as **Bessie Smith.** Lucille, however, was petite and sweet-voiced. She sang in church as a child and at the age of 15 joined a touring minstrel company. When the company ran out of money and folded, she went to Chicago and sang in clubs, where she became known as the Georgia Peach. She then married her accompanist, Bill Hegamin.

Besides performing in clubs in Los Angeles and New York, Lucille Hegamin appeared in vaudeville and revues, among them *Shuffle Along, Creole Follies,* Lew Leslie's *Plantation Revue* with Florence Mills, and *Liza* with Gertrude Saunders.

Over the years she recorded with Victor, Paramount, Cameo, and Arto labels. Her biggest hit was "He May Be Your Man, but He Comes to See Me Sometimes." At the height of her career she was featured at the Cotton Club, from which she broadcast on the radio each week. The Depression, however, brought her career to an end. During the lean years from the 1930s to the 1950s she worked as a nurse.

In 1962, when Lucille Hegamin was 68, Victoria Spivey recorded her on the Spivey label singing her hit "He May Be Your Man, but He Comes to See Me Sometimes," as well as Spivey's song "Number 12 Train."

The songs Lucille Hegamin wrote include "Mississippi Blues" and "Lonesome Monday Mornin' Blues."

She died in Harlem on March 1, 1970.

SOURCES
Harris, Sheldon. *Blues Who's Who.*
Stewart-Baxter, Derrick. *Ma Rainey and the Classic Blues Singers.*
Southern, Eileen. *Music of Black Americans.*

HILL, BERTHA "CHIPPIE" (1905–1950)   "Charleston Blues"

Born in Charleston, South Carolina, on March 15, 1905, Bertha Hill was 1 of 16 children. She sang in church as a child. By the age of 14 she had left home to work as a dancer. She toured with the Rabbit Foot Minstrels and played the TOBA circuit as a singer and dancer. In 1925 she recorded with Louis Armstrong and also with **Lovie Austin**'s Blues Serenaders. In New York she sang with Kid Ory's Band, in Chicago with King Oliver's. She also worked briefly with **Ma Rainey.** At the age of 24 she married John Offett and retired to raise a family of seven children.

In 1946 she made a comeback, recording blues on the Circle label. Two years later she was a sensation at the Paris Jazz Festival.

Some of her compositions are "Atomic Blues," "Blackmarket Blues," "Pratt City Blues," and "Charleston Blues."

Her life was cut short on May 7, 1950, when she was killed by a hit-and-run driver in New York City.

SOURCES
Harris, Sheldon. *Blues Who's Who.*
Oliver, Paul. *Story of the Blues.*
Stewart-Baxter, Derrick. *Ma Rainey and the Classic Blues Singers.*

HUNTER, ALBERTA (1895–1984)   "The Love I Have for You"

Alberta Hunter was an international star of musicals and supper clubs, famous in London and Paris as well as in New York. Born a year after **Bessie Smith,** on April 1, 1895, in Memphis, Tennessee, she sang in local school programs as a child and wrote songs when she was very young.

She wrote "Downhearted Blues" when only ten. In 1907, at the age of 12, she ran away from home, taking a train to Chicago. She had heard that girls there were paid $6 a week to sing. Fortunately she met someone she had known in Memphis, and this friend looked after her.

When she was older, Alberta Hunter did get jobs singing, first in a house of prostitution, then in clubs, and then in Dreamland, where Louis Armstrong and **Lil Hardin** played with King Oliver's Band. At last she was making big money, $17.50 a week plus tips, and in those freewheeling, speakeasy days in Chicago sometimes tips were $100 to $200 a night. When she could afford to do so, she brought her mother to Chicago to live with her.

Alberta Hunter recorded on the Paramount label, backed by such fine musicians as Louis Armstrong, Eubie Blake, Fats Waller, **Lovie Austin,** and Fletcher Henderson. Her first hit record was her own song "Down Hearted Blues" (1922), which was the best-selling version until Bessie Smith recorded it. Bessie's version was an enormous hit that sold 800,000 copies.

Alberta Hunter's performance in the 1923 musical comedy *How Come* made her a Broadway star.

Performing in Cincinnati in 1927, she met and married Willis Saxbe Townsend, a waiter, but the marriage last only a few weeks. Alberta found out that she wasn't interested in being a housewife.

The following year she went to Europe and became an international success. In London she played opposite Paul Robeson in *Show Boat* and sang "Can't Help Lovin' Dat Man." In Paris she replaced Josephine Baker at the Folies Bergère and later performed at Chez Florence, where she entertained the Prince of Wales and Cole Porter. Porter liked her singing so much he wrote the song "I Travel Alone" just for her.

When she returned to the United States, the stock market had crashed and the Depression made work hard to find. She knew she could work in Europe, so she returned there. From Stockholm to Athens to Cairo, she toured in her own cabaret act, singing songs in seven languages. In 1934 she sang at a club in London and the following year appeared in a film singing the song "Black Shadows." With World War II approaching, she returned to New York. There she sang on her own radio show and in clubs like Connie's Inn, where she sang with Louis Armstrong. In 1939 she appeared on Broadway with **Ethel Waters** in *Mamba's Daughters.*

During the war years she toured with the United Service Organizations, the USO, entertaining servicemen and women in Europe and the Far East. She was in Korea in 1954 on her seventh tour when she learned that her mother had died. Returning to the United States, she was unable to find a singing job. She was now 59. So she enrolled in nursing school and became a practical nurse. For 20 years thereafter she worked as a nurse in a New York City hospital, keeping her age a secret. She worked until she was 82.

Retired and bored, Alberta Hunter was delighted when she received an offer to perform again at a club in Greenwich Village. She had lost none of her charm, and New Yorkers flocked to hear her. And so at 82 the legendary Alberta Hunter was a hit again. After this she recorded with Columbia, appeared on television in the United States and Scandinavia, and sang in clubs and at jazz festivals. She did television commercials and sang blues on the soundtrack of Robert Altman's 1978 film *Remember My Name*. President Carter invited her to sing at the White House. In 1988 a documentary about her, *My Castle's Rockin'*, was shown on Public Television. **Victoria Spivey**'s record company recorded Alberta singing her own songs, "I Got Myself a Working Man" and "Got a Mind to Ramble."

Nat Shapiro and Nat Hentoff's book *Hear Me Talkin' to Ya* includes an interview with Alberta Hunter in which she talks about writing the blues. The blues had always been a part of her life, she said. Often a new song would came to her at night. "I might have an idea, and lyrics will come to me. And the tune will come right along with it. And I'll get up early and go downtown and have somebody take the music down and put the words with it" (Shapiro and Hentoff, *Hear*, pp. 247–48). Like many others who wrote blues, she was paid a flat fee for her songs and never paid any royalties.

Alberta Hunter wrote a great number of songs, many blues, some religious, some ballads. Among her songs are "I Got a Mind to Ramble," "I Got Myself a Working Man," "I Want a Two-Fisted, Double-Jointed, Rough and Ready Man," "Mistreated Blues," "Chirping the Blues," "Streets Paved with Gold," "What's the Matter Baby?" "Remember My Name," "My Castle's Rockin'," "You Got to Reap Just What You Sow," "I Want to Thank You Lord for My Blessings," "Will the Day Ever Come When I Can Rest?" "The Love I Have for You," and "Now I'm Satisfied."

In October 1984 Alberta Hunter died in her easy chair.

SOURCES
Albertson, Chris. *Bessie.*
Bogle, Donald. *Brown Sugar.*
Dahl, Linda. *Stormy Weather.*
Harris, Sheldon. *Blues Who's Who.*
Lynn Farnol Group. *ASCAP Biographical Dictionary.*
Oakley, Giles. *Devil's Music.*
Oliver, Paul. *Story of the Blues.*
Placksin, Sally. *American Women in Jazz.*
Shapiro, Nat. *Hear Me Talkin' to Ya.*
Southern, Eileen. *Music of Black Americans.*
Stewart-Baxter, Derrick. *Ma Rainey and the Classic Blues Singers.*

JOHNSON, EDITH NORTH (c. 1905–   )   "Beat You Doing It"

It is believed that Edith North was born in St. Louis, Missouri, in 1905. Before becoming a singer she worked as a saleslady in a music store. She married Jessie Johnson, who owned the music store and who also worked as a talent scout for a record company. With her husband's help she began to record for the Paramount, OKeh and QRS labels.

Her husband was so enthusiastic about her career that he once hired a plane to drop leaflets advertising her latest record onto a crowd of spectators at a baseball game. Unfortunately, after they were married, her husband changed his mind and persuaded her to give up her career.

Nevertheless, Edith Johnson wrote a number of songs, among them "Nickel's Worth of Liver," "Eight Hour Woman," "Beat You Doing It," "That's My Man," "Cornet Pleading Blues," "Good Chib Blues," "Honey Dripper Blues," "Whispering to My Man," and "Can't Make Another Day."

SOURCES
Harris, Sheldon. *Blues Who's Who*.
Oliver, Paul. *Story of the Blues*.

JOHNSON, MARY "SIGNIFYIN" (c. 1900–   )   "Tornado Blues"

Born in Eden Station, Mississippi, about 1900, Mary Johnson spent most of her life in St. Louis, Missouri, where she had moved in her teens. As she grew older she sang in clubs and bars in St. Louis. In 1925 she married blues singer Alonzo Johnson and raised a family of six children.

Her singing career began in 1929 when she won a blues contest, in which the prize was a record contract. She first recorded with Paramount and then Decca, but her steady income came from working in a hospital.

Over the years Mary Johnson wrote many songs, primarily blues, among them "Baby Please Don't Go," "Prison Cell Blues," "Tornado Blues," "Black Gal Blues," "Rattlesnake Blues," "Mean Black Man Blues," "Key to the Mountain Blues," "Mary Johnson Blues," "Barrelhouse Flat Blues," and "Dream Daddy Blues."

SOURCES
Dahl, Linda. *Stormy Weather*.
Harris, Sheldon. *Blues Who's Who*.

JONES, MAGGIE (1899–   )   "Northbound Blues"

She was born Fae Barnes in Hillsboro, Texas, in 1899. In her twenties she was singing in clubs in New York, touring on the TOBA circuit, and performing in vaudeville. In New York City she appeared in Lew Leslie's *Blackbirds of 1928*. During the 1920s she recorded on the Black Swan, Victor, Paramount, and Columbia labels with Louis Armstrong and Fletcher

Henderson. She first sang under the name of Fae Barnes and then as Maggie Jones. As the Depression deepened in the 1930s, she returned to Texas to perform in her own revue. The times were bad, and after this she dropped out of show business altogether.

Among the songs Maggie Jones wrote are "Undertaker's Blues," "Screamin' the Blues," "Single Woman's Blues," and "Northbound Blues."

SOURCES

Harris, Sheldon. *Blues Who's Who.*
Stewart-Baxter, Derrick. *Ma Rainey and the Classic Blues Singers.*

JOPLIN, JANIS   *See* Pop Rock.

LEE, JULIA (1902–1958)   "Gotta Gimme Whatcha Got"

Julia Lee was a blues and jazz singer, a pianist, and a songwriter.

Born in Boonville, Missouri, on October 31, 1902, she sang with her father's trio at the age of four. As a child she played violin in her father's string band; she also studied piano.

In her teens Julia Lee was featured in the Novelty Singing Orchestra of her brother, George E. Lee. She toured with the band as a vocalist and pianist. When the band broke up, she toured as a soloist. Various record companies recorded her singing blues and playing her boogie-woogie piano, among them OKeh, Brunswick, and Capitol.

From 1934 to 1948 she resided in Kansas City. In 1948, President Harry Truman invited her to sing at a command performance.

Later in Hollywood she sang at Ciro's Nightclub, and other opportunities came her way. For the movie *The Delinquents* (1957), she sang "Dirty Rock Boogie."

Besides performing, she wrote a number of songs, among them "Julia's Blues," "That's What I Like," "Dream Lady Blues," "Julia's Boogie," "Gotta Gimme Whatcha Got," and "Come On Over to My House."

After returning to Kansas City, she died of a heart attack on December 8, 1958.

SOURCES

Chilton, John. *Who's Who of Jazz.*
Harris, Sheldon. *Blues Who's Who.*
Oliver, Paul. *Story of the Blues.*
Southern, Eileen. *Biographical Dictionary of Afro-Americans.*

LISTON, VIRGINIA (c. 1890–c. 1932)   "Jealous Hearted Blues"

Another of the early blues singer-songwriters was Virginia Liston. She was born about 1890. By 1912 she was singing blues in Philadelphia and Washington. She performed on the TOBA circuit and in vaudeville as Liston and Liston, with her first husband, Sam H. Gray, a musician and actor. They later settled in New York, where she performed in Harlem theaters from the early 1920s. In 1925 she toured the South in a revue, *Eliza Scandals*. Her recording career, which began in the early 1920s, lasted only three years.

By 1929 her marriage to Gray had ended, and she married Charles Harry Lee Smith. They moved to St. Louis, Missouri, where Virginia Liston retired. It is believed that she died in St. Louis in 1932.

Most of the songs she wrote were blues, among them "Bed Time Blues," "Don't Agitate Me Blues," "Jealous Hearted Blues," "Night Latch Key Blues," "Sally Long Blues," "Bill Draw," "Happy Shout," "Oh What a Time," "Put Your Mind on No One Man," and "You Thought I Was Blind but Now I Can See." She wrote "You Don't Know My Mind" with Samuel Gray and Clarence Williams.

SOURCES
Harris, Sheldon. *Blues Who's Who.*
Shirley, Kay. *Book of the Blues.*
Stewart-Baxter, Derrick. *Ma Rainey and the Classic Blues Singers.*

MARTIN, SARA (1884–1955)   "Death Sting Me Blues"

Sara Martin was one of the early classic blues singers. Her contemporaries were Mamie Smith and **Ma Rainey.** She was born Sara Dunn on June 18, 1884, in Louisville, Kentucky.

Sara Martin began her career on the vaudeville and TOBA circuits. Her opening was always very theatrical. Standing on a candle-lit stage in a darkened theater, Sara would begin to moan and wail the opening lines of her song. She would clutch the curtains, then throw herself down, and end up rolling on the stage overcome with emotion. The audience loved it.

In the early 1920s she began making recordings with Clarence Williams, Fats Waller, and her own Brown Skin Syncopators for OKeh and Columbia Records. Her greatest hit was a song she wrote herself, "Death Sting Me Blues," recorded with King Oliver.

Sara Martin went on to write a great number of songs, mostly blues, among them "Good Bye Blues," "Got to Leave My Home Blues," "Mistreating Man Blues," "Sweet Man's the Cause of It All," "I'm Gonna Hoodoo You," "Daddy Ease This Pain of Mine," "Your Going Ain't Giving Me the Blues," "Uncle Sam Blues," and "Trouble Blues." She and Clarence Williams wrote "Mama's Got the Blues."

Between 1927 and 1929 she toured in *Get Happy Follies* and appeared in New York in revues like *Bottomland* and *Sun-Tan Frolics*. She also appeared in the film *Hello Bill*.

She was married to Hayes Withers.

For a time when the Depression hit, she worked in clubs and theaters; but finally unable to make a living in music, she started her own private nursing home in Louisville, where she lived the rest of her life. She died there of a stroke on May 24, 1955.

SOURCES

Harris, Sheldon. *Blues Who's Who.*
Heilbut, Tony. *Gospel Sound.*
Oliver, Paul. *Story of the Blues.*
Stewart-Baxter, Derrick. *Ma Rainey and the Classic Blues Singers.*

McDANIEL, HATTIE (1895–1952)   "I Wish I Had Somebody"

Hattie McDaniel was a singer and songwriter, but she is probably best remembered for her Oscar-winning performance in the film *Gone with the Wind* (1939).

She was born on June 10, 1895, in Wichita, Kansas, into a family of 13 children. Her father was a minister who also owned a touring company where Hattie McDaniel began her early training as a performer. When she was older, she became a singer in vaudeville. In the mid-1920s OKeh Records recorded her with **Lovie Austin**'s Serenaders. By 1929 she had a part in the touring company of *Show Boat.*

Drawn to the movies, Hattie McDaniel moved to Hollywood in the early 1930s and began her long film career there. The height of her acting career came with her role in *Gone with the Wind*. In 1939 she was the first African-American to win an Academy Award. She continued to appear in films, nearly 80 of them, sometimes in a singing role, but more often as a maid or nanny.

Between motion pictures she appeared on radio and television shows. She did the "Amos 'n' Andy Show" for a time, and in the early 1950s starred in "Beulah" on television.

She was married twice, first to Lloyd Crawford and in 1949 to Larry C. Williams.

Hattie McDaniel wrote a number of songs, including "Any Kind of a Man Would Be Better Than You," "I Wish I Had Somebody," "That New Love Maker of Mine," and "Boo Hoo Blues."

She died in Hollywood on October 26, 1952, at the age of 57.

SOURCES
Block, Maxine. *Current Biography.*
Harris, Sheldon. *Blues Who's Who.*

MEMPHIS, MINNIE (1897–1973)   "Meningitis Blues"

Memphis Minnie was born Lizzie Douglas on June 3, 1897, on a farm in Algiers, Louisiana. One of 13 children, she learned to play both banjo and guitar as a child.

At the age of 11 she ran away from home and went to Memphis, Tennessee. She found work in the Ringling Brothers Circus and remained with them four years. Then she started singing in saloons along Beale Street in Memphis. In her thirties she began recording her own songs with several record companies. For a time she had her own vaudeville troupe. Later she sang in clubs in Chicago.

Over the years she married three times.

Some of the songs she wrote were "Bumble Bee," "I Want to Do Something for You," "Meningitis Blues," "Nothing in Rambling," and "Queen Bee."

Her health became bad in the 1950s. After living in Detroit for some years, she returned to Memphis, where she died on August 6, 1973.

SOURCES
Harris, Sheldon. *Blues Who's Who.*
Lieb, Sandra. *Mother of the Blues.*
Southern, Eileen. *Music of Black Americans.*

MOORE, MONETTE (1902–1962)   "Show Girl Blues"

Monette Moore was born in Gainesville, Texas, on May 19, 1902. She sang as a child and taught herself to play the piano. One of her first jobs was playing piano to accompany the silent movies in the local movie house.

By the time she was 21, Monette Moore had recorded with Paramount; later she recorded with George Lewis's Ragtime Band on Vocalion.

She sang in musical comedies and in films. In her fifties she appeared in the Judy Garland remake of *A Star Is Born* (1954) and later in the film *The Outsider* (1961). On television she sang with Louis Armstrong.

Two of the songs Monette Moore wrote are "Show Girl Blues" and "Treated Wrong Blues."

She died of emphysema in Garden Grove, California, on October 21, 1962.

SOURCES
Dahl, Linda. *Stormy Weather.*
Harris, Sheldon. *Blues Who's Who.*

PIERCE, BILLIE (1907–1974)   "Billie's Gumbo Blues"

Billie Pierce was born Willie Madison Goodson in Marianna, Florida, on June 8, 1907. Born into a large musical family, she taught herself to play the piano by the age of seven. When she was older, she worked as a dancer in the local theaters, but it was her ability to play the piano that got her a job accompanying **Bessie Smith.**

In 1922 when Bessie Smith's accompanist, Clarence Williams, quit the tour, Bessie hired Billie Pierce to replace him, although Pierce was only a youngster. Billie later became an accompanist for other great blues singers as well, among them **Ma Rainey** and **Ida Cox.** In the mid-1920s she toured the South in a revue, performing as a singer, dancer, and pianist.

She married cornetist De De Pierce and continued to play in and around New Orleans.

Probably her greatest claim to fame was in forming the Preservation Hall Jazz Band in New Orleans, where she worked from the 1960s through the 1970s. She appeared in a PBS television show about New Orleans Jazz in 1964 and in ABC-TV's "Anatomy of Pop" in 1966. She also played at the Newport Folk Festival and at Fillmore East and West with the Dixieland Jazz Quintet.

Some of the songs Billie Pierce wrote are "Billie's Gumbo Blues," "Good Tonk Blues," "Freight Train Moanin' Blues," "In the Racket," and "Going Back to Florida."

SOURCES
Dahl, Linda. *Stormy Weather.*
Harris, Sheldon. *Blues Who's Who.*

RAINEY, GERTRUDE "MA" (1886–1939)   "Blues Oh Blues"

The first great classical blues singer was Ma Rainey. Born Gertrude Pridgett in Columbus, Georgia, on April 26, 1886, she was the second of five children. When she was 14, she made her first stage appearance at the Springer Opera House in Columbus in a local talent show called a Bunch of Blackberries. After this she performed in tent shows.

In 1904 she married William "Pa" Rainey, who was a song-and-dance man and a comedian. Thus, at the age of 18 she became known as "Ma" Rainey. She and Will toured the South in a traveling show as the team of Rainey and Rainey, the Assassinators of the Blues. In the following years she worked in Silas Green's minstrel shows, Tolliver's Circus, and the celebrated Rabbit Foot Minstrels. By 1917 she was the star of her own show, Madame Gertrude Rainey and Her Georgia Smart Sets.

Perhaps as early as 1902 Gertrude Rainey had added a new kind of song to her performances, the blues. In later years she told the story of how she first heard the blues. When Ma Rainey was performing in a tent show in a small Missouri town, a local girl came to the tent and sang for her one morning. The song was so plaintive and strange that Ma Rainey couldn't forget it. She learned the song, adding it to her performances as an encore. Audiences responded so well that she was encouraged to include more of these songs, which she called the blues. Ma Rainey didn't originate the blues, which was a kind of folk music sung privately everywhere by African-Americans. She was, however, the first to give this music public recognition and validity by performing it in her shows. For this reason, she is known as the Mother of the Blues.

Ma Rainey performed almost entirely for black rural audiences in the South. In this era before television and movies, the tent show undoubtedly provided the only excitement and glamor for those who lived in small towns and agricultural communities. Ma Rainey understood very well that her show provided her audiences with a magical escape from the raw drudgery of field work and farm labor. So Ma gave them a show to remember.

The stage lights would come up on a huge Victrola. Ma's voice would be heard singing from inside the Victrola. Then the cabinet doors would open and Ma would sashay out in all her feathers and finery, wearing a sequined black dress and a beaded headband, all the while fanning herself with ostrich plumes, her gold-capped teeth sparkling through her smile. She was short, dark, and chubby, never described as good looking; but when she sang, it didn't matter. She was the kind of singer who held her audience spellbound. She didn't need any words. When she would moan, the audience would moan with her. Jazz critic Ralph Gleason described her in his book Celebrating the Duke as "a singer of amazing power and capable of evoking deep, almost mystical emotion" (Gleason, p. 8).

It wasn't until 1923, when she was 37, that record companies finally located Ma Rainey and began recording her. Over the next five years she recorded 92 songs for the Paramount label. To these she brought the rough, gritty, low-down sounds of the country blues. She was accompanied by a rough jazz band or a jug band with such country instruments as a banjo, musical saw, kazoo, and slide-whistle. Ma Rainey's voice, also, was a departure from the sweet voices of blues singers from the musical stage like Mamie Smith or Ethel Waters. It was heavier and her articulation was less distinct, but there was a quality in the voice that touched the heart.

Although she recorded in Chicago and New York, Ma Rainey's live performances were almost entirely in the South for rural black audiences. These were her people, and it was for them that she sang and wrote her songs.

> My head goes round and around, Babe, since my baby left town
> And I don't know if the river runnin' up or down
> But there's one thing certain, Mama's gonna leave town.
> —"Moonshine Blues" by Ma Rainey

The blues Ma Rainey wrote conveyed strong emotions. In "Moonshine Blues" the woman is drunk because her lover left town. She is "Counting the Blues" to get her mind off her troubles. In "Little Low Mama" she's going to hang herself because her man doesn't love her. In "Rough and Tumble Blues" she killed the woman who stole her lover. Two songs concern homosexuality. In "Sissy Blues" her man left her for another man, and in "Prove It on Me Blues" they say she likes women, recalling Ma's own bisexual nature. Two other songs are comic: "Those Dogs of Mine," about her tired feet, and a popular dance with a double entendre in the title, "Ma Rainey's Black Bottom." Other songs written by Ma Rainey include "Hear Me Talking to You," "Chain Gang Blues," "Runaway Blues," "Southern Blues," "Broken Hearted Blues," and "Bo-Weevil Blues," the latter written with **Lovie Austin.**

Ma Rainey wrote songs with members of her band, such as accompanists Thomas A. Dorsey and Lovie Austin. She also wrote with the manager of the Race Records division at Paramount Records, J. Mayo Williams, and with his secretary, Althea Dickerson, who used the pseudonym Selma Davis. Ma Rainey's most famous collaborator was **Bessie Smith,** with whom she wrote "Don't Fish in My Sea" and "Weepin' Woman Blues."

The origin of some of Ma Rainey's songs is not clear. "See See Rider" is often attributed to Ma Rainey, but some authorities consider it to be a folk song of very old origin and of unknown authorship. Sandra Liebe, author of the biography of Ma Rainey, *Mother of the Blues,* found that the song had been copyrighted by Lena Arrant, but she suggests that Arrant probably wrote only the introduction. Also, "Hustlin' Blues" is credited to Malissa Nix and Thomas Dorsey. Malissa was Ma Rainey's sister.

Ma Rainey didn't write all the songs she recorded, but she did write nearly half of the songs she recorded each year. In 1928, her last year of recording, she wrote 12 of the 21 records she cut. Although not all of these songs were blues, the majority were in traditional blues forms. Ironically, as the record companies and listening public were becoming less interested in blues, Ma Rainey was moving more deeply into the country blues sound.

With the competition of sound movies and live radio music, record companies were having a difficult time trying to keep up with the changes in musical taste. So in 1928 Paramount Records didn't renew Ma Rainey's recording contract. They thought her rustic country style had gone out of fashion. The following year the stock market crashed. The Depression years that followed put most of the blues singers out of work, but Ma Rainey was still popular on the touring circuit. She toured through the South with her own Arkansas Swift Foot Revue and also performed with the Al Gaines Carnival Show. Even through the dark days of the Depression she had employment.

The details of Ma Rainey's personal life are sketchy. After she married William Rainey, they adopted a son, Danny, who was a dancer. The marriage, apparently, was short lived. It was thought that some years later Ma married a younger man not in show business.

In 1935 both her sister, Malissa, and her mother died. That year, at the age of 49, Ma Rainey quit performing and moved back to Columbus, Georgia, to keep house for her brother, Thomas. There she ran two theaters, one in Columbus and one in Rome. She joined the Friendship Baptist Church, where her brother was a deacon. It was in Columbus that she died of a heart attack on December 22, 1939, at the age of 53, just two years after Bessie Smith's death. Ma Rainey is buried in the family plot in Porterdale Cemetery.

SOURCES

Albertson, Chris. *Bessie.*
Bogle, Donald. *Brown Sugar.*
Brooks, Edward. *Bessie Smith Companion.*
Collier, James. *Making of Jazz.*
Gleason, Ralph. *Celebrating the Duke.*
Harris, Sheldon. *Blues Who's Who.*
Jones, Hettie. *Big Star Fallin' Mama.*
Lieb, Sandra. *Mother of the Blues.*
Moore, Carman. *Somebody's Angel Child.*
Morgenstern, Dan. *Ma Rainey. Milestone* album notes.
Oakley, Giles. *Devil's Music.*
Oliver, Paul. *Story of the Blues.*
Placksin, Sally. *American Women in Jazz.*

Southern, Eileen. *Music of Black Americans.*
Stewart-Baxter, Derrick. *Ma Rainey and the Classic Blues Singers.*

RAITT, BONNIE   *See* Pop Rock.

SCRUGGS, IRENE (1901–   )   "You Got What I Want"

Born in Mississippi on December 7, 1901, Irene Scruggs began her singing career by winning an amateur contest. Then she toured on the TOBA
circuit. About 1920 she married and had a daughter, "Baby" Scruggs, who
later became a dancer.

By 1924 Irene Scruggs had a recording contract with the OKeh label.
She later recorded with King Oliver's Creole Jazz Band for the Vocalion
label. Around 1935 she retired in St. Louis.

However, in 1953 the British Broadcasting Corporation (BBC) located
her and presented her on their radio program "Ballads and Blues."

Irene Scruggs wrote a number of songs, including "Cherry Hill Blues,"
"Everybody's Blues," "Home Town Blues," "Sorrow Valley Blues," "Back
to the Wall," "Borrowed Love," "Cruel Papa but a Good Man to Have
Around," "My Daddy's Calling Me," and "You Got What I Want."
SOURCE
Harris, Sheldon. *Blues Who's Who.*

SMITH, BESSIE (c. 1894–1937)
"Please Help Me Get Him off My Mind"

Known as the Empress of the Blues, Bessie Smith is considered to have
been the greatest of all the women blues singers. She was fortunate to have
begun her career in a traveling show that featured the great **Ma Rainey**
and was therefore able to observe and learn from the Mother of the Blues.
They became good friends and even wrote some songs together. But it was
Bessie Smith's talent and personality that made her a great artist and an
enormous influence on subsequent generations.

Born on April 15, c. 1894, in Chattanooga, Tennessee, Bessie Smith was
one of the seven children of an impoverished, part-time Baptist minister
and his wife. Unfortunately both parents died before she was nine years
old. Her older sister, Viola, kept the family together and raised her siblings
as best she could. To earn money Bessie and her brother sang and danced
for pennies on the streets of Chattanooga.

Her brother Clarence got a job as a dancer and comedian in the Moses Stokes traveling show. When the show came through Chattanooga, he was able to get Bessie, age 18, a job as a dancer in the show with him. One of the featured acts of the Moses Stokes traveling show was Ma and Pa Rainey.

By 1913 Bessie Smith was singing in a show and earning $10 a week and several more dollars in tips thrown on the stage every day. Then she teamed with Buzzin' Burton as Smith and Burton in a song-and-dance act. About 1915 she joined the Rabbit Foot Minstrels with Ma and Pa Rainey and toured the South. She went on touring with many other tent shows, the *Florida Cotton Blossoms* minstrel show, Silas Green's minstrel show, *Liberty Belles Revue,* and other touring shows throughout the South.

It wasn't until 1923 when Bessie Smith was 28 and had spent more than ten years in touring shows that she was put under contract by Columbia Records. Her first recording, "Down Hearted Blues" backed by "Gulf Coast Blues," was a huge success, selling 780,000 copies in less than six months. She continued to make recordings for the next ten years, working with such artists as Benny Goodman, Louis Armstrong, Joe Smith, Jack Teagarden, and others. For each recording she was paid a flat fee, at the most $200, but no royalties—not a penny more no matter how well the record sold. This is particularly ironic, since it was the popularity of her records that helped save Columbia Records from bankruptcy in the lean years. It was her public appearances that brought in the money, as much as $2,000 a week at the peak of her career.

Of the 180 songs she recorded, about one-fourth of them were her own compositions. Most of her songs were about love, mostly unhappy love, and the rest had to do with pain, suffering, poverty, prison, alcohol, and death—the usual subject matter of the blues. Bessie Smith's blues were earthy and full of double meanings, like the one she wrote with Ma Rainey: "Don't Fish in My Sea."

> If you don't like my ocean, don't fish in my sea
> If you don't like my ocean, don't fish in my sea
> Stay out of my valley, and let my mountain be.
>
> Ain't had no lovin' since God knows when
> Ain't had no lovin' since God knows when
> That's the reason I'm through with these no good triflin' men.
> —"Don't Fish in My Sea," words by Bessie Smith and
> music by Gertrude Rainey

Her blues classic "Back Water Blues" came from her personal experience of being stranded by a flood while traveling by train with her touring company. Everyone had to be taken off the train in rowboats. But their problems were not as bad as those of the people who lived in the low, backwater areas that were intentionally flooded to relieve pressure on the river embankments. The people in these backwaters lost everything. When Bessie Smith got home, the song just came to her, according to her sister-in-law. "Bessie came in the kitchen one day, and she had a pencil and paper, and she started singing and writing. That's when she wrote the 'Back Water Blues,' " as Chris Albertson reported in his biography *Bessie* (p. 127). Her recording of the song became famous partially because it was released in 1927 at the time of one of the worst floods in Mississippi's history.

Many of her songs were written on the spot at recording sessions. In Ralph Gleason's book *Celebrating the Duke*, Louis Armstrong told of seeing Bessie Smith writing songs: "Like Bessie Smith. I remember she just stayed in the studio and wrote the blues there. She finish one, she write another" (p. 45). She would write the words and sing the tune; then someone else, usually her pianist, would write down the notes. It was in this manner that many of Bessie Smith's songs were written.

Bessie Smith's artistry is still apparent on the old recordings. Dan Morgenstern, writing for *Downbeat* magazine, described her talent and her legacy. "Bessie Smith's magnificent voice, majestic phrasing, clear and unaffected diction, and incomparable rhythmic sureness have had a far-reaching influence on the development of jazz singing" (Morgenstern, "Hall of Fame Winner," *Downbeat*, August 24, 1967, p. 22). Biographer Chris Albertson considered her to be the greatest of all female blues singers.

Some of the songs Bessie Smith wrote included "Death Valley Moan," "Dirty No Gooder Blues," "Good Feelin' Blues," "Hard Time Blues," "He's Gone Blues," "It Makes My Love Come Down," "My Man Blues," "Poor Man's Blues," "Preachin' the Blues," "Please Help Me Get Him off My Mind," "Shipwreck Blues," "Wasted Life Blues," and "Young Woman's Blues." She wrote several with Clarence Williams: "Jail House Blues," "Jot 'Em Down Blues," and "Cake Walkin' Babies," the latter with A. Troy and Clarence Williams. With Irving Johns, her accompanist, she wrote "Pinchbacks, Take 'Em Away," "Rocking Chair Blues," and "Sorrowful Blues." Three songs credited to Jack Gee, her husband, are "Cold in Hand Blues," "Dying Gambler's Blues," and "Woman's Trouble Blues." She also wrote "Spiderman Blues" with Harold Gray.

Bessie Smith was a legendary personality. Stories abound about her exploits, her drinking, her bisexual adventures. She had an intimidating presence. She stood five feet, nine inches tall and weighed 210 pounds, and she was famous for punching people who annoyed her. On one occasion

Bessie Smith, 1928. (Frank Driggs Coll.)

some Klans men arrived to disrupt one of her tent shows. Bessie glowered at them, told them what she thought of them, and they fled.

She was never comfortable with society people. At a party in the New York apartment of author-photographer Carl Van Vechten, Bessie Smith drank too much and became irritated with all the fancy white people. When she started to leave, petite Mrs. Van Vechten attempted to kiss her good-bye. Bessie roared, "Get the - - - away from me. I ain't never heard of such - - -!" and gave her hostess a shove that sent her to the floor while Bessie staggered off (Albertson, *Bessie*, p. 143).

Bessie Smith had a low tolerance for pretense and for white people in general. One thing that angered her was producers who hired only light-skinned African-Americans. She herself had been excluded from jobs for being too dark. In her own shows she hired only dark-skinned people. Although some people found Bessie Smith's behavior scandalous, others admired her for being a powerful black woman who said and did what she wanted without pretense and without fear.

Bessie appeared to be so indestructible that her sudden death in an auto accident on September 26, 1937, seemed impossible. The car in which she was a passenger crashed into a truck that had stopped on a dark country road in Coahoma, Mississippi, near Clarksdale. She was taken to a hospital in Clarksdale, where she died the next morning. Some say she died because she had been refused treatment at a whites-only hospital. Others say that no ambulance driver in those days of segregation would have taken a black woman to a whites-only hospital. A doctor who saw her at the accident said that he thought she must have had serious internal injuries. (For more about this controversy see Chris Albertson's *Bessie*.)

Whatever the truth may be about the circumstances of her death, certainly the world had lost a great blues singer many years too soon.

The short 16-minute film *The St. Louis Blues* (1929), in which Bessie Smith sings, is now available on videocassette.

SOURCES

Albertson, Chris. *Bessie.*
Bogle, Donald. *Brown Sugar.*
Brooks, Edward. *Bessie Smith Companion.*
Chase, Gilbert. *America's Music.*
Collier, James. *Making of Jazz.*
Feinstein, Elaine. *Bessie Smith.*
Gleason, Ralph. *Celebrating the Duke.*
Hammond, John. *On Record.*
Harris, Sheldon. *Blues Who's Who.*
Hitchcock, H. Wiley. *New Grove Dictionary of American Music.*
Lieb, Sandra. *Mother of the Blues.*
Moore, Carman. *Somebody's Angel Child.*
Oakley, Giles. *Devil's Music.*
Oliver, Paul. *Story of the Blues.*
Placksin, Sally. *American Women in Jazz.*
Shirley, Kay. *Book of the Blues.*
Stewart-Baxter, Derrick. *Ma Rainey and the Classic Blues Singers.*

SMITH, CLARA (c. 1894–1935)   "Every Woman's Blues"

Known as Queen of the Moaners, Clara Smith was one of the early classic blues singers, like the other famous **Smiths—Bessie, Trixie,** and Mamie—none of whom was related to the other. She also sang under the name of Violet Green.

Clara Smith was born in Spartanburg, South Carolina, about 1894. In her teens she performed in vaudeville and by 1918 had become a headliner on the TOBA circuit. In New York's Harlem she sang in clubs and speakeasies. She sang blues and popular songs, and she performed boisterous comedy routines.

Her recording career began in 1923 and lasted ten years during which she recorded 123 songs and sang with the top blues musicians, including Louis Armstrong. She also recorded duets with Bessie Smith in the mid-1920s. Her first record was one of her own songs, "Every Woman's Blues." Some of her other songs were "So Long Jim," "Whip It to a Jelly," "Deep Sea Blues," and "Court House Blues."

She married ex–baseball manager Charles Wesley in 1926 and settled in New York, where she appeared in her own revues *Black Bottom* and *Clara Smith Revue*. In 1931 she appeared in an all-black musical western called *Trouble on the Ranch*. The following year she sang at the Harlem Opera House.

However, the Depression brought an end to her career. She retired to Detroit, and there on February 2, 1935, Clara Smith, in her early forties, had a heart attack and died.

SOURCES
Harris, Sheldon. *Blues Who's Who.*
Oakley, Giles. *Devil's Music.*
Placksin, Sally. *American Women in Jazz.*
Stewart-Baxter, Derrick. *Ma Rainey and the Classic Blues Singers.*

SMITH, TRIXIE (1895–1943)

"The World's Jazz Crazy and So Am I"

Known as the Southern Nightingale, Trixie Smith was born in Atlanta, Georgia, in 1895. She attended Selma University in Selma, Alabama. About 1918 she began touring on the TOBA circuit, after which she sang in clubs, theaters, and revues in New York City.

In January 1922 she won a blues-singing contest at the Inter-Manhattan Casino by singing her own song, "Trixie's Blues." For this she won a silver loving cup and a contract to record with Black Swan Records. Her recording of "Trixie's Blues" became a hit, but her most famous record was the 1925 recording she made with Louis Armstrong of her own "Railroad Man Blues." Other songs of hers were "The World's Jazz Crazy and So Am I," "Freight Train Blues," and "Mining Camp Blues."

She appeared in a 1932 film, *The Black King,* and had roles in stage shows, some of which were nonsinging roles.

She died in New York City on September 21, 1943.

SOURCES

Dixon, Robert. *Recording the Blues.*
Harris, Sheldon. *Blues Who's Who.*
Oliver, Paul. *Story of the Blues.*
Stewart-Baxter, Derrick. *Ma Rainey and the Classic Blues Singers.*

SPIVEY, VICTORIA (1906–1976)   "Black Snake Blues"

Known as the Queen, Victoria Spivey was probably the most productive of the women blues singer-songwriters. During her career of more than 50 years, she wrote nearly 1,500 songs, in addition to performing and running a record company.

Born on October 15, 1906, in Houston, Texas, into a family of musicians and band leaders, she was destined for a career in the music business. Both her father and her uncles had string bands. Her cousin, **Sippie Wallace,** was a great blues singer. Victoria and her sisters—Addie, known as Sweet Peas, Elton, known as Za-Zu, and Leona Spivey—all became singers. As a child Victoria Spivey learned to play a variety of musical instruments, and by the time she was 12 she had a job playing piano to accompany the silent movies in a Houston theater.

Derrick Stewart-Baxter in his book *Ma Rainey and the Classic Blues Singers* tells the story of how Victoria Spivey decided to become a singer. She saw a performance by Mamie Smith, who was the first black woman to record the blues, and in that moment Victoria decided she would become a blues singer too. "Miss Smith walked on that stage and I could not breathe for a minute . . . then she sang—she tore the house apart" (Stewart-Baxter, *Ma,* p. 16).

Victoria Spivey began singing with blues bands in clubs and gambling houses in Texas. In 1926 she made her first recording on the OKeh label. She accompanied herself on her own composition, "Black Snake Blues." The record was a hit and sold 150,000 copies the first year. Later other blues artists such as Leadbelly and Josh White also recorded the song. On the flip side of her record was "T. B. Blues," another of her compositions, about a childhood playmate who had died of tuberculosis.

Victoria Spivey's songs dealt with harsh realities—alcohol, drugs, prison, and suicide. Writing in *Rolling Stones,* Jim O'Neal said of her songs, "Many of her blues were grim tales of death, despair, cruelty, and agony, underscored by her somber piano and stark Texas blues moans" (O'Neal, p. 26).

Songwriting had been part of Victoria Spivey's life since childhood, and so in 1927 she became a staff writer for a St. Louis music-publishing company and wrote more than 100 songs for them. After that she went back to touring in vaudeville and appearing in musical revues such as Olsen and Johnsen's *Hellzapoppin*. She had a singing part in the 1929 all-black film *Hallelujah!*

On her recordings she worked with many of the greats, such as Louis Armstrong, King Oliver, Clarence Williams, and Blind Lemon Jefferson. She recorded extensively from 1926 to 1937.

In the 1930s she toured with dancer Billy Adams and also with Louis Armstrong. Then in the 1940s she moved to New York, where she sang in jazz clubs. She quit performing in 1952 and turned her energies to church activities, but in 1961 she was back touring the United States and Europe.

Finally, in 1962 she formed her own jazz and blues recording company, Spivey Record Company, and recorded the surviving classic blues singers: Lucille Hegamin, Alberta Hunter, Hannah Sylvester, as well as male country blues singers Big Joe Williams, Muddy Waters, Otis Spann and others. Two years later she returned to Europe in the *American Folk Blues Festival*.

According to Derrick Stewart-Baxter, who interviewed her in the 1960s, she was a woman of tremendous energy and enthusiasm for life. In her sixties she was running a recording company, doing concerts, and still writing songs. She had also married four times and had a daughter, Jackie Lynn Wilson. In her later years she performed in blues festivals throughout the United States and Europe; she also made television appearances on the BBC and on PBS. But on October 3, 1976, a few days short of her seventieth birthday, she died of an internal hemorrhage.

In *Devil's Music*, Giles Oakley quotes Victoria Spivey on her feelings about singing the blues: "To pay too much heed to standardized blues tones and bars spoils the emotional impact inwardly for yourself. . . . You must feel in your heart most of all, not in your brains or in the interest of your pocket" (Oakley, p. 36).

Among the more than 1,500 songs Victoria Spivey wrote were "Alligator Pond Went Dry," "Black Cat Blues," "Black Snake Blues," "Blood Hound Blues," "Blood Thirsty Blues," "Bum Can't Do You No Good," "Dirty Women's Blues," "Don't Trust Nobody Blues," "Dope Head Blues," "Go Tell My Other Man," "Hoodoo Man Blues," "I Got Men All over Town," "I'm a Red Hot Mama," "Jook House Blues," "Murder in the First Degree," "Steady Grind," "T.B. Blues," "You Done Lost Your Good Thing," and "You're Going to Miss Me When I'm Gone."

SOURCES
Chilton, John. *Who's Who of Jazz.*
Claghorn, Charles. *Biographical Dictionary of American Music.*
Harris, Sheldon. *Blues Who's Who.*
Hitchcock, H. Wiley. *New Grove Dictionary of American Music.*
Jones, Leroi. *Black Music.*
Oakley, Giles. *Devil's Music.*
Oliver, Paul. *Story of the Blues.*
Stewart-Baxter, Derrick. *Ma Rainey and the Classic Blues Singers.*

TAYLOR, KOKO (1935–   )   "Baby, Please Don't Dog Me"

Koko Taylor is a blues singer in the tradition of the classic blues women. Born Cora Walton in Memphis, Tennessee, on September 28, 1935, she sang in the church choir as a youngster. In 1953 she moved to Chicago and was making her living there as a domestic when she was discovered in the 1960s by bluesman Willie Dixon.

She sang in clubs through the 1960s and appeared on local television. From 1963 on she recorded on various labels, including Spivey, USA, Checker, and Alligator. She sang at blues festivals in the United States and Europe, including the Montreux Jazz Festival in 1972. During the 1970s she appeared in the film *The Blues Is Alive and Well in Chicago* and on Public Television's "Soundstage." She toured with her own group, The Blues Machine, playing at colleges and festivals.

In 1984 she shared a Grammy with other performers for Best Traditional Blues Recording for the album *Blues Explosion.* Her 1990 album was *Jump for Joy.*

Some of the songs Koko Taylor has written include "Be What You Want to Be," "Voodoo Woman," "Nitty-Gritty," "Honkey Tonkey," "Baby, Please Don't Dog Me," and "What Kind of Man Is This?"

She married Robert Taylor and had a daughter.

Koko Taylor continues to perform on television, in clubs, and at blues festivals.

SOURCES
Clarke, Donald. *Penguin Encyclopedia of Popular Music.*
Dahl, Linda. *Stormy Weather.*
Harris, Sheldon. *Blues Who's Who.*

THOMAS, HOCIEL (1904–1952)   "Tebo's Texas Boogie"

Hociel Thomas was born into a large musical family in Houston, Texas,
on July 10, 1904. Her father was musician, songwriter, and publisher George
W. Thomas, Jr. Her aunt was blues singer **Sippie Wallace.** Another rela-
tive was **Victoria Spivey.** From her early teens Hociel was raised by her
aunt, Sippie Wallace, and it was with her that she began her performing
career.

In the 1920s she worked in Storyville, New Orleans, and Chicago. She
recorded with Louis Armstrong on OKeh Records. Two of the songs she
recorded at this time were her own, "Shorty George Blues" and "Tebo's
Texas Boogie."

She married Arthur Tebo and had a child.

In the 1940s she began a comeback, singing with Kid Ory's Band in San
Francisco, but her return was cut short by tragedy. She and her sister got
into a ferocious fight with each other that resulted in the blinding of Hociel
and the death of her sister. Hociel Thomas was acquitted of manslaughter,
but she never fully recovered from this tragedy and died on August 22,
1952, in Oakland, California. Aunt Sippie Wallace, who had raised Hociel,
then raised her child.

SOURCES
Harris, Sheldon. *Blues Who's Who.*
Oliver, Paul. *Story of the Blues.*

THORNTON, WILLIE MAE "BIG MAMA" (1926–1984)
"Ball and Chain"

She was known as Big Mama Thornton. Although she was primarily a
performer in the classic blues shouter tradition, she also wrote songs, one
of which became a hit for **Janis Joplin** in the 1960s, "Ball and Chain."

Born on December 11, 1926, in Montgomery, Alabama, Willie Mae
Thornton was the daughter of a minister. At the age of 14 she won first
prize singing in an amateur show. Inspired by blues singers **Bessie Smith,**
Memphis Minnie, and **Ma Rainey,** Willie Mae Thornton got a job in Sammy
Green's *Hot Harlem Review* as a singer, dancer, and comedienne. The
show toured the South, but she left the show and settled in Houston in
1948. There she sang in local clubs. In the 1950s she toured with Johnny
Otis's Rhythm and Blues Caravan.

She had begun recording in 1950, scoring a hit with "Hound Dog," which became a rhythm and blues (R&B) classic. She later appeared at the Apollo Theater in New York and at the folk, blues and jazz festivals in Monterey, Berkeley, Newport, and San Francisco; and she performed in Europe as well. Eventually she settled in Los Angeles.

Unfortunately, an auto accident injured her so severely that she never fully regained her health. Nevertheless, she continued performing until a month before her death on July 25, 1984, of heart failure in Los Angeles. She was 57.

Some of the songs she wrote include "Big Change," "Big Mama's New Love," "Don't Need No Doctor," "Down-Home Shakedown," "Everybody's Happy (but Me)," "Everything Gonna Be Alright," "Guide Me Home," "I Feel the Way I Feel," "I'm Feeling Alright," "I'm Lost," "Jail," "Just Can't Help Myself," "Lost City," "Private Number," "Sassy Mama," "Sometimes I Have a Heartache," "Swing It on Home," "They Call Me Big Mama," "Willie Mae's Blues," and "Your Love Is Where It Ought to Be."

SOURCES

Dahl, Linda. *Stormy Weather.*
Oakland Tribune. Obituaries, July 28, 1984, p. B6.
Southern, Eileen. *Biographical Dictionary of Afro-American Music.*

WALLACE, BEULAH "SIPPIE" (1898–1986)   "Woman Be Wise"

Known as the Texas Nightingale, Sippie Wallace was one of the great blues singers. She was born Beulah Thomas in Houston, Texas, on November 11, 1898. One of 13 children, she came from a musical family. Two of her brothers, Hersal and George, Jr., were professional musicians, and her niece, **Hociel Thomas,** became a blues singer.

Sippie Wallace's father was a church deacon, and it wasn't long before Sippie began to play the organ at church. When she was older, she got a job singing and playing with the local tent shows and on the TOBA circuit throughout the South. Then she moved to Chicago and about 1923 began recording blues on the OKeh label with Louis Armstrong and King Oliver, recording many of her own songs. She had a rich, powerful voice and was a fine blues pianist. After her brother had settled in Detroit, she moved there in 1933.

During the Depression years she retired from professional work but continued to play the organ and sing in church. She married Frank Seals and later Mass Wallace. While in her early teens Hociel Thomas lived with Sippie Wallace, her aunt, and after Hociel's death in 1952, Sippie raised Hociel's child.

In the early 1960s her cousin, **Victoria Spivey,** began recording all the surviving classic blues singers, including Sippie Wallace herself. Then in 1966 Sippie Wallace began her comeback in a European tour of *American Folk Blues,* which played the Albert Hall in London. She also made recordings while in Europe. In her eighties she was a featured singer at the Kool Jazz Festivals of 1980 and 1981.

Sippie Wallace wrote a number of songs, including "Baby I Can't Use You No More," "Can Anybody Take Sweet Mama's Place?," "He's the Cause of My Being Blue," "Lonesome Hours Blues," "Murder Gonna Be My Crime," "Suitcase Blues," "Trouble Everywhere I Roam," "Special Delivery Blues," and "Woman Be Wise."

She died on November 1, 1986, in Detroit, Michigan.

SOURCES
Chilton, John. *Who's Who of Jazz.*
Dahl, Linda. *Stormy Weather.*
Harris, Sheldon. *Blues Who's Who.*
Jones, Hettie. *Big Star Fallin' Mama.*
Oliver, Paul. *Story of the Blues.*
Southern, Eileen. *Music of Black Americans.*
Stewart-Baxter, Derrick. *Ma Rainey and the Classic Blues Singers.*

WATERS, ETHEL (1896–1977)   "Kind Lovin' Blues"

Ethel Waters is probably best remembered for her performance in the film *The Member of the Wedding* (1952) as the kindly, grandmotherly caretaker of two children portrayed by Brandon de Wilde and Julie Harris. But acting was only one facet of Ethel Waters's long and varied career. Besides being a singer, dancer, actress, and author, she was a songwriter.

She was born Ethel Howard in Chester, Pennsylvania, on October 31, 1896. Her parents never married, and she was raised by her mother. As a child she was so poor that she stole food to keep from going hungry. She began work at an early age, and in later years she said that she had never had a childhood. At the age of five she began her singing career in a local church, where she was known as Baby Star. She also won many dance contests, and at 13 Ethel Waters dropped out of school to work.

She started singing professionally at the age of 17. By the time she was 21, she had a job singing and dancing in vaudeville as Sweet Mama Stringbean. Tall, slender, and sweet-voiced, Ethel Waters often began her show by telling the audience, "I ain't no Bessie Smith" (Oliver, *Story of the Blues,* p. 69). Although she did not have the large voice of a blues shouter, she became a fine versatile singer of blues, jazz, music hall tunes, and popular music.

In her early days she toured the United States performing in theaters, tent shows, and clubs, including a tour with the Rabbit Foot Minstrels. By 1919 she was working on Broadway in a musical comedy. Among the first shows she appeared in was the *Plantation Revue* (1925). When so many performers found themselves out of work during the Depression years, Ethel Waters kept right on working, spending much of 1929 in London.

When she returned, there were more Broadway shows for her: Lew Leslie's *Blackbirds of 1930* and *Rhapsody in Black* (1930). In 1933 Irving Berlin cast her in *As Thousands Cheer*, making her the black star of an all-white Broadway musical. She appeared in dramatic roles as well, *Mamba's Daughter* (1939), *Cabin in the Sky* (1940), and *The Member of the Wedding*, in which she toured in 1950 and appeared in again in 1964 and 1970. She won the 1950 New York Drama Critics Award for Best Actress for her role in this play.

Ethel Waters was among the first black women vocalists to be recorded. In the early 1920s she recorded on Cardinal and Black Swan labels with Cordy Williams's Jazz Masters. Her recording of "Shake That Thing" (1925) became a hit record.

Interspersed with her other activities, she made guest appearances on a number of radio shows, among them "The Rudy Vallee Show," "The Bing Crosby Show," "Kraft Music Hall," "The Tex and Jinx Show," and "Amos 'n Andy."

In Hollywood she appeared in a dozen movies. She made two early films, *On with the Show* in 1929 and *Southern Blues* in 1939. But in the 1940s she began to have better roles. She made *Cairo* (1942) with Jeanette MacDonald and Dooley Wilson, and *Tales of Manhattan* (1942) with Rita Hayworth, Charles Boyer, and Paul Robeson. She sang in *Stage Door Canteen* (1943) during the war years, and in *Cabin in the Sky* (1943) with Lena Horne and Louis Armstrong. In the latter film she introduced the song "Happiness Is Just a Thing Called Joe."

It was a straight acting role in *Pinky* (1949) with Ethel Barrymore and Jeanne Crain that earned her an Academy Award nomination. Her second Oscar nomination came for her role in the film *The Member of the Wedding* (1953). She also appeared in the 1959 film version of *The Sound and the Fury*.

On television she appeared on every kind of show, from "The Ed Sullivan Show" to "The General Electric Theater" to "Break the $250,000 Bank." She also sang at the White House for President Richard Nixon.

By the late 1950s she began appearing on evangelist Billy Graham's religious crusades, which she continued to do even more frequently in the 1960s, including his Hawaiian, London, and Canadian Crusades.

In her private life she did not have an easy time with either marriage or money. She married three times, first at the age of 13. Although she worked continuously all her life and reportedly earned more than $1 million, in the latter part of her life she was in trouble with the Internal Revenue Service.

The two books she wrote were her autobiography, *His Eye Is on the Sparrow* (1951), and *To Me It's Wonderful* (1972).

In addition to writing books and performing, Ethel Waters wrote a number of songs, among them "Kind Lovin' Blues," "You'll Want Me Back," "Chinese Blues," "Maybe Not at All," "Ethel Sings 'Em," "Satisfyin' Papa," "Go Back Where You Stayed Last Night," "Stop Myself from Worrying over You," and "Tell 'Em 'bout Me." She also wrote gospel songs, such as "With the Help of the Lord I Will Overcome" and "There Is Nothing My God Cannot Do."

Ethel Waters died on September 1, 1977, in Chatsworth, California, near Los Angeles, at the age of 81 after a long and successful career.

SOURCES

Bogle, Donald. *Brown Sugar.*
Dixon, Robert. *Recording the Blues.*
Feinstein, Elaine. *Bessie Smith.*
Harris, Sheldon. *Blues Who's Who.*
Jackson, Irene. *Afro-American Religious Music.*
New York Times. Obituaries, September 2, 1977, p. 1.
Oliver, Paul. *Story of the Blues.*
Stewart-Baxter, Derrick. *Ma Rainey and the Classic Blues Singers.*

WELLS, VIOLA (1902–   )   "Long, Tall, Tan and Terrific"

Billed as Miss Rhapsody, Viola Gertrude Wells was a singer-songwriter. She was born on December 14, 1902, in Newark, New Jersey, where she sang in the church choir as a youngster.

She began singing professionally in clubs in Philadelphia and Baltimore. In 1937 she toured the TOBA circuit with blues singer Ida Cox and the Harlem Strutters. She played the Apollo Theatre with Bunny Berigan and also Cafe Society Downtown in New York City. On radio she sang with Art Tatum, Benny Carter, and Count Basie. During World War II she did USO tours of Europe to entertain the troops.

For a time Viola Wells retired from show business and ran a restaurant. In the mid-1960s **Victoria Spivey** recorded Viola Wells singing her own song, "Long, Tall, Tan and Terrific." After this Viola Wells did radio and television shows in New York and Paris, touring Europe again in the late 1970s.

She married twice and had a daughter.

Among the songs that Viola Wells wrote are "I Fell for You," "Don't Rush Me Baby," "Long, Tall, Tan and Terrific," "My Lucky Day," and "Grooving the Blues."

SOURCES
Harris, Sheldon. *Blues Who's Who.*
Stewart-Baxter, Derrick. *Ma Rainey and the Classic Blues Singers.*

WILSON, EDITH (1896–1981)
"Put a Little Love in Everything You Do"

Edith Wilson was a singer, actress, and songwriter. She was born Edith Goodall in Louisville, Kentucky, on September 2, 1896, and was the great-granddaughter of John C. Breckenridge, a vice-president of the United States.

In her teens she moved to Chicago and began singing in clubs and cabarets. For a time she sang on the TOBA circuit. In 1921 she appeared in the musical *Put and Take* in New York, the same year she made her first recording. The following year Edith Wilson appeared as a headliner in Lew Leslie's revue *Nighttime in Dixieland*. After this she sang with the Duke Ellington Orchestra at the Cotton Club in New York City. She toured Europe in revues, *Plantation Revue* and *Rhapsody in Black* (1935), and toured the United States and Europe with the bands of Cab Calloway, Noble Sissle, and Jimmy Lunceford.

After moving to the West Coast, Edith Wilson appeared in several films, *I'm Still Alive* and *To Have and Have Not* (1944), with Humphrey Bogart and Lauren Bacall. On the radio she appeared as Kingfisher's mother-in-law on the "Amos 'n Andy Show." She made guest appearances on the Garry Moore and Jackie Gleason television shows. For a time Edith Wilson toured as Aunt Jemima for the Quaker Oats Company.

In 1966 she retired from music, but in the early 1970s she came back to record with Eubie Blake and to sing at various folk festivals. She appeared in the 1976 BBC television show "A History of the Blues."

She was first married to pianist Danny Wilson and later to Millard Wilson.

Some of the songs Edith Wilson wrote include "Rainy Day Friend," "Daddy Change Your Mind," "Put a Little Love in Everything You Do,"

"She Knew All Along It Was Wrong," "To Keep from Twiddling Your Thumbs," "Carrie," and "Let's Get Back to the Old Times."

Edith Wilson died March 31, 1981, in Chicago.

SOURCES

Cook, Bruce. *Listening to the Blues.*
Harris, Sheldon. *Blues Who's Who.*
Oakley, Giles. *Devil's Music.*
Southern, Eileen. *Biographical Dictionary of Afro-Americans.*
Stewart-Baxter, Derrick. *Ma Rainey and the Classic Blues Singers.*

YANCEY, ESTELLA "MAMA" (1896–1986)   "Santa Fe Blues"

Blues singer and songwriter Estella Yancey was born Estella Harris on January 1, 1896, in Cairo, Illinois. Her mother loved to sing and play the guitar, and Estella learned from her.

Estella Yancey sang traditional blues in clubs, at concerts, and at folk festivals around the country with her husband, pianist Jimmy Yancey. She recorded for the Riverside, Folkways, and Verve labels.

She appeared on the PBS television show "Jazz Alley" in 1969 and was still performing at the age of 85 at the Kool Jazz Festival in New York City in 1981.

Some of Mama Yancey's songs are "Death Letter Blues," "Four o'Clock Blues," "Good Package Blues," "Mama Yancey's Blues," "Monkey Woman Blues," "Santa Fe Blues," "Sweet Lovin' Daddy," "Good Conductor," "Cabbage Patch," "Every Day of the Week," and "Get Him out of Your System."

She died May 4, 1986, in Chicago.

SOURCES

Dahl, Linda. *Stormy Weather.*
Harris, Sheldon. *Blues Who's Who.*
Southern, Eileen. *Biographical Dictionary of Afro-Americans.*

V | JAZZ

INTRODUCTION

New Orleans is usually considered the birthplace of jazz. The city was always exceptionally musical with several opera companies, symphony orchestras, and numerous brass bands. The musical instruments left by the departing military bands after the Civil War may account for the large number of brass bands that developed in the city.

Bands played for every occasion, not only for dances and parades but also for store openings, picnics, and funerals. Small bands even worked in Storyville, the red-light district of New Orleans, playing music in the bordellos. Jazz was created by these African-American musicians, most of whom could not read music but developed jazz from a blending of the blues, ragtime, spirituals, marches, and popular dance music that they knew.

When Storyville was closed down in 1917, many jazz musicians went north to find work in Chicago. Among them was King Oliver, who moved there with his Creole Jazz Band; Louis Armstrong joined them a few years later. They performed in speakeasies, which during the Prohibition era provided patrons with illegal alcohol and jazz.

The first jazz recording was made by a white band, the Original Dixieland Jazz Band, who had learned their music from listening to black bands in New Orleans. Through radio broadcasts and live performances, jazz became so pervasive and so popular in the 1920s that the era became known as the Jazz Age.

In the 1930s and 1940s jazz took the form of swing and became the music of the big band era. Such bands as those of Benny Goodman, Tommy Dorsey, Woody Herman, and Count Basie toured the country playing dance music. This was the music of World War II.

In the 1940s during the big band era a new style of music was developing, moving jazz away from commercial dance music and in a new direction. The music was called bebop. Musicians such as Dizzy Gillespie and Charlie Parker began experimenting with the structure of jazz, changing chords, changing the beat, producing new and often discordant sounds. Others like Stan Kenton and Claude Thornhill took their big bands in the direction of classical music, strongly influenced by Debussy and Stravinsky.

In the 1960s some musicians such as John Coltrane and Miles Davis took the experiment begun with bebop one step further and developed a new movement called free jazz. It had even less structure than bebop, and it often seemed to be total cacophony.

At this point jazz began to lose some of its audience partly throught the inaccessibility of the new jazz forms and partly due to the popularity of rock music, which had begun in the 1950s. Some musicians, including Miles Davis, saw what was happening and began incorporating elements of rock into their music, developing jazz fusion, which began to bring new listeners to jazz.

Contemporary jazz music has fragmented into many different styles, and seemingly all the styles of the past continue to coexist, from dixieland to fusion.

The women songwriters included here who worked in jazz were either vocalists or pianists with jazz bands. Billy Holiday and Dinah Washington were vocalists in the big band era of the 1940s. Mary Lou Williams was a pianist and arranger with many big bands, but she became part of the New York bebop movement as an arranger for Dizzy Gillespie. Betty Carter is associated with free jazz. The songs written by these women reflect the times in which they worked.

CARTER, BETTY (1929–   )   "I Can't Help It"

Jazz singer Betty Carter was born Lillie Mae Jones in Flint, Michigan, on May 16, 1929. Her father was the choir director at her church. She grew up in Detroit and was interested in music from childhood. In high school she played in the band and loved to play bebop on the piano. As early as 16 she was going to jazz clubs to listen to bebop. For a time she studied piano at the Detroit Conservatory of Music.

When she was 18, Lionel Hampton hired her as a vocalist, and she toured with the band for two years singing as Lorene Carter, then as Betty Carter.

From one of the musicians she learned how to arrange music, and in 1957 she left Lionel Hampton to work on her own. After that she moved to New York and sang in various clubs, working on a free jazz vocal style that often made her voice sound like another instrument in the group.

In 1953 she recorded with Epic and later with other labels, but she was dissatisfied and finally in 1971 set up her own label, Bet-Car Productions.

Before then, however, in 1963, she toured Japan with Sonny Rollins. She played London the following year. She also worked with Miles Davis and Thelonious Monk, and others. Later, in the 1970s, she toured the college circuit, sang at New York's Lincoln Center, and performed at the Newport Jazz Festival. She also appeared in an acting-singing role in *Don't Call Me Man*, produced at the Billie Holiday Theater in Brooklyn. During the Reagan presidency she was asked to sing at the White House.

With her considerable vocal ability, Betty Carter undoubtedly could have had a larger following and a more prosperous career singing popular music, but jazz was what interested her and developing her own jazz vocal style was what she chose to do. Concerned that there are few young jazz vocalists coming along today, she has conducted jazz workshops at colleges and universities to help develop new talent.

She was married and has two sons, whom she raised after the marriage ended.

Some of the songs Betty Carter has written are "Happy," "Tight," "We Tried," "Sounds," "Fake," "What Is It?," "I Can't Help It (That's the Way I Am)," "Jumps," "Open the Door," and "Droppin' Things." She wrote a song for Billie Holiday called "Don't Weep for the Lady."

Betty Carter's home is in Brooklyn.

SOURCES
Dahl, Linda. *Stormy Weather.*
Gourse, Leslie. *Louis' Children.*
Moritz, Charles. *Current Biography*, 1982.
Placksin, Sally. *American Women in Jazz.*
Southern, Eileen. *Biographical Dictionary of Afro-Americans.*

FITZGERALD, ELLA   *See* Pop Rock.

HOLIDAY, BILLIE "LADY DAY" (1915–1959)
"God Bless the Child"

The legendary jazz vocalist Billie Holiday was born Eleanor Fagan on April 7, 1915, in Baltimore, Maryland, to teenagers Sadie Fagan and Clarence Holiday. Though in later years she became a famous and glamorous singer, Billie Holiday never overcame the effects of her brutal childhood of physical abuse, poverty, prostitution, reform school, and racial degradation. Even during her successful years, her personal life was always tormented, and she succumbed at the age of 44 to the effects of alcoholism and heroin addiction. Her extraordinary life was documented in a 1956 autobiography, *Lady Sings the Blues*, written with William Dufty. A film based on this book was made in 1972 starring Diana Ross.

Billie Holiday began her professional singing career in desperation when her mother was sick and they were about to be evicted for not paying the rent. Teenager Billie Holiday walked into a Harlem night club and auditioned as a singer. She was hired on the spot.

From singing in small clubs in Harlem she came to sing with many great bands, including those of Benny Goodman, Teddy Wilson, Count Basie, and Artie Shaw. As a black vocalist with a white band she was often subjected to threats and verbal abuse. Eventually she was hired to sing in the chic supper clubs of New York City.

Her recording career began when she cut her first record at 18 with Benny Goodman and was paid $35. She made very little from her early recordings, as she explained in her autobiography. "I made over 200 sides between 1933 and 1944, but I don't get a cent of royalties on any of them. They paid me 25, 50 or a top of 75 bucks a side, and I was glad to get it" (Holiday and Dufty, p. 168). But she didn't receive any other compensation, no matter how big a hit the song became.

Although Billie Holiday didn't write many songs, she did write some memorable ones: "God Bless the Child," "Don't Explain," and "Fine and Mellow."

While she was singing at Cafe Society, poet Lewis Allen brought her a poem he had written. He was hoping to make a song of it for her to sing. From this encounter came the song most closely identified with her, "Strange Fruit." It is the story of lynchings in the South. Billie was so moved by the poem that she, Allen, and Sonny White, her accompanist, turned it into a song, according to Billie's autobiography, although the song is copyrighted in Allen's name alone. "Strange Fruit" became her blockbuster song. It always left the audience in stunned silence and left Billie feeling sick. Indeed, she had trouble finding a record company that would cut it. Finally Commodore Records accepted it, and she made the record in 1939, with "Fine and Mellow" on the flip side. The record became Billie's first pop hit.

Her song "God Bless the Child" came after she had an argument with her mother, who had refused to loan Billie some money. Billie was angry for several weeks. One day the whole song popped into her head. She sang it to Arthur Herzog, who picked out the music on the piano. "God Bless the Child" became another hit.

"Don't Explain" was written after her husband, Jimmy Monroe, came home with lipstick on his collar and gave a long explanation of how it got there. Billie said, "Don't explain." Soon she was singing phrases to herself and suddenly she had a whole song.

In the 1930s she began to receive movie offers. She appeared in *Symphony in Black* (1939), *New Orleans* (1947), and short films with Count Basie and Duke Ellington. She hated her part in *New Orleans,* in which she played a maid. All her life she had struggled to escape working as a maid, and now that she was a successful singer she felt humiliated to play such a role. As a result she vowed never to make another film.

During the last years of her life Billie Holiday struggled to overcome her drug addiction. She was hounded from one club date to the next by federal narcotics agents. In 1947 she served ten months in jail for drug possession, after which she made a spectacular comeback, but it was only temporary.

Although her 1956 autobiography ends on a hopeful note, her life did not end happily. Three years later she was arrested again for illegal drug possession in a New York City hospital, where she lay on her deathbed. She died there on July 17, 1959, at the age of 44. It was a sad loss of an original and enormously influential jazz vocalist.

SOURCES

Berendt, Joachim. *Jazz Book.*
Bogle, Donald. *Brown Sugar.*
Chilton, John. *Who's Who of Jazz.*
Dahl, Linda. *Stormy Weather.*
Feather, Leonard. *New Encyclopedia of Jazz.*
Holiday, Billie. *Lady Sings the Blues.*
Whitman, Wanda. *Songs That Changed the World.*

KITCHINGS, IRENE WILSON (n.d.)   "This Is the Moment"

Irene Kitchings was a jazz pianist and songwriter. Born in Marietta, Ohio, she was raised by an aunt in Detroit from the age of 13. By the time she was 18 she was working as a jazz pianist in Chicago clubs as Irene Eadie. Respected as a musician, she led her own band (all men) in the 1920s.

About 1931 she married jazz pianist Teddy Wilson and retired from performing. They moved to New York, where Teddy worked with the Benny Carter Band. It was Carter who encouraged her to write songs. Later when Teddy Wilson worked for Benny Goodman, she met Goodman's vocalist,

Billie Holiday, and they became friends. Through Billie Holiday she met Arthur Herzog, Jr., who became Irene's lyricist. "Anything she wrote, I could put words to, and that doesn't happen very often," Arthur Herzog explained in Sally Placksin's book *American Women in Jazz.*

Her song "Some Other Spring" was written after her separation from Teddy Wilson. Irene later married Elden Kitchings.

Other songs by Irene Kitchings include "Ghost of Yesterday," "Some Other Spring," "What Is This Gonna Get Us?" and "I'm Pulling Through." Probably her best-known song is "This Is the Moment." Her friend Billie Holiday recorded many of Irene Kitchings's songs.

SOURCES

Bogle, Donald. *Brown Sugar.*
Dahl, Linda. *Stormy Weather.*
Holiday, Billie. *Lady Sings the Blues.*
Placksin, Sally. *American Women in Jazz.*

LINCOLN, ABBEY (1930–   )   "People in Me"

Abbey Lincoln is a singer, actress, teacher, and songwriter. Born Anna Marie Wooldridge on August 6, 1930, in Chicago, Illinois, she was the tenth of 12 children. When she was young, her family moved to Calvin Center, Michigan, where she attended Kalamazoo High School. For a time she worked as a domestic, but soon she found she could make a living singing.

In the 1950s she began singing in nightclubs. First, in 1951, she moved to California and sang as Gaby Lee. From there she went to Hawaii, where she sang for two years.

Returning to Hollywood, she recorded as Abbey Lincoln with Benny Carter's orchestra and appeared in the film *The Girl Can't Help It* (1956). Then she recorded with a group that included Max Roach, whom she married in 1962. (They are now divorced.) Through him she met many leading figures in the world of jazz: Thelonious Monk, Coleman Hawkins, Charles Mingus, and John Coltrane.

Abbey Lincoln began writing songs in the late 1950s and 1960s. Many of her songs, such as "We Insist! Freedom Now Suite," show the influence of the civil rights movement. Among her songs are "People in Me," "Straight Ahead," "In the Red," "Retribution," "Let Up," and "Blue Monk," the latter written with Thelonious Monk. In the 1970s she recorded the album *People in Me.*

Her film career began in 1964 when she co-starred with Ivan Dixon in the film *Nothing but a Man*. For her acting in this film she received many awards, including Best Actress at the First World Festival of Negro Arts. She subsequently starred in *For Love of Ivy* (1968) with Sidney Poitier. In 1975 she was inducted into the Black Filmmakers Hall of Fame. More recently she had the role of Denzel Washington's mother in Spike Lee's film *Mo' Better Blues*.

On a visit to Africa in 1975, she was given the names Aminata Moseka, which she took as her professional name for a number of years afterward.

In the 1980s she taught and directed at the African-American Theater of the California State University at Northridge, California.

In 1990 she recorded the album *The World Is Falling Down* and followed that with *You Gotta Pay the Band* (1991).

Abbey Lincoln lives in New York City.

SOURCES

Cloyd, Iris. *Who's Who among Black Americans.*
Dahl, Linda. *Stormy Weather.*
Hitchcock, H. Wiley. *New Grove Dictionary of American Music.*
Leland, John. "You Gotta Pay Respect." *Newsweek*, January 6, 1992, pp. 50–51.
Southern, Eileen. *Biographical Dictionary of Afro-Americans.*

SIMONE, NINA (1933–   )   "Backlash Blues"

Jazz pianist and composer Nina Simone is known as the High Priestess of Soul. She was born Eunice Kathleen Waymon in Tryon, North Carolina, on February 21, 1933. She was the sixth of eight children. The family was poor, but musical.

Because Eunice showed considerable talent, a local piano teacher offered to teach her free of charge. The teacher also helped to raise money for Eunice's education. Eunice Waymon was class valedictorian when she graduated from high school. After this she studied at the Juilliard School of Music in New York until her money ran out. Then she taught piano and attended the Curtis Institute of Music in Philadelphia. She found a job playing for a club in Atlantic City, but the manager wanted her to sing too, so she chose a new name, Nina Simone, and began her singing career.

Her recording of Gershwin's "I Love You Porgy" in 1959 was a hit, which led to performances at the Apollo Theater, the Newport Jazz Festival, and a concert at Carnegie Hall. After that there were tours of the United States and Europe.

In the 1960s Nina Simone was active in the civil rights movement, and her song "Mississippi Goddam" comes out of that experience. Some of her other songs were set to the words of black poets, such as those of Paul

Dunbar in her song "Compensation." "The Backlash Blues" and "To Be Young, Gifted and Black" were based on the poems of Langston Hughes. The latter has become the anthem of the Congress of Racial Equality.

Nina Simone began composing at a recording session. When two songs were cancelled, she quickly wrote two new ones. From this experience she discovered that composing songs came easily to her. Since then she has written many more. Some of the more than 500 songs she has written are "Central Park Blues," "If You Knew," "Return Home," "African Mailman," "Go Limp," "Blackbird," "Children Go Where I Send You," "Nina's Blues," "Flo Me La," "Sugar in My Bowl," and "Backlash Blues." To accompany a Langston Hughes poem she wrote "Four Women," which is about the stereotyped roles African-American women play.

In 1987 she appeared in the film *Someone to Watch over Me*.

Nina Simone has been married twice and has a daughter. She now lives in the Netherlands.

SOURCES

Bogle, Donald. *Brown Sugar*.
Cloyd, Iris. *Who's Who among Black Americans*.
Dahl, Linda. *Stormy Weather*.
Lynn Farnol Group. *ASCAP Biographical Dictionary*.
Moritz, Charles. *Current Biography*, 1968.
Southern, Eileen. *Biographical Dictionary of Afro-Americans*.
Stambler, Irwin. *Encyclopedia of Pop, Rock and Soul*.

WASHINGTON, DINAH (1924–1963)   "Fast Movin' Mama"

Dinah Washington was a great jazz and popular song vocalist in the 1940s who had considerable influence on later generations of singers.

She was born Ruth Lee Jones on August 29, 1924, in Tuscaloosa, Alabama. When she was a child, her family moved to Chicago, where she grew up and went to school. Her mother taught music, so she learned to play the piano as a youngster and soon was the church pianist, then the choir director. When she was 15, she won an amateur talent show. Shortly after this she became the accompanist for the Sallie Martin Gospel Singers.

By the 1940s she had left the gospel circuit and was singing with some of the top bands. In 1942, for example, she sang with Fats Waller in Chicago. The following year she toured with Lionel Hampton, and later she sang with Count Basie and Duke Ellington. She brought to her music a blending of gospel, soul, blues, and improvisational jazz. No longer singing religious music, she took a new name, Dinah Washington.

She sang at Birdland, the Apollo Theater, Carnegie Hall, and the other top clubs and halls in the United States and Europe. She appeared at U.S. jazz festivals and also sang on television. From 1955 to 1958 she sang at the Newport Jazz Festival. Her last appearance there was documented in a film, *Jazz on a Summer's Day* (1959).

As a recording artist, she cut at least 24 albums for the Decca, Roulette, and Mercury labels. Her recording of "What a Diff'rence a Day Makes" won her a Grammy in 1959.

Dinah Washington's personal life was complex. She had many lovers, men and women, married seven times (some sources say nine), and had two children. In many ways she seemed to have had two distinct personalities, that of the sweet-tempered Ruth Jones and that of the hard, tough-talking Dinah Washington. To control her weight she took diet pills, which kept her so "wired" that she couldn't sleep and would stay up all night partying. She seemed to attract a rough crowd, and occasionally she carried a gun. Once she threatened her landlady with it and spent the night in jail.

In addition to all her other activities, Dinah Washington also wrote songs. Some of them are "Fast Movin' Mama," "Fine Fat Daddy," and "Juice Head Man of Mine."

Her untimely death on December 14, 1963, in Detroit, Michigan, at the age of 39 was apparently accidental, the result of ingesting diet pills with alcohol. It cut short the career of a unique and distinctive song stylist.

SOURCES
Gourse, Leslie. *Louis' Children.*
Harris, Sheldon. *Blues Who's Who.*
Southern, Eileen. *Biographical Dictionary of Afro-Americans.*
Southern, Eileen. *Music of Black Americans.*

WILLIAMS, MARY LOU (1910–1981)

"Black Christ of the Andes"

The great jazz keyboard artist, Mary Lou Williams was born Mary Elfrieda Scruggs in Atlanta, Georgia, on May 8, 1910. She was born into a poor family of eight children, whom her mother supported by doing housework. Her mother played the organ and taught her to play at the age of four. The family moved to Pittsburgh, Pennsylvania, where Mary Lou Williams grew up. Her elementary school principal introduced her to classical music and opera, but jazz was always her main interest.

By the time she was 15, she had a job playing in vaudeville shows. One of her early inspirations was seeing **Lovie Austin** play in a local theater.

When she was 21, Mary Lou Williams began an 11-year association with the Andy Kirk Band in the Kansas City area as soloist, arranger, and composer. In the early 1940s she moved to New York and became an arranger for Benny Goodman, Duke Ellington, Louis Armstrong, Earl Hines, Tommy Dorsey, Glen Gray, Bob Crosby, and others.

Her early marriage at the age of 16 to saxophonist John Williams ended, and she married Harold "Shorty" Baker, a trumpeter. Together they led a small combo in the early 1940s. Then they moved on to work with Duke Ellington. For a time she was an arranger for Ellington and during that period wrote for him "Trumpet No End." In 1944 Mary Lou started a residency at Cafe Society, which lasted a number of years and gave her time to do her own composing. She began writing orchestral works, cantatas, chamber music, and piano pieces. She introduced her composition "The Zodiac Suite" at a town hall concert in 1945, and it was performed by the New York Philharmonic Orchestra the following year at Carnegie Hall.

By the 1950s Mary Lou Williams had become involved in the New York bebop movement, writing arrangements for Dizzy Gillespie's band. In the early 1950s she went to Europe and toured for two years. After she returned home, she stopped performing and began religious studies that led to her conversion to Catholicism. After this, she began composing religious works. In 1969 she was commissioned to write a mass, which became *Mary Lou's Mass*. This work was later choreographed as a ballet for the Alvin Ailey Dance Company. She also wrote "Black Christ of the Andes," a jazz hymn, and "Anima Christi: Praise the Lord."

Her retirement was partially a result of her disillusionment with jazz, with the direction it had taken after the Bud Powell and Charlie Parker era. She hated the commercialism and the avant-guard movement that she felt had taken over. She believed that jazz was moving away from its roots in spirituality, love, and suffering. However, a priest persuaded her to return to music and make her contribution there. She established a foundation to teach the history of jazz to children so as to perpetuate jazz. Another foundation she established was the Bel Canto Foundation, which she created to help rehabilitate musicians who had become alcoholics or drug addicts. She funded these foundations through her concerts and royalties.

In 1972 Mary Lou Williams came out of retirement briefly to perform at the Newport Jazz Festival. The last years of her life were spent teaching jazz history as artist in residence at Duke University from 1977 on.

In 1977 she recorded a song she wrote for her mother, "My Mama Pinned a Rose on Me." Some of her other songs include "Little Joe from Chicago," "Morning Glory (What's Your Story)," written with Paul Webster and Jack Lawrence, and "Walkin'," written with Lindsay Steele. Among her religious choral works are "Black Christ of the Andes" (St. Martin de Porres), with lyrics by Father Antony Woods, "Anima Christi: Praise the Lord," and "The Devil."

Over the years she received many honors, including a Guggenheim Foundation grant for composition and several honorary doctorates. Yet Mary Lou Williams had never had formal piano lessons. She had avoided classical training, for she believed that it harmed the ability to be spontaneous which she felt was essential to jazz. Jazz, she said, "comes from the heart."

She died of cancer at her home in Durham, North Carolina, on May 28, 1981, at the age of 71.

SOURCES

Bogle, Donald. *Brown Sugar.*
Chilton, John. *Who's Who of Jazz.*
Claghorn, Charles. *Biographical Dictionary of American Music.*
Cohen, Aaron. *International Encyclopedia of Women.*
Hitchcock, H. Wiley. *New Grove Dictionary of American Music.*
Jacques Cattell Press. *ASCAP Biographical Dictionary.*
Lyons, Len. *Great Jazz Pianists.*
Moritz, Charles. *Current Biography,* 1966.
Placksin, Sally. *American Women in Jazz.*
Shirley, Kay. *Book of the Blues.*
Simon, George. *Best of the Music Makers.*

VI | FOLK

INTRODUCTION

Folk songs range from long narrative tales to melancholy ballads. But folk songs also have a long tradition of expressing social and political protest.

In the early 1930s in the United States many folk songs were written to protest the inhumane conditions in mining communities and to support labor unions. Aunt Molly Jackson, who lived in a coal-mining town, wrote songs about the poverty and death that she saw around her. Florence Reece, another woman from the coal fields, wrote the haunting labor song "Which Side Are You On?"

During the McCarthy era of the 1950s many folksingers and songwriters were blacklisted for their political views. Unable to get a job teaching because of her politics, Malvina Reynolds turned to writing folk songs. Her best-known song, "Little Boxes," is about mindless conformity. Some of her other songs are about poverty, ecology, and peace.

Folk songs became popular again in the 1960s and became a means of expressing civil rights and anti–Vietnam War sentiments. Bob Dylan, the leading folk songwriter of the 1960s, began with traditional folk music but later blended folk with blues, country, and rock and roll to make his own commentaries about contemporary issues. Many women singer-songwriters of this era, such as Joan Baez, Judy Collins, and Barbara Dane, were also active participants in the civil rights and antiwar movements.

In the 1990s some contemporary singer-songwriters such as **Suzanne Vega** and **Tracy Chapman** are writing songs of social criticism, blending elements of folk and rock music. Their profiles are to be found in the section titled "Pop Rock."

Of course, not all folk songs are protest songs. Many of the folk songs women wrote were romantic ballads, like Joan Baez's "Diamonds and Rust."

BAEZ, JOAN (1941–   )   "Diamonds and Rust"

Folksinger, peace activist, author, and songwriter, Joan Baez was one of the leading figures in the 1960s folk song revival. She was born on Staten Island, New York, on January 9, 1941. After attending high school in Palo Alto, California, she entered Boston University.

She started singing folk songs in the coffee houses around Boston in 1958. Subsequently, she played other folk clubs around the country, including the Gate of Horn in Chicago. Her career took off a year later after a performance at the Newport Folk Festival.

At the age of 20 she cut her first album, which became the highest-selling individual-female folk album in the history of long-playing records. She has since recorded 29 albums, 8 of them gold.

During the 1960s Joan Baez was active in the civil rights movement and in Vietnam War protests. Arrested for acts of civil disobedience, she served time in jail. In 1968 she married peace activist and draft resister David V. Harris and had a son. (They are now divorced.) Her interest in peace and human rights led her to form two organizations, the Institute for the Study of Nonviolence in 1965 and Humanitas in 1979.

Songwriting came late to Joan Baez. For a long time she was dissatisfied with her own compositions. However, in 1975 she wrote "Diamonds and Rust," a recollection of a youthful romance with folksinger Bob Dylan, and the song became a hit. Since then she has written many other songs, including "Honest Lullaby," "Love Song to a Stranger," "A Song for David," "Altar Boy," "Thief," "Dida," "Gabriel and Me," "Blessed Are . . . ," and "Winds of the Old Days." Her main collaborator has been Ennio Morricone.

Joan Baez has also written several books: *The Joan Baez Songbook* (1964), *Daybreak* (1968), *And Then I Wrote* (1979), *Coming Out*, co-authored with David Harris, and *A Voice to Sing With* (1987).

She has toured widely in the United States, Europe, and Japan and has also made many television appearances.

Joan Baez lives in Woodside, California.

SOURCES
Jacques Cattell. *ASCAP Biographical Dictionary.*
Lawless, Ray. *Folksingers and Folksongs in America.*
Stambler, Irwin. *Encyclopedia of Folk, Country, and Western Music,* 1969.
Stambler, Irwin. *Encyclopedia of Pop, Rock and Soul.*
Who's Who of American Women, 1989.

CHAPMAN, TRACY   *See* Pop Rock.

COLLINS, JUDY (1939–   )   **"Since You Asked"**

Judy Collins was one of the major figures in the folk music revival of the
1960s. She was born Judy Marjorie Collins in Seattle, Washington, on May
1, 1939. Her father, Chuck Collins, though blind, was a successful singer
and entertainer on radio and television.

As a child Judy Collins studied classical piano music, and when her family moved to Denver, Colorado, she studied with Antonia Brica. However,
at 16 Judy's desire to become a concert pianist waned when she became
interested in folk music and learned to play the guitar. After high school
she attended MacMurray College in Illinois for a year.

Then at the age of 18 she married Peter Taylor and had a child. To help
put her husband through school, she began playing the guitar and singing
in a pizza parlor in Denver five nights a week. In the summer she played
at the Gate of Horn, a folk music club in Chicago. In the 1960s the family
moved to Connecticut, where her husband taught. Judy sang in a folk music club in New York, spending the weekends at home with her family.
Occasionally she sang in other cities. Although she wanted to quit, the
necessity of supplementing the family income kept her performing and away
from her family. After a few years, the marriage ended. And so to make a
living she continued singing in clubs and doing commercials.

In 1961 Elektra signed her to a recording contract, and she made her
first album, *A Maid of Constant Sorrow.* Other albums followed. The album made at her Town Hall concert, *The Judy Collins Concert,* in 1964
was one of the best-selling albums of the year. She continued on at Elektra
for more than 20 years and recorded 22 albums, 6 of them gold, selling
500,000 copies.

When she wasn't recording she was touring the United States, Europe,
or Japan, singing in concert halls or at folk festivals or on television. Her

schedule had her singing too many concerts, 40 to 50 a year, which was hard on her vocal cords. She also was concerned about social issues and went to Mississippi during the civil rights movement to help register blacks to vote. She sang at the Kent State memorial for the students killed in an antiwar protest on campus.

In 1967 she had a hit with her recording of Joni Mitchell's song "Both Sides Now." It also won a Grammy. The following year she had a hit with "Someday Soon." Then in 1969 she tried something entirely new, an acting-singing role in the Shakespeare in the Park Festival in New York City. She played Solveig with Stacy Keach as Peer in *Peer Gynt*. A few years later she ventured into yet another new area, that of filmmaking. She produced and co-directed a documentary about the life of her former piano teacher and renown conductor Antonia Brica. The film, *Antonia: A Portrait of the Woman*, was highly acclaimed and won many awards, including a nomination for an Academy Award.

One of her big hits in the 1970s was the gospel song "Amazing Grace." The other was Stephen Sondheim's song "Send in the Clowns" from his Broadway musical *A Little Night Music*. Many other singers had recorded it, but it was Judy Collins's rendition that became the huge success.

At the height of her success Judy Collins suddenly had severe health problems that threatened her whole singing career. For years she had overcommitted her energies. She sang too many concerts a year, got too little rest, smoked too much, and drank too much, and the stress had taken its toll on her vocal cords. In 1977 she started on a big tour of the United States, but she had a problem with her voice and had to cancel the tour. Although her doctor wanted her to have a complete rest, she still had commitments, such as television's "The Muppet Show," which she was unwilling to give up. After remaining silent for one month to rest her voice, she performed on "The Muppet Show" and then immediately after had the throat operation. Afterward she gave up smoking but was still drinking to excess. Finally realizing how serious the situation was, she agreed to go through an alcohol recovery program.

After her recovery, her life changed. She developed a healthy lifestyle and swam frequently to strengthen her lungs. As her health improved, so did her creativity. For the first time in years she was able to write songs again.

It was in 1966 that she wrote her first song, "Since You Asked." Her subject matter is mostly of a personal nature about her family and her own inner life. For example, she wrote "The Wedding Song" for her brother's wedding in 1979. Among her other songs are "My Father," "Secret Gardens," "Albatross," "Open the Door," and "Houses." She collaborated with

Dave Grusin on "Shoot First," about handguns, and with Stacy Keach on "Easy Times," a theme for one of his movies, *The Repeater*.

In 1987 Judy Collins published an autobiography, *Trust Your Heart*, and released an album by the same name.

She lives in New York City.

SOURCES

Collins, Judy. *Trust Your Heart*.
Hitchcock, H. Wiley. *New Grove Dictionary of American Music*.
Jacques Cattell Press. *ASCAP Biographical Dictionary*.
Lawless, Ray. *Folksingers and Folksongs in America*.
Stambler, Irwin. *Encyclopedia of Folk, Country, and Western Music*, 1969.
Stambler, Irwin. *Encyclopedia of Pop, Rock and Soul*.
Who's Who of American Women, 1986.

COTTEN, ELIZABETH (1892–1987) "Freight Train"

Born in Chapel Hill, North Carolina, in January 1892, Elizabeth "Libba" Cotten achieved fame late in life. Although she had written songs and played the guitar and banjo all her life, she had worked as a housekeeper for a living. It wasn't until she was 60 years old and became the housekeeper for ethnomusicologist Charles Seeger (Pete Seeger's father) and his family that her musical talents were discovered.

Pete Seeger invited her to perform with him at various folk festivals in the United States and Canada in the 1960s. She had a Carnegie Hall concert in 1978, still playing the guitar the way she had taught herself to play it as a child, fingering with the right hand and strumming with the left.

Various recording companies signed her to cut albums, among them Vanguard, Folkways, and Arhoolie. She won a Grammy in 1984 for her album *Elizabeth Cotten Live!*

Her most famous song was "Freight Train," which she composed as a child. Although the song had been performed and recorded by many other singers, Elizabeth Cotten had never received credit or royalties for writing it. Only when she became a performer herself did she finally received recognition as the composer of "Freight Train." Other songs that she wrote were "I'm Going Away," "Washington Blues," "Sugaree," and "Babe, It Ain't No Lie."

In her early years she had married Frank Cotten and had a child. Elizabeth Cotten was still performing in her nineties, a charming, sweet, unassuming, grandmotherly woman. She lived to the age of 95 and died on June 29, 1987, in Syracuse, New York.

SOURCES
Harris, Sheldon. *Blues Who's Who.*
Lanker, Brian. *I Dream a World.*
Lawless, Ray. *Folksingers and Folksongs in America.*

DANE, BARBARA (1927–   )   "Working Class Woman"

Born Barbara Spillman in Detroit, Michigan, on May 12, 1927, Barbara Dane showed an early interest in music. As a youngster she sang in church and played the piano and guitar. She attended college in West Virginia and Wayne University in Detroit.

She began performing folk songs in 1946 and played with Pete Seeger in Detroit. Moving to the West Coast, she worked in radio and on television in San Francisco and played at clubs in Hollywood. By 1952 she had a folk music program on KPFA radio in Berkeley and in 1956 began performing with Turk Murphy's band in San Francisco, singing folk songs, spirituals, and the blues.

Barbara Dane then appeared with Louis Armstrong on CBS-TV in 1959, which gave her career a boost. Following that she performed at the Newport Folk Festival the same year. In 1962 she sang on Johnny Carson's "Tonight Show," on the "Steve Allen Show," and in the film *The Blues.* She sang at many political demonstrations in the 1960s, as well as performing in women's music festivals and folk festivals. Like a number of other folksingers, during the civil rights movement she helped register black voters in the South.

Although she is primarily a blues and folksinger, Barbara Dane has also written songs. Among them are "Working Class Woman," written with Jane Felczer, "I Just Can't Make It by Myself," "Wild Cat Blues," and "Factory Girl."

Barbara Dane has three children and lives with her husband, Irwin Silber, in Oakland, California.

SOURCES
Harris, Sheldon. *Blues Who's Who.*
Lawless, Ray. *Folksingers and Folksongs in America.*
Stambler, Irwin. *Encyclopedia of Folk, Country, and Western Music,* 1969.
Who's Who of American Women, 1972.

HAWES, BESS (1921–   )   "The M.T.A. Song"

She was born Bess Lomax in Austin, Texas, and was the daughter of folklorist John Lomax and the sister of Alan Lomax. She graduated from high school at the age of 15 and then studied at the University of Texas and Bryn Mawr College. Before the age of ten she had studied piano and had also taught herself to play the guitar. Woody Guthrie taught her to play the mandolin. Because of her father's work at the Archive of Folksong of the Library of Congress, Bess knew most of the great names in folk music.

She joined the Almanac Singers and later married Butch Hawes of that group. They had three children. When the Almanac Singers broke up, she worked for the Office of War Information during World War II.

After the war, the family moved to Boston and later to California. She became a professor of anthropology at San Fernando Valley State College and, in the summer, a professor of folk music at the Idyllwild School of Music and the Arts. She has also performed at concerts and folk music events.

Bess Hawes wrote "The M.T.A. Song" with Jacqueline Steiner, and it became a hit for the Kingston Trio.

SOURCES
Claghorn, Charles. *Biographical Dictionary of American Music.*
Stambler, Irwin. *Encyclopedia of Folk, Country, and Western Music,* 1969.

JACKSON, AUNT MOLLY (1880–1960)   "Poor Miner's Farewell"

Aunt Molly Jackson was an early union organizer, singer, and songwriter in the coal-mining country of Kentucky. She was born Mary Magdalene Garland in Clay County, Kentucky, in 1880.

Her people had been farmers and early settlers in the region. Later coal was discovered in the area, and Clay County became an important mining center. However, before there were unions, the miners' wages were so low that people starved. In fact, Aunt Molly's mother died of starvation in 1886. After that her father became a union organizer, and Molly helped him. She was just ten years old the first time she went to jail with the union organizers. At the age of 14, she married. Later she became a nurse. Then a mine accident blinded her father and brother. Later on Aunt Molly's husband, son, and another brother were killed in a mine accident.

Aunt Molly's songs came out of her life experience. She wrote "Poor Miner's Farewell" three weeks after her brother's death in the mines. Her song "The Coal Miner's Child" was based on the true story of an orphan child was was refused help by a mine owner and died as a result. Her protest song "Hard Times in Colman's Mines" condemned the mine owner and urged the miners to strike for higher wages. Some of her other songs are more like traditional English folk songs, such as "The Birth of Robin Hood" and "The Dishonest Miller." But many of her songs of the 1930s, such as "The Death of Harry Simms," recount the effects of the Depression—unemployment, starvation, and riots. When it became impossible for her to stay, Aunt Molly left Kentucky and moved to New York, where she continued singing at union meetings.

During the 1930s and 1940s John Lomax recorded her for the Archive of Folksong of the Library of Congress. She made several hundred recordings during this period before her health began to fail. When she was elderly and living in poverty on an old-age pension, folk song collectors often visited her to learn her songs. She would sometimes ask them how she could make a little money from the songs. Although they had been translated and recorded in five languages, she had never received a penny for any of them.

Shortly before her death, plans had been made for her to make her first commercial album; but on September 1, 1960, the week before the recording session, she passed away. In 1961 Folkway Records released an album of her songs sung by John Greenway, *The Songs and Stories of Aunt Molly Jackson.*

They leave their dear wives, and little ones too,
To earn them a living, as miners all do.
Poor hardworking miners, their troubles are great—
So often, while mining, they meet their sad fate.—Chorus

Chorus:
Only a miner killed under the ground;
Only a miner and one more is found,
Killed by some accident; there's no one can tell—
Your mining's all over, poor miner, farewell.

Poor orphaned children, thrown out on the street
Ragged and hungry with nothing to eat.
Their mothers are jobless and their fathers are dead;
Poor fatherless children, left a-crying for bread.—Chorus

When I'm in Kentucky so often I meet
Poor coal miner's children out on the street.
"How are you doing?" to them I said,
"We're hungry, Aunt Molly we're begging for bread."—Chorus
                    —"Poor Miner's Farewell" by Aunt Molly Jackson

Aunt Molly's half-sister was Sarah Elizabeth Gunning, who was also a songwriter and wrote "I Am a Girl of Constant Sorrow."

SOURCES
Baggelaar, Kristin. *Folk Music More than a Song.*
Harker, David. *One for the Money.*
Stambler, Irwin. *Encyclopedia of Folk, Country, and Western Music,* 1969.
Whitman, Wanda. *Songs That Changed the World.*

MacCOLL, PEGGY (1935–   )   "I'm Gonna Be an Engineer"

Born on June 17, 1935, in New York City, Peggy Seeger grew up in a household devoted to music. Her father musicologist Charles Seeger and her mother composer Ruth Crawford Seeger both worked in the Archive of Folksong of the Library of Congress. The family sang and played music together at home, and they often had folksingers as guests. Both her brother Mike Seeger and half-brother Pete Seeger became folksingers.

Peggy attended Radcliffe College, then married Ewan MacColl, an English folksinger and songwriter. She moved to England and became an English citizen. The MacColls have two children. Daughter Kirsty MacColl is a singer-songwriter.

Like the songs of **Malvina Reynolds,** Peggy Seeger MacColl's songs often express social criticism. Some of her songs are "Darling Annie," "That Bomb Has Got to Go," "L.B.J.," "Come Fill Up Your Glasses," "An Affair of State," "Harold the Bootblack," "Springhill Mine Disaster," "Song of Myself," and "I'm Gonna Be an Engineer." The latter is about a young girl who wants to be an engineer when she grows up.

SOURCES
Lawless, Ray. *Folksingers and Folksongs in America.*
Stambler, Irwin. *Encyclopedia of Folk, Country, and Western Music,* 1969.
Wenner, Hilda. *Here's to the Women.*

RAITT, BONNIE   *See* Pop Rock.

REECE, FLORENCE (1900–1986)   "Which Side Are You On?"

Born in 1900, Florence Reece was a social activist and a writer of short stories, poetry, and songs. She was best known as the author of the song "Which Side Are You On?" which became an anthem for the labor movement. She wrote the song in the 1930s when her husband and other miners in Harlan County, Kentucky, were preparing for a strike. She set her words to the tune of the old hymn "Lay the Lily Low." Folksinger Pete Seeger recorded the song in 1941. It continues to be sung at gatherings for labor and other social causes throughout the world.

Florence Reece wrote many other labor songs and also wrote a book of short stories and poems, *Against the Current*. When Ronald Reagan, who enjoyed jellybeans, was president, Florence Reece wrote a poem entitled "You Can't Live on Jellybeans," criticizing the president's cuts in programs for the poor and needy.

In 1978 her husband died, but Florence Reece continued to live in the Kentucky coal fields until a heart attack caused her death in Knoxville, Tennessee, on August 3, 1986.

SOURCES

New York Times. Obituaries, August 6, 1986, II, p. 4.
Wenner, Hilda. *Here's to the Women*.
Whitman, Wanda. *Songs That Changed the World*.

REYNOLDS, MALVINA (1900–1978)   "Little Boxes"

One of the top writers of folk songs during the folk music revival of the 1950s and 1960s was Malvina Reynolds.

Born Malvina Milder in San Francisco, California, on August 23, 1900, she earned a Ph.D. in English literature from the University of California at Berkeley, where she graduated Phi Beta Kappa. In 1934 she married William Reynolds and had a daughter.

Because she was blacklisted for her politics, she couldn't get a teaching position. While making a living as a tailor, social worker, and steelworker in the 1940s, she got a guitar and tried her hand at songwriting. In the early 1950s her first songs were published in *Sing Out!* The songs were so appealing that they were subsequently recorded by many of the leading folk artists, including Pete Seeger, Woody Guthrie, and the Almanac Singers. Recognizing that other singers were having success with her songs, Malvina started recording and performing her own songs at concerts and folk festivals, despite her rather raspy singing voice.

She gave many performances in the United States, Japan, and Europe. Politically active, Malvina Reynolds also often performed at antiwar rallies, civil rights demonstrations, and concerts for the women's movement. She was still singing at political rallies in her seventies.

In 1963 she published a collection of her songs, *Little Boxes and Other Handmade Songs*. Although her songs had the simplicity of children's songs, they dealt with the serious problems of the world—peace, poverty, the ecology, conformity—but the subject matter was always treated with hope

Malvina Reynolds. (Virginia Grattan)

and humor. She had no regrets about her career choice. She once told an interviewer that she would rather be a songwriter than a college professor.

Among her more than 500 songs are "Little Boxes," "What Have They Done to the Rain," "No Hole in My Head," "It's up to You," "I've Got a Song," "Don't Push Me," "Upside Down," "This World," "Bury Me in My Overalls," and "God Bless the Grass." She wrote "Let It Be" and "From Way up Here" with Pete Seeger, "Turn Around" with Alan Greene, and

"Sally, Don't You Grieve" with Woody Guthrie. She recorded on Cassandra Records, Columbia, and Folkways.

Malvina Reynolds died on March 17, 1978, in Berkeley, California.

> Little Boxes on the hillside,
> Little Boxes made of ticky tacky,
> Little Boxes on the hillside,
> Little Boxes all the same.
>
> There's a green one and a pink one
> And a blue one and a yellow one,
> And they're all made out of ticky tacky,
> And they all look just the same.
>
> And the people in the houses
> All went to the university,
> Where they were put in boxes
> And they came out all the same,
> And there's doctors and lawyers,
> And business executives,
> And they're all made out of ticky tacky,
> And they all look just the same.
>
> And they all play on the golf course
> And drink their martinis dry,
> And they all have pretty children
> And the children go to school,
> And the children go to summer camp,
> And then to the university
> Where they are put in boxes
> And they come out all the same.
>
> And the boys go into business
> And marry and raise a family
> In boxes made of ticky tacky
> And they all look just the same.
> There's a green one and a pink one
> And a blue one and a yellow one,
> And they're all made out of ticky tacky,
> And they all look just the same.
>
> —"Little Boxes," words and music by Malvina Reynolds*

SOURCES

Claghorn, Charles. *Biographical Dictionary of American Music.*
Hitchcock, H. Wiley. *New Grove Dictionary of American Music.*

*© Copyright 1962 Schroder Music Co. Renewed 1990 N. Schimmel. Used by permission. All rights reserved.

Lynn Farnol Group. *ASCAP Biographical Dictionary.*
Stambler, Irwin. *Encyclopedia of Folk, Country, and Western Music*, 1969.
Whitman, Wanda. *Songs That Changed the World.*

RITCHIE, JEAN (1922–   )   "Mountain Born and Country Gentle"

The Ritchie family was a well-known singing group in the Cumberland Mountains of Kentucky. Jean grew up singing the family songs and learning to play the guitar and the dulcimer. In later years she became an author, a folk music authority, and songwriter.

Born in Viper, Kentucky, in the Cumberland Mountains, on December 8, 1922, Jean Ritchie was the youngest of 14 children. The children were encouraged to obtain good educations, and Jean graduated Phi Beta Kappa from the University of Kentucky in Lexington intending to go into social work. During World War II she taught school in her home area because there was an extreme shortage of teachers. For a time she was superintendent of the elementary schools in Perry County. Then she went to New York and worked as a music counselor in a settlement house, using her vocal and instrumental talents. She began performing in schools and colleges and was pleased to find people interested in her songs and tales from the Kentucky Mountains.

She met folklorist Alan Lomax, who invited her to sing on his radio show. In 1948 she sang at Columbia University and at Town Hall in New York. Then in the 1950s she sang on a New York radio station and began making recordings. She has since recorded on the Elektra, Folkways, and Prestige labels.

In 1950 she married photographer George Pickow, and they had two children.

She also wrote song books: *The Swapping Song Book* of folk songs and *A Garland of Mountain Song.* Then in 1952 she received a Fulbright grant for folk song research in the British Isles. There she researched the origins of American folk songs. While in London, she sang on the British Broadcasting Corporation (BBC) station and made recordings.

After returning to the United States, she wrote several more books. In 1955 she wrote the history of her family and its heritage of folk music from colonial times to the present, called *Singing Family of the Cumberlands.* A later book of hers is *Celebration of Life.* Over the years Jean Ritchie has also compiled many collections of folk songs.

In the 1960s when folk music came into mainstream popularity, Jean Ritchie began performing at folk music festivals, singing and playing her

mountain dulcimer. She was one of the seven original directors of the Newport Folk Festival, where she has performed many times.

In 1979 she was a visiting professor of folklore at the California State
University at Fresno.

Besides performing traditional folk songs, Jean Ritchie has written the
score for the television film *Blue Diamond Mines,* as well as many songs.
Among her songs are "The L&N Don't Stop Here Anymore." "Sweet Sorrow in the Wind," "Black Waters," "West Virginia Mine Disaster," "Now
Is the Cool of the Day," "One, I Love," and "Come Fare Away (Marnie)."
She publishes her music through her own Geordie Music Publishing Company.

SOURCES

Jacques Cattell Press. *ASCAP Biographical Dictionary*
Lawless, Ray. *Folksingers and Folksongs in America*
Moritz, Charles. *Current Biography,* 1959.
Shapiro, Nat. *Popular Music.*
Stambler, Irwin. *Encyclopedia of Folk, Country, and Western Music,* 1969, 1984.

VEGA, SUZANNE   *See* Pop Rock.

VII

COUNTRY

INTRODUCTION

Country music has its roots in the Scottish, Irish, and English songs brought to this country by the earliest settlers. These old songs survived the longest in the inaccessible mountain regions of Kentucky and West Virginia, where they were passed down from generation to generation.

In the 1920s recording companies, which had found a profitable new market in blues, decided to record country music. In 1927 the Victor Talking Machine Company sent out a crew to record country music in the field. They placed ads in the local papers, and people came down from the hills to audition. In this way Jimmie Rodgers and the Carter Family were first discovered and recorded.

With the advent of radio, local stations in Nashville, Atlanta, and Fort Worth began broadcasting country music. Most stations had a barn dance program on which local talent could perform and many country singers got their start on such programs. The barn dance show on WSM later became the "Grand Ole Opry," a showcase for the best country artists.

Motion pictures in the 1930s brought country-western music to the nation through the popular films of such cowboys as Gene Autry and Roy Rogers. These early motion picture cowboys always played the guitar and sang, and they were usually joined by a singing cowgirl. Patsy Montana frequently sang with Gene Autry, for example, and Dale Evans with Roy Rogers. Both of these women were songwriters as well as performers. Dale

Evans's song "Happy Trails to You" was Roy Rogers's television theme song and has since become their signature song.

Another factor that helped disseminate country music was World War II. The war caused great shifts of population to the battlefields overseas and to centers of war industry at home. Country music lovers took their music with them and thus helped popularize it throughout the United States and abroad.

After the war, from the 1950 to the 1970s, Nashville grew into the recording and talent center of country music. As larger commercial interests moved in, they began changing country music to appeal to the larger pop music audience. Producers took control of the recordings by choosing the songs, singers, and arrangers, and by controlling the style of the performance. The nasal country twang in singing voices was removed. Strings and horns were added to give the music a lush sound like popular music. Records with this "Nashville Sound" began to regularly cross over to the pop charts, and that was where the big money was. Country music continued to grow, and even with these changes the music was able to keep both the older audiences and the younger. By the 1960s Nashville had become a big recording center like Los Angeles.

In the early days country music was a a masculine world where women could play only a supporting role. They could be comediennes like Aunt Minnie Pearl or be part of a singing group, but men were the stars. In the 1930s, however, Patsy Montana through her work in movies and on radio became a star in her own right. Her success opened more opportunities for women in country music, not only as performers but also as songwriters. Most of the women included here are singer-songwriters who are recognized primarily as performers. Dolly Parton, however, is almost equally well known for her songs. For some, like Felice Bryant and Cindy Walker, songwriting is their primary career, and they leave the singing to others.

Country music today has a worldwide audience. It has absorbed the influences of rock and other popular music styles, but it still maintains a respect for its country origins. Today women continue to make important contributions to country music both as singers and as songwriters.

BRYANT, FELICE (1925–   )   "Wake Up Little Susie"

Felice Bryant and her late husband, Boudleaux Bryant, were a songwriting team of both pop and country-western songs.

Felice was born in Milwaukee, Wisconsin, on August 7, 1925. She met Boudleaux in 1945 when he was playing fiddle with a group in Milwaukee and she was an elevator operator at a hotel there. After their marriage she traveled with him when he toured, and sometimes they made up songs just for fun. They sent one of their songs to Fred Rose of Acuff-Rose in Nashville. He bought the song, and it became a top ten hit. He urged them to move to Nashville and write songs professionally, which they did. From then on their songs were often hits on the top ten charts.

Many performers have recorded their songs, including Carl Smith, Frankie Laine, Eddy Arnold, the Everly Brothers, and Jim Reeves. Their songs helped the Everly Brothers dominate the pop field in the late 1950s.

Some of the songs that Felice and Boudleaux Bryant wrote were "Wake Up Little Susie," "All I Have to Do Is Dream," " Bye Bye Love," "Country Boy," "Hey Joe," "It's a Lovely, Lovely World," "Our Honeymoon," "Just Wait 'Til I Get You Alone," "Back Up, Buddy," "I've Been Thinking," "Bird Dog," "Blue Boy," "Let's Think about Living," "Richest Man," "Baltimore," and "I Love to Dance with Annie."

Felice and Boudleaux Bryant had two sons. Boudleaux died in 1987 at the age of 67. In 1991 Felice and her late husband were inducted into the Country Music Hall of Fame. Now in her sixties, Felice Bryant is still writing songs.

SOURCES
Mattfeld, Julius. *Variety Music Cavalcade.*
Stambler, Irwin. *Encyclopedia of Folk, Country, and Western Music,* 1969.

CARSON, MARTHA (1921–   )   "I Can't Stand Up Alone"

Singer, guitarist, and songwriter, Martha Carson was born in Neon, Kentucky, on March 19, 1921.

As a teenager she played guitar and sang at dances and other local events. When she was 18, she sang on a radio station in Bluefield, West Virginia. After this she was featured on several of the top country-western radio shows, and she began touring.

By the 1950s she had become a well-known performer. She appeared on the "Tennessee Barn Dance" radio show from Knoxville and in 1952 was asked to join the "Grand Ole Opry." She made guest appearances on the television shows of Ed Sullivan, Jimmy Dean, and Ernie Ford. In addition, she performed at country fairs, supper clubs, and colleges.

She recorded on RCA Victor, Capitol, Cadence, and Decca labels. Her recording of her own song "Satisfied" was a hit, so she continued to write songs as well as perform. Martha Carson has written more than 100 songs, including "I'm Gonna Walk and Talk with My Lord" and "I Can't Stand Up Alone."

SOURCRS
Claghorn, Gene. *Women Composers and Hymnists.*
Stambler, Irwin. *Encyclopedia of Folk, Country, and Western Music,* 1969.

CARTER, CARLENE (1955–   )   "Me and the Wildwood Rose"

Born in 1955, singer-songwriter Carlene Carter comes from a long line of country singers. She is the daughter of **June Carter** and Carl Smith, and the granddaughter of **Mother Maybelle Carter.** It was her grandmother who first taught Carlene to play the guitar.

Coming from such a background should have made success in the music world easy for Carlene Carter, but it wasn't. For her early recordings she was encouraged to sing country-pop music, but her records were not hits. Discouraged, she left the music scene and moved to London in the late 1970s. There she lived with her third husband, British rocker Nick Lowe, who produced her country-rock album *Musical Shapes* (1980).

She wrote songs that became hits for other performers, however, songs such as "One Step Closer," "I'm the Only One," and "Easy from Now On," the latter written with Susanna Clark.

While she was living in London, Carlene Carter's mother and two of her aunts did a Carter Family show there, and when one of the aunts became ill, Carlene took her place. Suddenly she was singing again the old familiar songs she had grown up with, the old Appalachian mountain harmonies. After that she began singing regularly with the Carter Family.

In 1988 she returned to the United States and continued singing the more traditional songs. She performed at the Grand Ole Opry and toured the United States in 1991.

Some of the songs Carlene Carter has written are "Me and the Wildwood Rose," " Come On Back," "One Step Closer," "I'm the Only One," and "Goodnight Dallas." With Susanna Clark she wrote "Easy from Now On." With Howie Epstein and Perry Lamek she wrote "One Love." Her song "Me and the Wildwood Rose" is about how she and her sister grew up at the knee of country legend Maybelle Carter. Generally her songs are about her childhood and her personal life. Like some of the other young country stars today, she has now returned to more a traditional country sound.

In 1990 she recorded a new album, *I Fell in Love,* and made an accompanying video. The title song, which she wrote with Howie Epstein, Beumont Tench, and Perry Lamek, ranked 13 on the country charts.

Carlene Carter has married three times and has two children. When she was just beginning in the music business, she had drug problems, but now she is chemically free. Her 18-year-old daughter studies art and lives with Carlene's former husband in London, and her 14-year-old son lives with his father in Los Angeles. Carlene lives in Nashville in the old family home that was her grandmother's.

SOURCES

Jerome, Jim. "In the Best Family Tradition." *People*, November 12, 1990, pp. 169–70.

Jones, Malcolm, Jr. "Country's New Traditionalist." *Newsweek*, August 17, 1990, p. 58.

CARTER, JUNE (1929–)   "Ring of Fire"

June Carter was born into a musical family on June 23, 1929, in Maces Spring, Virginia. Her mother, **Maybelle Carter,** taught her to play the autoharp.

In 1943 she sang with her sisters Helen and Anita as the Carter Sisters. With their mother they toured and sang on radio shows. In 1950 they were invited to join the Grand Ole Opry and so moved to Nashville. After the group broke up, June went solo and sang on the shows of Tennessee Ernie Ford, Jack Paar, and Garry Moore. As an actress she appeared on several television series and also had a part in the movie *Country Music Holiday.*

June Carter made records both solo and with her family. With Homer and Jethro she made a comedy version of "Baby, It's Cold Outside," which became a top ten hit in 1949. She also wrote songs. "The Matador," which she wrote with Johnny Cash in 1963, became one of his big hits. Her song "Ring of Fire," written with Merle Kilgore, became a standard. In 1966 she, Cash, and Kilgore wrote "Happy to Be with You," which became a top ten hit.

That same year she and Johnny Cash performed in Liverpool, England. The following year they were married. Johnny's daughter, **Rosanne Cash,** is also a singer-songwriter, as is June Carter's daughter, **Carlene Carter.**

In 1971 June and Johnny Cash made a film in Israel about Christianity; it was called *Gospel Road.*

June Carter Cash now often performs with her sisters as the Carter Family, and sometimes they are joined by her daughter, Carlene Carter.

SOURCES
Claghorn, Charles. *Biographical Dictionary of American Music.*
Stambler, Irwin. *Encyclopedia of Folk, Country, and Western Music,* 1969.

CARTER, MOTHER MAYBELLE (1909–1978)
"A Rose-Covered Grave"

Maybelle Carter was one of the members of the Original Carter Family singers. Born Maybelle Addington in Nikelsville, Virginia, on May 10, 1909, she grew up in a musical family and learned to play the guitar, banjo, fiddle, and autoharp in her childhood.

At the age of 16 she married Ezra Carter, who also came from a musical family. They settled in Poor Valley, Virginia, near Bristol, Tennessee.

In 1927 when RCA Victor sent a talent scout to Bristol, Tennessee, to audition country singers, Maybelle and her brother-in-law, A. P. Carter, and his wife, Sara, went to Bristol to audition. The first recordings they made became hits and launched their professional careers. From this point on they toured and recorded as the Original Carter Family.

Radio also helped spread their popularity. For several years they broadcast from a radio station in Texas; then they broadcast from Richmond, Virginia; Knoxville, Tennessee; and Springfield, Missouri.

The divorce of A. P. Carter and Sara Carter broke up the Original Carter Family. After that Maybelle Carter formed a new group with her three daughters, June, Anita, and Helen. The family moved to Nashville in 1950. There they became stars of the "Grand Ole Opry." Later on two of the daughters left to get married. **June Carter** decided then to be on her own as a singer and actress. Meanwhile Mother Maybelle Carter decided to stay on at the Opry. In 1965 she appeared at the Newport Folk Festival and toured the country music circuits. She also recorded for the Smash, Columbia, and Briar labels.

Some of the songs the Carter family performed and recorded were songs Maybelle had written, among them "Lonesome Homesick Blues," "A Jilted Love," and "Walk a Little Closer." She also co-authored "Don't Wait," "Storms Are on the Ocean," "The Kneeling Drunkard's Plea," "A Rose-Covered Grave," and "I've Got a Home in Glory."

Maybelle Carter's daughter June married Johnny Cash, and the Carter Family, consisting of Maybelle, Helen, Anita, and June, often appeared together on Johnny Cash's television show.

The Carter Family was elected to the Country Music Hall of Fame. At the age of 69 Maybelle Carter died in Nashville, Tennessee, on October

23, 1978. Her daughters and granddaughters carry on the family musical tradition.

SOURCES
Dellar, Fred. *Illustrated Encyclopedia of Country Music.*
Stambler, Irwin. *Encyclopedia of Folk, Country, and Western Music,* 1969.

CASH, ROSANNE (1955–   )   **"Blue Moon with Heartache"**

Singer, songwriter, and actress, Rosanne Cash is the daughter of country singer Johnny Cash and half-sister of singer **Carlene Carter.**

She was born in Memphis, Tennessee, on May 24, 1955, but grew up in southern California, where her family had moved. After high school Rosanne Cash toured with her father's show for three years, first working as a wardrobe assistant, but finally becoming a soloist.

After this experience Rosanne wasn't sure what she wanted to do, so she went to London for several months. When she returned, she decided to be an actress. She studied drama at Vanderbilt University in Nashville for three years. Then she moved to Los Angeles to study further at the Lee Strasberg Theater Institute. While she was there, a demo tape she had made in 1978 brought her a contract with a European record company, and she cut her first album for the European market. Columbia Records signed her the following year. Her album *Right or Wrong* (1980) contained two hit singles, "Couldn't Do Nothin' Right" and "Take Me, Take Me."

With success on the way, she married her record producer, Rodney Crowell, and had a baby.

Her next album was *Interiors*, which was also produced by her husband, who wrote some of the songs with her. Her 1981 album, *Seven Year Ache*, featured two of her own songs, the title song, "Seven Year Ache," and "Blue Moon with Heartache."

Most of the songs Rosanne Cash writes are about personal relations between men and women and the difficulties of making relationships work. Among the songs she has written are "Hold On," "Halfway House," "Tennessee Flat Top Box," and "Looking for a Corner to Back My Heart Into," the latter written with Rodney Crowell. She also wrote "If You Change Your Mind," with Hank De Vito.

Rosanne Cash was awarded a Grammy in 1985 as the Best Female Country Vocalist of the year.

SOURCES
Pollock, Bruce. *Popular Music*, vol. 9, 1986.
Pollock, Bruce. *Popular Music*, vol. 10, 1986.

Pollock, Bruce. *Popular Music*, vol. 13, 1989.
Selvin, Joe. "Rosanne Cashes in on Her Humanity," *San Francisco Chronicle*, December 17, 1990, p. F3.
Stambler, Irwin. *Encyclopedia of Folk, Country, and Western Music*, 1984.

COOPER, WILMA LEE (1921–   )   "Big Midnight Special"

Wilma Lee Cooper is a singer, guitarist, banjoist, organist, and songwriter. She was born Wilma Lee Leary on February 7, 1921, in Valley Head, West Virginia. The Leary Family was a well-known musical group that sang in churches and at local festivals. It was with this group that she began singing and performing at the age of five. In 1938 the Leary Family was featured at a national folk festival sponsored by Eleanor Roosevelt.

After high school Wilma Lee Cooper went on to college and earned a BA degree in banking at Davis and Elkins College, West Virginia. She married Stoney Cooper, a guitarist and singer with the Leary Family.

She and Stoney toured and performed together throughout the United States. They also sang on the Wheeling, West Virginia "Jamboree" for ten years, and in 1957 joined the regular cast of the "Grand Ole Opry," where they remained for another decade. They played at state and county fairs in the United States and toured Canada and Europe.

They recorded many best-selling records for Columbia, Hickory, and Decca. Some of the songs written by Wilma Lee and Stoney Cooper include "Cheated Too," "Loving You," "I Tell My Heart," "Tomorrow I'll Be Gone," "Heartbreak Street," "He Taught Them How," and "My Heart Keeps Crying." Their songs the "Midnight Special," "Come Walk with Me," and "There's a Big Wheel" were all top ten hits in 1959. In 1961 they scored another hit with "Wreck on the Highway."

In the mid-1970s Stoney Cooper became ill and subsequently died. Wilma Lee continued on at the Opry. Many honors came to her. The Smithsonian Institution in Washington asked her to record and be a part of the library's collection of great country singers. And in 1979 she was featured on the "Bluegrass Spectacular" on Public Television. In the 1980s she remained one of the stars of the "Grand Ole Opry."

SOURCES

Dellar, Fred. *Illustrated Encyclopedia of Country Music*.
Stambler, Irwin. *Encyclopedia of Folk, Country, and Western Music*, 1984.

DAVIS, SKEETER (1931–)

"There's a Fool Born Every Minute"

Singer-songwriter Skeeter Davis was born Mary Frances Penick in Dry Ridge, Kentucky, on December 30, 1931. She grew up on a farm, one of seven children in a musical family.

In her teens she sang with Betty Jack Davis as the Davis Sisters. They performed in small clubs in Kentucky and on local radio stations. In 1953 they were signed to record with RCA Victor Records, but they were involved in a car accident coming home from a performance. Betty Jack Davis was killed, and Skeeter Davis was seriously injured. When she recovered from her injuries, Skeeter joined with Betty Jack's sister, Georgia Davis, and began singing again.

In 1955 Skeeter Davis went solo. She toured with the RCA Caravan of Stars and worked with Eddy Arnold and Elvis Presley. *Cash Box* magazine voted her the Most Promising Female Country Vocalist of 1958. The following year she became part of the "Grand Ole Opry" cast, as her recordings began to hit the top ten charts. She continued to perform at fairs and rodeos in the United States, and Canada, and she also toured Europe and Japan.

In the 1960s Skeeter Davis sang in New York's Carnegie Hall and made guest appearances on television, including the "Steve Allen Show," the "Jimmy Dean Show," "Oral Roberts" programs, the "Midnight Special," and "Hee Haw."

The songs Skeeter Davis has written include "My Last Date (with You)," "There's a Fool Born Every Minute," and "Bus Fare to Kentucky." She co-authored the song "Homebreaker."

She lives on a large farm in Brentwood, Tennessee.

SOURCES
Claghorn, Charles. *Biographical Dictionary of American Music.*
Stambler, Irwin. *Encyclopedia of Folk, Country, and Western Music,* 1984.

EVANS, DALE (1912–)

"Happy Trails to You"

Famous as Roy Rogers's co-star in numerous westerns, Dale Evans is also an author and a songwriter.

She was born Frances Octavia Smith on October 31, 1912, in Uvalde, Texas, and attended high school in Osceola, Arkansas, where her family had moved. They later settled in Memphis, Tennessee. There she studied at a business school and began singing on a local radio station as Dale Evans. Later she sang with the Anson Weeks Band in Chicago. After this she was hired to sing on a weekly CBS radio show called "News and Rhythm."

In 1941 she went to Hollywood and was signed to a motion picture contract by Twentieth Century Fox, but she still kept up her radio appearances, singing on the shows of Edgar Bergen, Jack Carson, and Jimmy Durante. Then in 1943 she made her first movie, *Swing Your Partner*. Over the next 20 years she made approximately 40 movies, primarily with Roy Rogers.

In 1947 she married her co-star, Roy Rogers. The song most frequently associated with them, "Happy Trails to You," was written by Dale Evans as a theme song for Roy Rogers's television show.

Dale Evans wrote many other songs, among them "Will You Marry Me, Mr. Laramie?," "Lo Dee Lo Di," "Aha, San Antone," "T for Texas," "Buckeye Cowboy," "No Bed of Roses," "I'm Gonna Lock You out a My Heart," and "Happy Birthday, Gentle Saviour."

In later years Dale Evans wrote several books, among them *Angel Unaware* (1953), which sold 400,000 copies, and *My Spiritual Diary* (1955). She also made more than 30 recordings, mostly western songs and religious songs for children.

Dale Evans had one son by a first marriage. She and Roy Rogers had three children and adopted two more. They live on a ranch in the San Fernando Valley.

SOURCES
Lynn Farnol Group. *ASCAP Biographical Dictionary.*
Candee, Marjorie Dent. *Current Biography,* 1956.
Stambler, Irwin. *Encyclopedia of Folk, Country, and Western Music,* 1969.

GENTRY, BOBBIE (1944–)   "Ode to Billie Joe"

A singer, guitarist, and songwriter, Bobbie Gentry was born Bobbie Street on July 17, 1944, on a farm in Chickasaw County, Mississippi. She grew up in Greenwood, Mississippi, then moved to Palm Springs, California, where she finished high school.

At 15 she was writing and performing songs; it was then that she took the stage name of Bobbie Gentry. In her teens she played guitar and later piano, vibraharp, banjo, and bass fiddle. After high school she studied philosophy at the University of California at Los Angeles and music at the Los Angeles Conservatory of Music. She also worked in small theater groups.

Bobbie Gentry started her professional career as a dancer in Las Vegas, but it was the recording of "Ode to Billie Joe" (1967), which she wrote and performed, that sent her career into orbit. The song became a million-selling single and won three Grammys. The album *Ode to Billie Joe* became a gold record as well. With this song Bobbie Gentry attained international recognition and received invitations to perform in Europe.

In 1969 she married William Harrah, a Nevada casino operator, but they divorced a year later.

Bobbie Gentry was very popular in Britain, where she had her own television show on the BBC in the early 1970s.

Among the songs she has written are "Chickasaw County Child," "Lazy Willie," "Papa Won't Let Me Go into Town with You," "Sweet Peony," "Ace Insurance Man," "Recollection," "Mornin' Glory," "Sunday Best," "Sittin' Pretty," "Mississippi Delta," "Oklahoma River Bottom Band," "Reunion," "Fancy," and "Tuesday's Child."

SOURCES

Claghorn, Charles. *Biographical Dictionary of American Music.*
Stambler, Irwin. *Encyclopedia of Folk, Country, and Western Music,* 1969.
Stambler, Irwin. *Encyclopedia of Pop, Rock and Soul.*
Who's Who of American Women, 1975.

JACKSON, WANDA (1937–   )   "Kicking Our Hearts Around"

Wanda Jackson is a singer, guitarist, and songwriter. She was born on October 20, 1937, in Maud, Oklahoma, where her father played in a small band. Wanda learned to play the guitar and piano when she was a child.

She entered a talent contest at a local radio station when she was 13 and won her own 15-minute radio show. Both of her parents encouraged her to perform. Her father managed her career and drove the car when she had to travel, and her mother made her costumes.

When Wanda Jackson was a junior in high school, Hank Thompson heard her and asked her to cut a record, singing a duet with Billy Gray. The song, "You Can't Have My Love," hit the top ten charts, and Decca signed her to a contract. She could have started singing professionally, but she decided to finish high school first. After she graduated, she went on tour with Elvis Presley, who was just becoming known. Since then she has toured Canada, Europe, and the Far East, and from 1950 on she played Las Vegas.

In 1961 Wanda Jackson married Wendell Goodman, a computer programmer. Since their marriage her husband has managed her career. They have two children.

For a time Wanda Jackson had her own television show, "Music Village." In the 1970s, however, she turned toward religious music and now often performs on evangelical tours.

Among the songs that Wanda Jackson has written are "Kicking Our Hearts Around," "Right or Wrong," and "In the Middle of a Heartache."

Her home is in Oklahoma City.

SOURCES

Claghorn, Charles. *Biographical Dictionary of American Music.*
Stambler, Irwin. *Encyclopedia of Folk, Country, and Western Music,* 1984.

JUDD, NAOMI (1946–   )
JUDD, WYNONNA (1964–   )   "Love Can Build a Bridge"

The Judds have been one of the most successful duos in country music, and one of the few mother-daughter teams.

Naomi Judd was born Diana Ellen Judd in Ashland, Kentucky, on January 11, 1946. Her father ran a gas station there. She married her high school sweetheart at 17, and they moved to Los Angeles. They had two daughters, Christina and Ashley, but the marriage ended. The older daughter, Christina Claire Ciminella, has been a singing partner with her mother for 17 years. When they began their singing career, they changed their names to Naomi and Wynonna Judd.

After her divorce Naomi Judd supported her two daughters and herself by working as a secretary and as a model. Finally she left Los Angeles and took her girls back to Kentucky to live. Naomi began taking courses and in the late 1970s became a nurse.

Wynonna Judd was always self-conscious. She cared only about music and would sit and play the guitar by the hour. Naomi used to harmonize with her, and their voices blended so well that they thought about a singing career. Naomi, by chance, had a patient whose father was a record producer, and he helped the Judds obtain an audition, which led to a record contract.

The Judds' first single in 1983 hit the top 20 charts. Their second single, "Mama He's Crazy," went to number one, and they won four Grammys. More hit singles followed, along with four platinum albums. The Judds' "Young Love" and "Let Me Tell You about Love" went to number one on the singles charts and the albums became platinum million sellers. Some of their other hits include "Why Not Me?," "Mama He's Crazy," and "Love Can Build a Bridge." They've sold more than 10 million records.

In 1990 they won their sixth consecutive duo-of-the-year award from the Country Music Association. Their eighth album, *Love Can Build a Bridge,* went to 13 on the country charts. Their other albums include *Why Not Me* and *Rockin' with the Rhythm,* both of which sold more than a million copies each, and *Heartland,* which went gold.

Then just before a tour, Naomi Judd found that she had hepatitis. She had been having very low energy and had not felt right for three years. After the initial diagnosis she cancelled the tour, but she felt obligated to keep some of the other engagements. Because she was the first country artist asked to host the American Music Awards, she wanted to be there. And because some of her upcoming concerts had huge audiences—10,000 in the Houston Astrodome and 22,500 in the Hoosier Dome in Indianapolis—she didn't want to disappoint so many fans. Her illness was finally diagnosed as chronic active hepatitis, which can be deadly. She is taking medication, and the disease is in remission now. As a consequence, the Judds decided that their 1991 tour would be their last.

Naomi Judd has also written some songs, among them "Change of Heart" and "Mr. Pain." She wrote "River of Time" with John Jarvis, "Cadillac Red" with Jarvis and Craig Bickhardt, and "Guardian Angel" with Jarvis and Don Schlitz. Her song "Love Can Build a Bridge," written with John Jarvis and Paul Overstreet, won a 1992 Grammy for Best Country Song.

Naomi married again in 1989. Her new husband, Larry Strickland, sang with the J. D. Stamps Quartet. They live in a log cabin in a valley near Franklin, Kentucky. Wynonna, who plans to continue on with a solo career, lives on a farm a few miles away. Naomi's other daughter, Ashley, was a French and history major at the University of Kentucky and is now a television actress.

The Judds' last concert together was in Nashville, Tennessee, in December 1991. It was telecast on pay-per-view television.

Naomi plans to write her autobiography after she retires.

SOURCES

Anderson, Nancy. "Here Come the Judds!" *Good Housekeeping,* June 1988, pp. 38–45.
Gleason, Holly. "What's Hot: Country Women." *Ladies Home Journal,* November 1988, pp. 142–46.
Sanderson, Jane. "Fighting to Cast Off Death's Shadow." *People,* November 26, 1990, pp. 90–94.
Who's Who of American Women, 1991.

LYNN, JUDY (1936–   )   "My Father's Voice"

Singer-songwriter Judy Lynn was born in Boise, Idaho, on April 12, 1936. She has been a singer since the age of ten. She won the Miss Idaho beauty contest in 1955 and was also the U.S. champion girl yodeler.

Judy Lynn has sung throughout the United States, and in the 1960s she had her own television show. She recorded with United Artists, producing a top ten hit in "Footsteps of a Fool."

Besides singing, she has written a number of songs, including "My Father's Voice," "Antique in My Closet," "Honey Stuff," and "The Calm before the Storm."

She married promoter John Kelly.

SOURCES

Claghorn, Charles Eugene. *Biographical Dictionary of American Music.*
Stambler, Irwin. *Encyclopedia of Folk, Country, and Western Music,* 1969.

LYNN, LORETTA (1935–   )   "Coal Miner's Daughter"

Loretta Lynn was born on April 14, 1935, in Butchers Hollow, Kentucky, into a poor coal-mining family.

She married at the age of 13 and was a mother at 14. Her husband was convinced she could be a successful singer and encouraged her to try. Even though at that time there were only two other women, Patsy Cline and Kitty Wells, who were major stars, her husband was convinced that she could be a star too. Loretta Lynn began singing at local clubs and on the radio; but times became hard, and when the mines closed she and her husband decided to move elsewhere to look for work. They went to the state of Washington, where Loretta Lynn formed her own band and sang in local nightclubs.

There a recording company offered her a contract, and the record she made, "I'm a Honky Tonk Girl," became a hit. After this Loretta Lynn and her family moved to Nashville, where she turned out a number of top ten hits in the early 1960s. She was invited to join the "Grand Ole Opry" cast and also made other guest appearances on television.

Loretta Lynn has won many honors. She won Country Music's Female Vocalist of the year in 1972 and Top Duet honors for four years, from 1972 to 1975. She won a Grammy in 1978. In 1980 the Academy of Country Music named her Entertainer of the Decade, and in 1988 she was inducted into the Country Music Hall of Fame.

The story of Loretta Lynn's journey from poverty to stardom was told in her autobiography, *Coal Miner's Daughter,* from which a movie was made starring Sissy Spacek.

Besides singing, Loretta Lynn has also written many songs, including "Don't Come Home A-Drinkin' with Lovin' on Your Mind," "You Ain't Woman Enough to Take My Man," "I Know How," "You Wanna Give Me a Lift?," "Woman of the World," "Here I Am Again," "Rated X," "Wings upon Your Horns," "One's on the Way," "Coal Miner's Daughter," "Ain't It Funny What Sundown Does to You," "Hey Loretta," "When the Tingle Becomes a Chill," "First City," "Adam's Rib," "Wouldn't It Be Great," "Your Squaw's on the Warpath," and "You're Looking at Country."

SOURCES

Morthland, John. *Best of Country Music.*
Stambler, Irwin. *Encyclopedia of Folk, Country, and Western Music,* 1969.
Who's Who in America, 1990–91.

McENTIRE, REBA (1955–   )   "I Don't Want to Be Alone"

Reba McEntire was born in Oklahoma on March 28, 1955. Her mother was a teacher, and her father, a rancher and champion roper at the rodeos. When she was little, her family followed the rodeo circuit. She made an early debut as a singer at the age of five when she sang "Jesus Loves Me" in the lobby of a hotel where her family was staying, and people gave her coins. Because her mother loved music, she saw to it that the children had singing lessons. Reba and her siblings performed at local dances and at the rodeos. At 19 Reba sang the national anthem at the opening of the national rodeo finals in Oklahoma City. This performance led to a demo tape and a contract in Nashville.

She has been making albums since 1986. They include *Whoever's in New England* (1986), *What Am I Gonna Do about You?* (1986), *The Last One to Know* (1987), *Reba* (1988), *Rumor Has It* (1990), and *For My Broken Heart* (1991). Some of her hits include "I Can't Even Get the Blues," "You're the First Time I Thought about Leaving," and "How Blue." She won her first Grammy for "Whoever's in New England." For four years in a row, from 1984 to 1987, Reba McEntire has been named the Female Vocalist of the Year by the Country Music Association. The American Music Awards also named her their favorite female country vocalist from 1987 to 1991.

Reba McEntire now manages her own career and produces her own records. She is a very upbeat, confident person. Undoubtedly this quality has contributed to her success. It may also have helped her carry on, after a plane crash in March 1991 killed seven members of her band. By chance Reba McEntire had taken a different flight. This tragedy left her very shaken, but she went on with her engagements.

Besides making recordings and giving live performances, Reba McEntire has also co-starred in a television drama with Kenny Rogers, "The Gambler IV" (1991). She often appeared on Johnny Carson's "Tonight Show" on television as well as on the "Grand Ole Opry."

Reba McEntire has written many songs, often collaborating with Don Schlitz. Among their songs are "Bobby," "Climb That Mountain High," "You Must Really Love Me," and "Am I the Only One Who Cares." She also wrote the words and music to "I Don't Want to Be Alone."

She has won many honors, including the Country Music Association's Female Vocalist Award each year from 1984 to 1987. She won a Grammy for Best Country Vocal Performance in 1987 and Entertainer of the Year from the Country Music Association in 1986.

Reba McEntire first married Charlie Battles, but she is now married to Narvel Blackstock, who is also her manager. They have a son. The family lives on an 80-acre farm outside Nashville.

SOURCES

Brady, James. "In Step with Reba." Parade, *Oakland Tribune*, October 27, 1991, p. 14.
Gareffa, Peter. *Newsmakers*, 1986.
Gleason, Holly. "What's Hot: Country Women." *Ladies Home Journal*, November 1988, pp. 142–46.
Stambler, Irwin. *Encyclopedia of Folk, Country, and Western Music*, 1969.

MONTANA, PATSY (1914–   )

"I Want to Be a Cowboy's Sweetheart"

Known as the Yodeling Cowgirl, Patsy Montana became one of the great country-western stars in the 1930s. Born Rubye Blevins on October 30, 1914, in Hot Springs, Arkansas, she grew up as the only girl in a family of ten brothers. After graduating from high school, she attended the University of Western Louisiana.

In 1934 she started singing with the Prairie Ramblers quartet on the WLS "National Barn Dance" from Chicago, and she continued for nearly 25 years. She later had her own radio show on ABC, "Wake up and Smile." In 1935 her recording of a song she wrote, "I Want to Be a Cowboy's Sweetheart," made her country music's first female million-seller.

She was one of the first women in country music to become an important solo singer. Before Patsy Montana, men were the stars of country-western music. Women did comedy or sang harmony in some kind of supporting role. But Patsy Montana was so successful that she became a star in her own right and made the way easier for other women.

Her recording career began in 1933. During that career she cut approximately 200 singles and a dozen albums on the RCA Victor, Surf, Vocalion, and Decca labels. Her records were enormously popular. She also made some western movies with Gene Autry.

Patsy Montana wrote many songs, most of them about cowboys and cowgirls: "My Poncho Pony," "Swing Time Cowgirl," "Cowboy Rhythm," "A Cowboy's Gal," "Me and My Cowboy Sweetheart," "The Buckaroo," "Sweetheart of the Saddle," "The Moon Hangs Low," "I'm a Little Cowboy Girl," "I've Found My Cowboy Sweetheart," "Put a Little Fuel on the Flame," and "My Baby's Lullaby."

She married Paul Rose in 1934 and had two daughters. When her children were small, they sometimes sang with her on stage as the Patsy Montana Trio. In 1959 Patsy Montana retired to Manhattan Beach, California, where she sold real estate; but now and then she still does personal appearances.

SOURCES

Claghorn, Charles. *Biographical Dictionary of American Music.*
Lynn Farnol Group. *ASCAP Biographical Dictionary.*
Morthland, John. *Best of Country Music.*
Stambler, Irwin. *Encyclopedia of Folk, Country, and Western Music.*

NELSON, TRACY (1944–   )   "Down So Low"

Singer-songwriter Tracy Nelson was born in Madison, Wisconsin, on December 27, 1944, and attended the University of Wisconsin.

As a youngster she loved singing folk music and blues. In the 1960s she knew that such singers as Janis Joplin and Grace Slick were working in San Francisco, so she thought that would be a good place for her to start her own career in music. She moved there but had a difficult time finding a band, so she formed her own. With her blues and soul band, Mother Earth, she made demo tapes that resulted in a contract with Mercury Records.

In 1965 she made her first album. Then she and the band toured the United States, ending up in Nashville. Tracy liked it there so much that she moved to Nashville in 1970. By that time she was singing more country music than rock. Atlantic Records signed her, and her duet with Willie Nelson, "After the Fire Is Gone," did well.

In the late 1970s she recorded several country albums for the MCA label and played the country circuit. She has also done television, including the "Lonesome Pine" on PBS.

Tracy Nelson continues to write country music songs. Her songs often do well for other performers, as witnessed by Linda Ronstadt's success with "Down So Low." Another of her songs is "I've Been There Before."

She lives in the country outside Nashville.

SOURCES
Hitchcock, H. Wiley. *New Grove Dictionary of American Music.*
Stambler, Irwin. *Encyclopedia of Folk, Country, and Western Music,* 1984.

OSLIN, K. T. (1942–   )   "I'll Always Come Back"

K. T. Oslin was born Kay Toinette Oslin in Crossett, Arkansas, in 1942. Her father died when she was five, and she was raised by her mother and grandmother.

When she was in her twenties, she went to New York to become an actress. She did commercials and bit parts, but her "big break" never materialized. When acting didn't work out, K. T. Oslin turned to songwriting and had some success. Many of her songs were recorded by other performers. K. T. herself, however, wasn't having much luck as a performer. Even her first record contract fell through. Discouraged but unwilling to give up, she borrowed money from an aunt, returned to Nashville, and started singing at a Nashville club. There a producer saw her, and that led to a record contract.

Her album *80's Ladies* was a hit in 1987, and she subsequently won a Grammy for Best Country Female Vocal Performance of the year. In fact, two singles on the album hit number one on the charts, "Do Ya" and "I'll Always Come Back." She completed the album *This Woman* in 1988 and *Love in a Small Town* in 1990.

In 1989 the Academy of Country Music voted K. T. Oslin Best Female Country Vocalist, and she also won an award for the Best Country Song, "Hold Me." She won Grammys in 1988 and 1989.

Some songs K. T. Oslin has written are "Come Next Monday," "Younger Men," "Jealous," "Hey Bobby," "Hold Me," "Money," and "Truly Blue." "Where Is a Woman to Go" and "Old Pictures" were written with Jerry Gillespie. "Round the Clock Lovin' " was written with Rory Michael Bourke.

SOURCES
"Country's '80s Lady, K. T. Oslin." *San Francisco Examiner-Chronicle,* Datebook,
      July 30, 1989, p. 35.
Gleason, Holly. "What's Hot: Country Women." *Ladies Home Journal,* November
      1988, pp. 142–46.
Vaughan, Andrew. *Who's Who in New Country Music.*
Who's Who of American Women, 1991.

OWENS, BONNIE (1932–   )   "Lead Me On"

She was born Bonnie Campbell into a poor family of nine children in Blanchard, Oklahoma, on October 1, 1932. When she was young, the family moved to Arizona, where she grew up during the Depression.

As a youngster Bonnie Owens had a stutter, but not when she sang, and she loved to sing. When she was in her teens, she sang and yodeled on a local radio show. After this she was hired to sing with Mac's Skillet Lickers band with Buck Owens, and she toured with them. She and Buck Owens did the "Buck and Britt Show" on a Mesa, Arizona, radio station.

Later she married Buck Owens and had two sons, but the marriage ended in divorce. After that Bonnie Owens moved to Bakersfield, California, where she worked as a car hop to support her family. There she sang on a local television show and was so successful that she continued on the show for ten years. When her father died, her mother came to live with her. With someone to look after her children, Bonnie was able to spend some time touring, which boosted her career.

In 1964 she recorded a hit single with Merle Haggard. Capitol Records signed her, and she continued recording duets with Haggard. They sang on radio and television, as well as at the "Grand Ole Opry," and in 1965 Bonnie Owens married Merle Haggard. They have since divorced.

She and Haggard began writing songs together for her first album, *Between the Two of Us* (1965). Some of their songs are "Hi Fi to Cry By," "Lead Me On," "Philadelphia Lawyer," and "That Little Boy of Mine."

In 1966 she and Merle Haggard toured the United States, Canada, and Europe with the Buck Owens Show. That year she was voted Best Female Vocalist by the Academy of Country and Western Music.

In 1975 Bonnie Owens retired from performing.

SOURCES
Claghorn, Charles. *Biographical Dictionary of American Music.*
Dellar, Fred. *Illustrated Encyclopedia of Country Music.*
Stambler, Irwin. *Encyclopedia of Folk, Country, and Western Music,* 1984.

PARTON, DOLLY (1946–   )   "Jolene"

Movie star, singer, and songwriter Dolly Parton came from humble beginnings. She was born on January 19, 1946, in Locust Ridge, Tennessee, in the foothills of the Great Smoky Mountains. Her father worked as a farmer and laborer to support his family of 12 children. Her mother was the daughter of a preacher, and it was in the small church of their grand-father that the Parton children first performed in public. The family loved music, and the children were encouraged to be musical.

From her early childhood, even before she could write, Dolly Rebecca Parton made up songs. Her mother would write the words down for her. When Dolly was six, she learned to play a broken mandolin she'd been given. Her uncle, Bill Owens, played in a band and helped her get singing jobs on the radio. He also helped her write one of her first songs, "Puppy Love." At 12 Dolly sang at the "Grand Ole Opry." After graduating from high school, she moved to Nashville to live with her uncle and his family and start her singing career.

It wasn't long until Monument Records signed Dolly Parton to a con-tract. Her career took off when she started recording her own songs, such as "Put It Off until Tomorrow," written with Bill Owens. She joined Porter Wagoner's popular television show and sang on it for seven years. All the while Dolly Parton continued to write songs and make records.

In 1974 she went on the road with her own Travelin' Family Band, which included her two brothers, two sisters, an uncle, and a cousin.

The next two years she was chosen Best Female Vocalist by the Country Music Association. As she began to gain in popularity, she made guest appearances on the television shows of Merv Griffin and Johnny Carson, and "Hee Haw." In 1976 she had her own television show, "Dolly."

After her considerable success in the country music world, Dolly Parton set out to cross over to the mainstream of popular rock. With a new group, Gypsy Fever, in 1977 she toured the United States and Europe.

Then in the 1980s she started making movies. Her first was the hit com-edy *9 to 5* (1980) with Jane Fonda and Lily Tomlin. This was followed by *The Best Little Whorehouse in Texas* (1982) in which she co-starred with Burt Reynolds. In 1984 she starred in *Rhinestone*, with Sylvester Stallone, and wrote 20 songs for it. Finally, in 1989 she co-starred in *Steel Magno-lias*.

In addition to being successful as a singer and an actress, Dolly Parton is also considered one of the top writers of country music. In fact, she writes most of the material she performs. In an interview with Jan Hod-enfield of the *New York Post*, she said of her songs that she wanted them to be simple enough to be understood, yet have enough depth to be ap-preciated. She explained that songwriting had been a part of her as long as she could remember, that it was a way for her to describe her feelings and memories. Much of the subject matter in her songs comes from her life growing up in Tennessee. For instance, her song "Coat of Many Colors" is about a coat her mother made for her out of many colored remnants she

Dolly Parton. (Frank Driggs Coll.)

pieced together. Other songs are about Dolly's childhood, like "My Tennessee Mountain Home" and "In the Good Old Days (When Times Were Bad)." Other songs Dolly Parton has written include "Joshua," "Daddy Was an Old Time Preacher Man," "Jolene," "We Used To," "Love Is like a Butterfly," "I Will Always Love You," "Something Fishy," "Dumb Blonde," "When the Sun Goes Down Tomorrow," "Shattered Image," "I'm a Drifter," "Falling Out of Love with Me," "Light of a Clear Blue Morning," and "Eagle When She Flies."

In 1966 she married Carl Dean, who owns a paving company. They live near Nashville in a 23-room mansion on 100 acres.

> Jolene, Jolene, Jolene, Jolene,
> I'm beggin' of you please don't take my man.
> Jolene, Jolene, Jolene, Jolene,
> Please don't take him just because you can.
>
> Your beauty is beyond compare
> With flaming locks of auburn hair
> With ivory skin and eyes of emerald green.
> Your smile is like a breath of spring,
> Your voice is soft like summer rain,
> And I cannot compete with you Jolene.
>
> He talks about you in his sleep
> And there's nothing I can do to keep
> From crying when he calls your name Jolene.
> And I can easily understand
> How you could easily take my man,
> But you don't know what he means to me Jolene.
>
> Jolene, Jolene, Jolene, Jolene,
> I'm beggin' of you please don't take my man.
> Jolene, Jolene, Jolene, Jolene,
> Please don't take him just because you can.
> You can have your choice of men
> But I could never love again;
> He's the only one for me Jolene.
> I had to have this talk with you,
> My happiness depends on you
> What ever you decide to do Jolene.
>
> Jolene, Jolene, Jolene, Jolene,
> I'm beggin' of you please don't take my man.
> Jolene, Jolene, Jolene, Jolene,
> Please don't take him even though you can
> Jolene.

—"Jolene" by Dolly Parton

SOURCES

Claghorn, Charles. *Biographical Dictionary of American Music.*
Hitchcock, H. Wiley. *New Grove Dictionary of American Music.*
Moritz, Charles. *Current Biography,* 1977.
Pollock, Bruce. *Popular Music,* vol. 9, 1986.
Pollock, Bruce. *Popular Music,* vol. 13, 1989.
Scobey, Lola. *Dolly Parton, Daughter of the South.*

WALKER, CINDY (n.d.)   "You Don't Know Me"

Cindy Walker may have inherited her songwriting talent from her grand-father, who was a noted hymn writer. Cindy was born in Mexia, Texas, where she began performing at the age of seven, singing and dancing in *Toy Land Review*.

When she was older, she got a job as a dancer at Billy Rose's showplace in Fort Worth. She also wrote a musical theme for the show, which was played on the radio by the Paul Whiteman Orchestra.

Cindy Walker was determined to be a songwriter and decided to take her new song, "Lone Star Trail," to Hollywood. There she was able to persuade Bing Crosby's brother to listen to it. He told her to make a demo (a demonstration tape) and send it to the record companies. She did just that. Decca liked her song and consequently signed her to a contract. While in Hollywood, Cindy Walker did do some performing and also appeared in movies, but she realized she preferred songwriting.

Her songs have been recorded by a variety of artists and have often been on the top ten charts. Eddy Arnold's recording of her song "Take Me in Your Arms and Hold Me" was her first hit. Hank Snow's recording of her song "Gold Rush Is Over" was another hit in the 1950s.

In 1954 Cindy Walker moved back to Mexia, Texas, and there she con-tinued to write songs. With Webb Pierce she wrote "I Don't Care." Pierce's recording of it was number one on the charts for many weeks. With Porter Wagoner she wrote "Trademark," and with Eddy Arnold she wrote another hit, "You Don't Know Me."

By the mid-1960s Cindy Walker had published more than 400 songs, among them "Leona," "This Is It," "Distant Drums," "Thank You for Call-ing," "China Doll," "Blue Canadian Rockies," "Fifteen Days," "I Was Just Walking out the Door," "Bubbles in My Beer," "In the Misty Moonlight," "The Night Watch," and "Till the Longest Day I Live."

SOURCES
Claghorn, Charles. *Biographical Dictionary of American Music.*
Stambler, Irwin. *Encyclopedia of Folk, Country, and Western Music*, 1984.

WELLS, KITTY (1919–   )   "I Can't Stop Loving You"

Born Muriel Ellen Deason in Nashville, Tennessee, on August 30, 1919, Kitty Wells became one of the reigning queens of country music.

She began performing at the age of 15 at local dances, playing the guitar and singing. Then she sang with her sisters as the Deason Sisters on a local radio show, WSIX in Nashville, starting in 1936.

When she was 18, Kitty Wells married singer Johnny Wright and toured with him. She also sang on many local radio shows and in 1947 appeared on the "Grand Ole Opry." After this she was hired as a regular on the "Louisiana Hayride" and so moved to Shreveport, Louisiana.

Her recording of "It Wasn't God Who Made Honky Tonk Angels" in 1952 sold more than a million records. The "Grand Ole Opry" signed her the following year. From 1952 to 1969 Kitty Wells had 25 songs in the top ten, almost twice as many as the nearest female country-western performer. The trade papers considered her the number one female country star from 1952 to 1965. Decca signed her to a lifetime contract, and she made more than 40 albums and 400 singles for them.

Kitty Wells also toured widely through the United States, Canada, Europe and the Far East. She made guest appearances on the "Jimmy Dean Show," "Ozark Jubilee," and the "Country Music Hall." She also appeared in the movie *Second Fiddle to a Steel Guitar*. In 1969 she and her husband had a television show, and their son Bobby Wright sometimes appeared with them.

At a time when most country-western songs were written from a male point of view, Kitty Wells's songs expressed the feelings and concerns of working-class women. Among the songs she has written are "I Can't Stop Loving You" and "Amigo's Guitar," written with John Loudermilk.

Kitty Wells was elected to the Country Music Hall of Fame.

SOURCES
Claghorn, Charles. *Biographical Dictionary of American Music.*
Dellar, Fred. *Illustrated Encyclopedia of Country Music.*
Morthland, John. *Best of Country Music.*
Stambler, Irwin. *Encyclopedia of Folk, Country, and Western Music*, 1984.

WEST, DOTTIE (1932–1991)   "Here Comes My Baby"

Singer-songwriter Dottie West was born Dorothy Marie Marsh on October 11, 1932, in McMinnville, Tennessee. She was the eldest of ten children in a poor farm family. She chopped cotton as a child and worked in the sugarcane fields. From part-time jobs she saved her money so that she could go to college and study music. She graduated in 1956 from Tennessee Technological University in Cookeville, Tennessee.

She married William West, a guitar-playing engineer whom she met in college. They started playing together in local clubs and on television. They also tried writing songs. In 1962 Dottie West had a chance to sing at the "Grand Ole Opry." Then they were offered a recording contract and recorded their own song, "Here Comes My Baby." It hit the top ten and won a Grammy in 1964. After that they wrote "Would You Hold It Against Me?" which was a 1966 hit. One of their four children, Dale, can be heard on the recording of their song, "Mommie, Can I Still Call Him Daddy?"

Dottie West has toured the United States, Canada, and Europe and also has sung with symphony orchestras in Atlanta, Denver, and New Orleans. On television Dottie West has appeared on the "Country Hit Parade," "Hee-Haw," "Barbara Mandrell," and the "Dukes of Hazzard." She has also appeared in the movies *Second Fiddle to a Steel Guitar* and *There's a Still on the Hill.*

She recorded several hits with Kenny Rogers, among them "Every Time Two Fools Collide" and "What Are We Doin' in Love?" Her other hits include "Paper Mansions," "A Lesson in Leavin'," and "Country Sunshine," the latter originally written for a Coca-Cola commercial. After this hit, "Sunshine" became her nickname.

Billboard magazine named Dottie West the number one female writer in 1974.

After her 20-year marriage to William West ended in 1972, she married drummer Byron A. Metcalf and later her road manager, Alan Winters. None of the marriages lasted.

In the 1990s she had financial problems that led to bankruptcy. She was still working and trying to pay off her debts when she was killed in an auto accident on her way to sing at the "Grand Ole Opry." She died on September 4, 1991, at the age of 58.

SOURCES

Claghorn, Charles. *Biographical Dictionary of American Music.*
Sanz, Cynthia. "Goodbye, Sunshine." *People,* September 16, 1991, pp. 38–39.
Stambler, Irwin. *Encyclopedia of Folk, Country, and Western Music,* 1984.

WILSON, KITTY (1927–   )   "We Lived It Up"

Kitty Wilson is a singer, songwriter, and bass player. She was considered one of the best bass players in country and western music for more than thirty years.

Born in Rome, Georgia, on December 11, 1927, Kitty went to school in Gladsden, Alabama. By the age of nine she was playing at local dances with a group called the Moonlight Ramblers. She dropped out of high school to marry country-western singer Smiley Wilson. In 1945 she joined the Circle

3 Ranch Gang with Smiley. Starting in 1949 she was on the "Louisiana Hayride" radio show and then joined the "Grand Ole Opry" two years later.

Kitty and Smiley Wilson have made recordings since 1947 on the Republic, Apollo, and MGM labels. In 1949 they were in the movie *Square Dance Jubilee*. They have also appeared on television.

In the 1960s both toured the United States with the Ferlin Husky Show.

Some of the songs Kitty Wilson has written include "Sing and Shout," "We Lived It Up," and "I Know."

SOURCE

Claghorn, Charles. *Biographical Dictionary of American Music.*
Stambler, Irwin. *Encyclopedia of Folk, Country, and Western Music,* 1969.

WYNETTE, TAMMY (1942–   )

"Your Good Girl's Gonna Go Bad"

Tammy Wynette was born Wynette Pugh on May 5, 1942, near Tupelo, Mississippi. Her father, who was musical, died when Tammy was an infant. Her mother moved to Birmingham, Alabama, to find work in the defense industry during World War II, and she left Tammy on the farm with her grandparents. After the war was over, she came back and took the child again, but the separation had been difficult for the little girl. Tammy Wynette inherited from her father some musical instruments—a guitar, a mandolin, a piano, an accordion, and a bass fiddle—which she learned to play.

She married early and by the age of 17 had three children. When the marriage ended, she supported her family by working as a beautician and singing on the side. During this time she appeared on Porter Wagoner's television show and sang at clubs in the area. She also began writing songs with Fred Lehner.

Hoping to break into the music business, Tammy Wynette moved to Nashville. After being turned down by four record companies, she was finally signed by Columbia/Epic Records. The record she cut in 1967 became one of the top hits of the year. The following year she had singles in the top ten again. Appearances at the "Grand Ole Opry" followed, and she became a star.

Besides writing with Fred Lehner, she has also written songs with music producer Billy Sherrill. Her song "The Ways to Love a Man" was written with Billy Sherrill and Glenn Sutton, and "Another Lovely Song" with Billy Sherrill and N. Wilson. Other songs she has co-authored include "I Don't Wanna Play House," "Your Good Girl's Gonna Go Bad," "Take Me to Your

World," and "D-i-v-o-r-c-e." Her hit "Stand by Your Man" made her famous. It was followed by her autobiography of the same name.

Tammy Wynette was the Country Music Association Female Vocalist of the Year for three years from 1968 to 1970.

She has been married and divorced five times.

SOURCES

Morthland, John. *Best of Country Music.*
Simon, George. *Best of the Music Makers.*
Stambler, Irwin. *Encyclopedia of Folk, Country, and Western Music,* 1984.

VIII

EARLY WOMEN SONGWRITERS

INTRODUCTION

Before there were records, tapes, CDs, and the like, songs were sold as sheet music to be played on the parlor piano when family and friends gathered to sing.

In order to sell their songs, publishers hired songpluggers to persuade or even bribe stars of the musical stage to sing their songs. A star occasionally would add a song to the show, whether it was relevant or not, and these "interpolations" often became hits.

Songs of the nineteenth century were melodic, sentimental, and sometimes even maudlin, like "Tis but a Little Faded Flower." Waltzes such as "Meet Me Tonight in Dreamland" and "Let Me Call You Sweetheart" were popular. Lyrics about girls left behind in the homeland beyond the sea were popular among the large immigrant population. Irish songs, such as "Mary from Tipperary" and "Sweet Rosie O'Grady," were popular. Some well-known children's songs, "Happy Birthday to You" and "Rock-a-bye Baby," are also from this period.

Stephen Foster, who was the leading songwriter of this era, set the style by writing sentimental songs with simple melodies and words that were easy to remember. Songs that imitated the African-American dialect, like "Mah Lindy Lou," and songs that idealized Indians living in the wilderness were also in vogue.

With the Civil War came an outpouring of patriotic songs. Fanny Crosby contributed "Dixie for the Union," and Mrs. E. Hundley, "Farewell to the

Star-Spangled Banner." However, the best-known song from the Civil War period was Julia Ward Howe's "The Battle Hymn of the Republic."

Not all patriotic songs were about war, however. Just before the turn of the century Katharine Bates wrote the song some consider to be the second national anthem, "America, the Beautiful."

BATES, KATHARINE (1859–1929)   "America the Beautiful"

Katharine Lee Bates was a teacher, scholar, and author. She was born in Falmouth, Massachusetts, in 1859. Educated at Wellesley College, she later taught there and become head of the English department. Besides teaching, she authored books on a variety of subjects, from travel books to children's books, as well as textbooks. She published six volumes of poetry during her lifetime, and two more were published posthumously. She was described as a large woman with a quick wit and an independent frame of mind.

Katharine Bates wrote "America the Beautiful" after she had taken a trip to the top of 14,110-foot Pike's Peak in Colorado. The view was breathtaking. She was awestruck by the vastness of the landscape. Pride in the beauty of her country overwhelmed her, inspiring her to write the poem.

She sent it to *The Congregationalist* magazine, where it was published in the July 4 issue in 1895. It was published again in the *Boston Evening Transcript* and received much favorable comment. The National Federation of Music Clubs wanted it to be the national anthem and sponsored a contest in 1926 for an original music composition to accompany the words. None was found to be as satisfying as Samuel A. Ward's hymn "Materna" (1888), which is the music that is used today. Congress eventually selected another song for the national anthem, but "America, the Beautiful" still has its fans. Even today some are trying to have it named as a second national anthem.

Katharine Bates received $4 or $5 for the poem's publication in the *The Congregationalist*, and although she copyrighted the poem, she never accepted royalties from it.

"America the Beautiful," words by Katharine Bates

> O beautiful for spacious skies,
> For amber waves of grain,
> For purple mountain majesties
> Above the fruited plain.
> America! America!

> God shed His grace on thee,
> And crown thy good with brotherhood
> From sea to shining sea.

SOURCES

Burgess, Dorothy. *Dream and Deed.*
Foote, Henry Wilder. *Three Centuries of American Hymnody.*
James, Edward. *Notable American Women.*
Krythe, Maymie. *Sampler of American Song.*
Mattfeld, Julius. *Variety Music Cavalcade.*
Spaeth, Sigmund. *History of Popular Music in America.*

BOND, CARRIE JACOBS (1862–1946)   "I Love You Truly"

Carrie Jacobs was born on August 11, 1862, in Janesville, Wisconsin. From her earliest childhood she wanted to be a songwriter. Her family loved music and encouraged her when at the age of four she began to pick out songs on the piano. However, her childhood was not a happy one, for her father died suddenly after he had lost all the family's money in bad investments. Widowed and without any means of support for herself and her child, Mrs. Jacobs returned to live with her father, who owned a hotel in Janesville.

At 18 Carrie Jacobs married Edward J. Smith. They had one child, Fred Jacobs Smith, born in 1881, but the marriage was not happy. Although in those days divorce was considered a scandal, Carrie divorced her husband, keeping the child with her. Two years later she married a doctor, Frank Lewis Bond, and they moved to a small mining and logging community in upper Michigan. Her life with Frank Bond was happy and he encouraged her to pursue her interest in songwriting. The marriage continued happily for seven years until one winter Frank Bond fell on the frozen ice and was injured so badly he died.

Due to poor investments, they had no savings. Carrie was left on her own to support herself and her child. Impoverished and in poor health, she moved to Chicago. There she found work running a rooming house and painting china for added income. When her other work was done, she found time to write songs. Despite her miserable circumstances, she held on to her dream of becoming a successful songwriter.

Finally she had some luck in selling two children's songs to a publisher. But that was all. Carrie decided then that she had to become her own songplugger and perform the songs at social gatherings, in concerts, and in vaudeville, wherever she could find an audience so that people would want to buy the sheet music. Although she lacked a beautiful singing voice, she presented the lyrics with such an expressive spoken manner that the songs were well received. From one of these presentations came an offer by a popular opera contralto, Jessie Bartlet Davis, to sing and promote Carrie's songs. In addition to this, Davis backed the publication of Carrie Jacob Bond's first collection of songs, *Seven Songs as Unpretentious as the Wild Rose,* published in 1901. This collection included two of Carrie Jacobs Bond's best songs, "I Love You Truly," for which she wrote both the words and music, and "Just A-Wearyin' for You," with lyrics by Frank Stanton. The collection sold more than a million copies.

With the success of her first collection, Carrie Jacobs Bond began setting up her own publishing company in her home. She not only wrote the words and music to most of the songs but also designed the artwork and printing on the cover of the sheet music. Her son helped her publish and sell the songs. In 1906 they opened an office in Chicago, Carrie Jacobs Bond and Son.

Friends arranged for Carrie to perform three recitals in New York, but they were not a success. She returned home ill and in debt. Then a friend, Walter Gale, bought an interest in her publishing business, and this enabled her to continue.

In 1910 she published her most successful song, "A Perfect Day." The song was inspired by a trip to the top of Mount Rubidoux in southern California. Watching the sun set from the mountain top, she reflected on what a perfect day it had been and the words came to her. The melody came later as she drove across the Mojave Desert by moonlight. "A Perfect Day" became enormously popular and sold over 5 million copies in a little more than ten years. Phonograph recordings and piano rolls of the piece also sold well.

When World War I broke out, Carrie Jacobs Bond entertained the troops with her songs.

Her later songs include "Roses in Bloom," "I've Done My Work," "His Lullaby," "A Little Pink Rose," and "God Remembers When the World Forgets." However, none of her later songs were ever as popular as "A Perfect Day." During her lifetime she wrote over 400 songs, although only about 170 of them were published. She was still writing songs at the age of 82.

In 1927 she wrote her memoir, *The Roads of Melody,* and in her later years she published a collection of her poems, *The End of the Road* (1940). She had finally achieved the success and prosperity for which she had worked so many years. Unfortunately, her later years were marred by the tragedy of her son's death. He had been with her through the long years of struggle, she doing the creative work and he managing the business. Then in a state of depression following an illness, he took his own life.

The last 30 years of her life Carrie Jacobs Bond lived in southern California, dying in Hollywood on December 8, 1946, at the age of 85. Condolences came from far and wide, including one from the president of the United States, Herbert Hoover.

SOURCES
Emurian, Ernest. *Living Stories of Favorite Songs.*
Hitchcock, H. Wiley. *New Grove Dictionary of American Music.*
James, Edward. *Notable American Women.*
Kinkle, Roger. *Complete Encyclopedia of Popular Music and Jazz.*
Lynn Farnol Group. *ASCAP Biographical Dictionary.*
Spaeth, Sigmund. *History of Popular Music in America.*

BURNS, ANNELU (1889–1942)   "I'll Forget You"

Annelu Burns was born in Selma, Alabama, on November 12, 1889. She attended Judson College, Boston College, Brenau College, and the Leopold Auer School. Later she became a teacher.

As a songwriter she collaborated with Ernest Ball. Together they wrote a number of popular songs. She wrote the lyrics to their 1921 hit "I'll Forget You" and to "For the Sake of Auld Lang Syne." She also wrote "Little Brown Shoes," "Shadows on My Heart," and "Little Spanish Villa by the Sea."

Annelu Burns died at Mt. Kisco, New York, on July 12, 1942.

SOURCES
Lynn Farnol Group. *ASCAP Biographical Dictionary.*
Spaeth, Sigmund. *History of Popular Music in America.*

CANNING, EFFIE (1857–1940)   "Rock-a-bye-Baby"

Effie Canning was a well-known actress and a leading lady for William Gillette, but she is probably most famous for a song she wrote when she was a teenager. A descendant of Davy Crockett, she was born Effie Crockett in 1857 in Rockland, Maine.

When she was 15 and babysitting with an infant in Winthrop, Massachusetts, she made up a song, "Rock-a-bye Baby," to sing to the child. When she played it for her music teacher, he encouraged her to have it published. He sent her to music publisher C. D. Blake in Boston. Blake published the song in 1887. Subsequently the song was used in a scene of a popular play, *The Old Homestead,* which led to its success. "Rock-a-bye Baby" sold over 300,000 copies of sheet music. Effie Crocket couldn't have been more pleased. However, when her music publisher died suddenly, her fortune changed. There was a dispute over the copyright of her song. The issue was never settled satisfactorily for Effie. Perhaps it was this disappointment that caused her to abandon a career as a songwriter.

When she was older, she became an actress known as Effie Canning. She married Harry J. Carlton, a character actor, and made her career in the theater.

Effie Canning died in Boston in 1940.

SOURCES
Emurian, Ernest. *Living Stories of Favorite Songs.*
Fuld, James. *Book of World-Famous Music.*
Spaeth, Sigmund. *History of Popular Music in America.*

EBERHART, NELLE (1871–1944)
"From the Land of the Sky-Blue Waters"

Lyricist Nelle Richmond Eberhart was born in Detroit, Michigan, on August 28, 1871. She was a teacher in Nebraska for a number of years.

The song for which she is best known comes from the "Four American Indian Songs": "From the Land of the Sky-Blue Waters," "The White Dawn Is Stealing," "Far Off I Hear a Lover's Flute," and "The Moon Drops Low." Nelle Eberhart wrote the words in 1909 to the music of Charles Wakefield Cadman, her longtime collaborator. The song "From the Land of Sky-Blue Waters" became famous years later when the lyrics were changed and it became a Hamm's beer commercial.

Other songs with lyrics by Nelle Eberhart include "At Dawning," "From Wigwam to Tepee," and "I Hear a Thrush at Eve," with music by Charles Wakefield Cadman.

Nelle Eberhart died in Kansas City, Missouri, on November 15, 1944.

SOURCES
Jasen, David. *Alexander's Ragtime Band.*
Kinkle, Roger. *Complete Encyclopedia of Popular Music and Jazz.*
Lynn Farnol Group. *ASCAP Biographical Dictionary.*
Mattfeld, Julius, *Variety Music Cavalcade.*
Spaeth, Sigmund. *History of Popular Music in America.*

FIRESTONE, IDABELLE (1874–1954)   "If I Could Tell You"

Idabelle Firestone was the wife of Harvey S. Firestone, founder of the Firestone Tire Company, and also was a songwriter in her own right.

Born Idabelle Smith on November 10, 1874, in Minnesota City, Minnesota, she was educated at Alma College in Ontario, Canada. She married Harvey S. Firestone on November 20, 1895, and they had six children.

The Firestone Tire Company sponsored a radio show of classical music, "The Voice of Firestone," which in later years was produced on television. The theme song for the show was "If I Could Tell You," which had been composed by Idabelle Firestone with the lyrics of Madeleine Marshall.

Some of the other songs Idabelle Firestone wrote include "In My Garden," "You Are the Song in My Heart," "Do You Recall?," "Bluebirds," and "Melody of Love."

She died on July 7, 1954, in Akron, Ohio.

Idabelle was not the only composer in the Firestone family. Her granddaughter Elizabeth Firestone (b. 1922) composed music for the film *Once More, My Darling* (1947), which starred Robert Montgomery and Ann Blyth.

SOURCES
Evans, Mark. *Soundtrack.*
Lynn Farnol Group. *ASCAP Biographical Dictionary.*
Smith, Sharon. *Women Who Make Movies.*
Who's Who in America, 1932–33.

HALE, SARAH JOSEPHA (1788–1879)

"Mary Had a Little Lamb"

Sarah Josepha Buell was born in Newport, New Hampshire, on October 24, 1788. Tutored at home by her mother, she later studied the books her brother had read at Dartmouth College and in this way became educated.

From 1806 until her marriage she ran a school for children. In 1813 she married David Hale, a lawyer. Nine years later he died, leaving her with five small children to support. She and her sister-in-law opened a millinery shop, and on the side Sarah wrote novels and poems to augment her income.

Juvenile Miscellany was the first to publish her poem "Mary Had a Little Lamb." It was based on a true story of a little girl named Mary whose father had given her a newborn lamb abandoned by its mother. The little girl was so fond of the lamb that she took it to school with her. Sarah Hale's poem "Mary Had a Little Lamb" was later included in her collection *Poems for Our Children* (1830). It wasn't until 1868 that it was set to music by H. R. Waite.

Financial security finally came to Sarah Hale when she was hired as editor of *The Ladies' Magazine* and later editor of Louis A. Godey's *Ladies' Book*, a popular women's magazine. She remained at that job 40 years, retiring when she was 90.

A woman of immense energy, Sarah Hale published 36 volumes of writing during her lifetime and wrote hymns as well, among them "Our Father in Heaven, We Hallow Thy Name." Over the years she also lobbied the government to create a Thanksgiving Day holiday. Abraham Lincoln finally did so by proclamation in 1863.

Sarah Hale died on April 30, 1879, in Philadelphia, Pennsylvania.

SOURCES

Claghorn, Gene. *Women Composers and Hymnists.*
Emurian, Ernest. *Living Stories of Favorite Songs.*
James, Edward. *Notable American Women.*
Reynolds, William. *Hymns of Our Faith.*
Spaeth, Sigmund. *History of Popular Music in America.*

HILL, PATTY (1868–1946)
HILL, MILDRED (1859–1916)   "Happy Birthday to You"

Born in Anchorage, Kentucky, on March 27, 1868, Patty Smith Hill was one of four daughters of a minister and college president. She became a distinguished educator at Columbia University and a leader in the kindergarten reform movement in the United States.

After graduating from the Louisville Collegiate Institute, where she studied to become a teacher, she taught at the institute's model kindergarten. She wanted the children to have a song to start the school day, a good morning song, but because she couldn't find one, she wrote "Good Morning to You." Her sister, Mildred Hill, who later became a concert pianist and music critic, wrote the music, and together they published it in their book *Song Stories for the Kindergarten* (1893). The children liked the song so much that they sang it at a birthday party, changing the words to "happy birthday." Patty Hill liked the idea and reworked the song to its now familiar version, "Happy Birthday to You."

Mildred Hill died in 1916, but Dr. Patty Smith Hill went on to become an expert in the field of early childhood education. She taught at Columbia University until 1935, when she retired. The author of many magazine and newspaper articles on child education, she was influential in introducing mental testing and medical care into kindergarten. She died on May 25, 1946, and was buried in Louisville, Kentucky.

"Happy Birthday to You" continues to make money today. In 1989 it was sold by the owners, Birchtree, Ltd., to music publisher Warner/Chappell for $25 million. The song generates $1 million a year in royalties.

SOURCES

Emurian, Ernest. *Living Stories of Favorite Songs.*
Lynn Farnol Group. *ASCAP Biographical Dictionary.*
Rothe, Anna. *Current Biography,* 1946.
Spaeth, Sigmund. *History of Popular Music in America.*
"Transitions." *Newsweek,* January 2, 1989. p. 55.

HOWE, JULIA WARD (1819–1910)
"The Battle Hymn of the Republic"

Julia Ward Howe was the bright, attractive daughter of a Wall Street banker. Born in New York on May 27, 1819, she was as a child educated by governesses and private tutors, and she attended the finest young ladies' schools when she was older. However, her personal life was not easy. Both her parents died when she was young, her mother when Julia was 5, and her father when she was 20. After her father's death she went to live with an aunt and uncle. It was at this time that she began to devote herself to writing.

At the age of 23 she married Dr. Samuel G. Howe, head of the Perkins Institution for the Blind. He was nearly 20 years older than she, and although he was an activist in the areas of prison reform, antislavery, and educating the retarded, he held conventional views about Julia's role as wife. Though they produced six children, their marriage was not a happy one. For Julia Ward Howe, it was the case of a talented woman trapped by the conventions of marriage and society. Dr. Howe resented his wife's writing and her interest in social causes. He felt that a wife's energies should be confined to the running of the home and the welfare of her husband and children. He was not pleased when her poems and articles began appearing in the leading newspapers and magazines or when her play *Leonora* was produced in New York in 1857. Although Julia Howe considered divorce, she chose to remain in the marriage and turned her interests to traveling, to studying religion and philosophy, to learning foreign languages, and to writing.

Her famous hymn, "The Battle Hymn of the Republic," was inspired by a visit to an army camp near Washington, D.C., at the time of the Civil War. There, she and her husband heard soldiers singing "John Brown's

Body." A minister friend with them remarked that the soldiers needed a more stirring song, one that would become a battle hymn for the republic. He suggested that since Julia was a writer, she might write such a song. That evening at the Willard Hotel in Washington where the Howes were staying, the poem came to Julia in her sleep. She got up and quickly wrote it down.

> Mine eyes have seen the glory of the coming of the Lord,
> He is trampling out the vintage where the grapes of wrath are stored.
> He hath loosed the fateful lightning of His terrible swift sword,
> His truth is marching on.

She sold her poem, "The Battle Hymn of the Republic," to the *Atlantic Monthly* for $10, and it appeared in the February 1862 issue of the magazine. It was published in the army hymn books set to the same music by William Steffe that was used for "John Brown's Body." It became the favorite Union hymn of the Civil War.

Julia Ward Howe continued writing plays, articles, and biographies. In addition, she worked in the peace movement, founded one of the first women's clubs in the United States, and worked for women's suffrage and for the establishment of women's colleges. She lectured widely on these subjects. Greatly respected and admired, in her later years she was given many honors. She received an honorary doctor of letters from Smith College and was the first woman elected to the American Academy of Arts and Letters. When she died on October 17, 1910 at the age of 91, the governor of Massachusetts led the funeral.

SOURCES
Hughes, Charles. *American Hymns Old and New*.
James, Edward. *Notable American Women*.
Spaeth, Sigmund. *History of Popular Music in America*.
Whitman, Wanda. *Songs That Changed the World*.

MORSE, THEODORA (1890–1953)

"Three O'Clock in the Morning"

Lyricist Theodora Morse was born Dorothy Terriss in Brooklyn, New York, on July 11, 1890. She also wrote under the name of Dolly Morse.

She and her husband, composer–music publisher Theodore F. Morse, wrote a number of popular songs together. Among their songs were "Another Rag" and "Sing Me Love's Lullaby" (1917).

However, Theodora Morse's best songs were written in collaboration with other composers. She and Julian Robledo wrote the hit song "Three O'Clock in the Morning" (1921). The following year she, Ferde Grofé, and Paul Whiteman wrote the lovely waltz "Wonderful One." She wrote "Baby Your Mother" with Joseph A. Burke, and "Siboney" with Ernesto Lecuona.

Theodora Morse died in New York City in 1953.

SOURCES
Claghorn, Charles. *Biographical Dictionary of American Music.*
Lynn Farnol Group. *ASCAP Biographical Dictionary.*
Shapiro, Nat. *Popular Music.*
Simon, William. *Reader's Digest Treasury of Best Loved Songs.*
Spaeth, Sigmund. *History of Popular Music in America.*

NUGENT, MAUDE (1874–1958)   "Sweet Rosie O'Grady"

Maude Nugent was a singer, actress, vaudeville performer, and songwriter. She was born in Brooklyn, New York, on January 12, 1874, and she married lyricist William Jerome.

In 1896 she introduced her song "Sweet Rosie O'Grady" at Johnny Reilly's musical hall, The Abbey, in New York City. The song became one of the most popular waltzes of the 1890s.

Many of Maude Nugent's songs had an Irish flavor: "Down at Rosie Riley's Flat," "Mamie Reilly," "My Irish Daisy," and "Mary from Tipperary." Some of her other songs are "There's No Other Girl like My Girl," "My Sweet Kimona," "My Little Creole Babe," "Somebody Wants You," "You'll Always Be the Same Sweet Girl to Me," "I Can't Forgive You Honey," and "My Pretty Little China Maid."

At the age of 28 Maude Nugent retired from the stage to raise a family. However, in her later years she returned to perform in Gay Nineties shows. Television discovered her in the early 1950s when she was in her eighties.

She died in New York on June 3, 1958, at the age of 85.

SOURCES
Claghorn, Charles. *Biographical Dictionary of American Music.*
Emurian, Ernest. *Living Stories of Favorite Songs.*
Fuld, James. *Book of World-Famous Music.*
Hitchcock, H. Wiley. *New Grove Dictionary of American Music.*
Mattfeld, Julius. *Variety Music Cavalcade.*
Spaeth, Sigmund. *History of Popular Music in America.*

ROMA, CARO (1866–1937)

"Can't You Heah Me Callin', Caroline?"

Caro Roma was the stage name of Carrie Northey, who was born in California in 1866. Her father had come to California with the gold rush pioneers.

Caro Roma began performing on stage at the age of three. As a youngster she studied at the New England Conservatory of Music in Boston. When she was still in her teens, she became the orchestra conductor of a French opera company on tour in Canada. Returning to Boston, she found a job singing with the Henry Savage Opera Company, where she later became prima donna. She then sang opera in San Francisco and later performed for royalty in Europe.

From early childhood she had written poetry and composed music, growing up equally adept at writing both words and music. Over the course of her lifetime she wrote more than 2,500 poems, some of which she set to music. She wrote many sea songs and composed a song cycle, "The Wandering One," with lyrics by Clement Scott. Her songs include "Faded Rose," "The Angelus," "I Come to Thee," "Thinking of Thee," "My One Hour," "Forbidden," "Resignation," "My Jean," "O, Lord Remember Me," and "Separation." Her most famous song, "Can't You Hear Me Callin', Caroline?" was written with lyrics by William H. Gardner. Collaborating with songwriter Ernest Ball, she wrote lyrics to "In the Garden of My Heart," "Love Me Today, Tomorrow May Never Come," and "Allah, Give Me Mine!" She wrote both words and music to "Somehow Mother's Different from the Rest."

In 1932, at the age of 71, Caro Roma gave a Golden Jubilee Concert in Los Angeles and sang 19 of her own compositions.

She retired in California, where she died in 1937.

SOURCES
Claghorn, Charles. *Biographical Dictionary of American Music.*
Spaeth, Sigmund. *History of Popular Music in America.*
Witmark, Isidore. *Story of the House of Witmark.*

STRICKLAND, LILY (1887–1958)   "Mah Lindy Lou"

Composer-writer Lily Teresa Strickland was born on January 28, 1887, in Anderson, South Carolina. She was educated at Converse College in Spartanburg, South Carolina, and won a scholarship to study at the Institute of Musical Art in New York. In 1924 she received a doctorate in music.

She was married to J. Courtenay Anderson, and for a number of years they lived in India.

Lily Strickland had been interested in music from childhood and began composing while in her teens. Over her lifetime she composed approximately 500 instrumental, vocal, and orchestral compositions. She also wrote operettas, musical plays for children, and sacred music.

However, she is probably best known for her song "Mah Lindy Lou," which was a hit in 1920. Some of her other songs are "My Lover Is a Fisherman," "At Eve I Heard a Flute," "Because of You," "St. John the Beloved," "My Shepherd, Thou," and "The Road to Home."

Lily Strickland retired to Hendersonville, North Carolina, where she died on June 6, 1958.

SOURCES
Claghorn, Charles. *Biographical Dictionary of American Music.*
Hitchcock, H. Wiley. *New Grove Dictionary of American Music.*
Lynn Farnol Group. *ASCAP Biographical Dictionary.*
Mattfeld, Julius. *Variety Music Cavalcade.*
Spaeth, Sigmund. *History of Popular Music in America.*
Who Was Who in America, 1966.
Wilder, Alex. *American Popular Song.*

WHITSON, BETH SLATER (1879–1930)
"Let Me Call You Sweetheart"

Lyricist Beth Slater Whitson was born in Goodrich, Tennessee, in 1879. She was educated at George Peabody College and wrote verse for magazines.

In 1909 she began writing songs with Leo Friedman. They made the mistake of selling their song "Meet Me Tonight in Dreamland" outright to the publisher for a flat fee and no royalties. The song became very popular and sold more than a million copies, which brought home to the songwriters how bad a bargain they had made. The following year when they sold "Let Me Call You Sweetheart," they insisted on royalties. It was a wise decision, for the song sold 5 million copies of sheet music. By the 1940s these two songs had sold close to 10 million copies.

Some of Beth Slater Whitson's other songs include "When the One You Love Forgets You," "Leaf by Leaf the Roses Fall," "Say but It's Lonesome Kid," "When the Roses of Summer Have Gone," and "My! But I'm Longing for Love," written with Leo Friedman. She also wrote the lyrics for "Don't Wake Me Up, I'm Dreaming," with Herbert Ingraham's music.

Beth Slater Whitson died in Nashville, Tennessee, in 1930.

SOURCES

Claghorn, Charles. *Biographical Dictionary of American Music.*
Ewen, David. *Panorama of American Popular Music.*
Fuld, James. *Book of World-Famous Music.*
Lynn Farnol Group. *ASCAP Biographical Dictionary.*
Spaeth, Sigmund. *History of Popular Music in America.*

WILLARD, EMMA (1787–1870)

"Rocked in the Cradle of the Deep"

Emma Hart Willard is known primarily as an educator and an early advocate of women's education, yet she wrote the words to one of the most popular basso solos of all time.

She was born on February 23, 1787, on a farm in Berlin, Connecticut, the sixteenth of 17 children. Although at that time education was considered more important for boys than girls, her father wanted her to be educated. In 1802 she entered the Berlin Academy, where she was such a good student that she was asked to stay on as a teacher.

In 1809 she married Dr. John Willard, nearly 30 years her senior. He incurred financial problems, so Emma decided to open a school, the Middlebury Female Academy, in their home. In 1821 they moved the school to Troy, New York, and renamed it the Troy Female Seminary. The school was one of the first in the United States to train young women to be teachers. Besides teaching and directing the school, Emma Willard also wrote the textbooks. Through her writing and lectures, she advocated the right of women to have equal educational opportunities.

Emma Willard was fond of writing poetry, and during an ocean voyage in 1839 she wrote the poem that became a famous concert song for bassos, "Rocked in the Cradle of the Deep." Basso Joseph P. Knight composed the music to the song and introduced it in a concert in New York City to great success.

Emma Willard lived to the age of 83.

> Rocked in the cradle of the deep . . .
> I lay me down in peace to sleep
> Secure I rest upon the wave . . .
> For thou Oh! Lord, hast power to save.

SOURCES
Claghorn, Gene. *Women Composers and Hymnists.*
Spaeth, Sigmund. *History of Popular Music in America.*

IX | HYMNS

INTRODUCTION

In the early nineteenth century there was an resurgence of religious revivalism. Evangelists touring the country gathered crowds together in huge tents to preach, sing, and save souls. It was soon apparent that traditional church hymns were not enthusiastic enough for such occasions and that new hymns were needed.

Also at that time many denominations were interested in improving the quality of their church music. Two of the reformers in this effort were Thomas Hastings and Lowell Mason, who in addition to writing and publishing hymns promoted music education and choir training. Mason wrote two of his best hymns with texts by women, "Work for the Night Is Coming," with Annie L. Walker, who was Canadian, and "Nearer, My God, to Thee," with Sarah Flower Adams, who was English. A number of ministers wrote hymns, sometimes with members of their own congregation, which was the case with Reverend Robert Lowry and Annie Sherwood Hawks. The wives and sisters of ministers were also enlisted to write hymns, as Harriet Beecher Stowe did for her brother, the Reverend Henry Ward Beecher. Because each denomination wanted its own hymnal, there was a demand for new hymns and hymn writers. As a result, many women became professional hymn writers employed by publishing companies. Such was the case with the remarkable Fanny Crosby, who could produce words for a hymn in a matter of minutes.

Many well-known hymns were written by American women, among them,

"I Love to Tell the Story," "I Need Thee Every Hour," "The Lord Bless Thee and Keep Thee," and the Sunday school song "Jesus Loves Me."

ASHFORD, EMMA (1850–1930)   "My Task"

Emma Ashford was a professional writer of sacred music. She was born Emma Louise Hindle on March 27, 1850, in Newark, Delaware.

Being the daughter of a music teacher, she learned to play music at an early age. By the time she was 12 she had become a church organist.

After she married John Ashford, they moved to Nashville, Tennessee. There she played the organ at church and wrote music for a publishing company in Ohio.

During her lifetime she composed over 250 anthems, 200 organ pieces, numerous solos, duets, trios, gospel songs, cantatas, and an organ instruction book. She is remembered primarily for the hymn "My Task," which she composed in 1903 with words by Maude Louise Ray. Another of her hymns was "O Son of Man, Thou Madest Known."

Emma Ashford died in Nashville on September 22, 1930.

SOURCES
Christ-Janer, Albert. *American Hymns Old and New.*
Claghorn, Gene. *Women Composers and Hymnists.*
Mattfeld, Julius. *Variety Music Cavalcade.*

BROWN, PHOEBE (1783–1861)   "I Love to Steal Awhile Away"

One of the early women hymn writers was Phoebe Hinsdale Brown. Born in Canaan, New York on May 1, 1783, she was orphaned at the age of two.

Poor and with no education, she was 18 years old before she learned to read. She married a painter and had a son who became a minister and missionary. However, she and her family always were in impoverished circumstances. Nevertheless, her faith sustained her.

Her private joy was writing hymns, four of which were published in an 1824 hymnal. Among them are "Yes,—When This Toilsome Day Is Gone," "Welcome, Ye Hopeful Heirs of Heaven," and "How Sweet the Melting Lay." Although she wrote many hymns during her lifetime, only one is still sung today, "I Love to Steal Awhile Away." The hymn refers to her pleasure in going into her garden to pray.

Phoebe Brown lived to the age of 78. She died in Marshall, Illinois on October 10, 1861.

SOURCES

Claghorn, Gene. *Women Composers and Hymnists.*
Foote, Henry. *Three Centuries of American Hymnody.*
Hatfield, Edwin. *Poets of the Church.*
Hughes, Charles. *American Hymns Old and New.*

CROSBY, FRANCES "FANNY" (1820–1915)

"Blessed Assurance"

One of the most respected and prolific of American hymnists was Frances Jane Crosby.

Born on March 24, 1820, in Putnam County, New York, Fanny, as she was called, had an eye infection in infancy that left her blind. As a child she was taught to memorize large portions of the Bible and other books, which gave her a prodigious memory. She enjoyed reading poetry and began writing it at the age of eight.

When she was 15 she entered the New York Institute for the Blind, where she obtained an excellent education and where her talent for writing poetry was encouraged. She became so quick at composing poems that she was often brought out to greet visitors to the school with a new poem she had just composed in their honor. At the institute she met many famous people, including William Cullen Bryant and Horace Greeley. She became so famous that she was invited to recite before President James Polk and Congress. Grover Cleveland became a good friend of hers when he worked at the institute as a young man.

After graduation, Fanny Crosby was asked to stay on at the institute and become a teacher. She remained there for the next 11 years. Some of her poems were accepted for publication in magazines like the *Saturday Evening Post*. When William B. Bradbury persuaded her to use her poetic talent to write hymns, Fanny Crosby was sure she had found the meaning of her life. Writing hymns became her mission and part of her religious commitment.

By the 1850s, when she was in her thirties, she began setting her words to music composed by the school's music teacher George F. Root, who became one of the leading songwriters of the era. In his memoir Root recalled that Fanny "had a great gift for rhyming, and better still, had a delicate and poetic imagination." He would tell her in prose what he wanted, hum enough of a melody to give her an idea of the meter and rhythm or play the music, and the next day she would have the poem and sometimes two or three of them. Her poems rarely needed any modification. At other times Root would work from her poem and write the music, sometimes on a streetcar while he was on his way to give a music lesson.

Fanny Crosby and George Root wrote many songs together, among them "The Honeysuckle Glen," "Hazel Dell," "There's Music in the Air," and "Rosalie, the Prairie Flower." Although the words were important to the success of a hymn or song, the writing of words was not highly remunerated. Fanny was paid $1, the usual rate; the words then became the property of the composer. On one of their collaborations, "Rosalie, the Prairie Flower," composer George Root earned $3,000.

Over the years Fanny Crosby collaborated with more than 20 composers and produced 50 or 60 popular songs, but it was in the writing of hymns that she was most productive. For many years she was employed by a publisher to write three hymns a week, which was not difficult because she often wrote six or seven hymns a day. Her publisher encouraged her to use many different pseudonyms so that it wouldn't be apparent that she had written half the selections in a hymnal. However, since she used more than 200 different pseudonyms, it has been difficult for historians to determine how many hymns she actually wrote. Some estimate that she may have written as many as 9,000 hymns.

Many of her best hymns were written with William Howard Doane: "Nearer the Cross" (1869), "Pass Me Not, O Gentle Savior" (1870), "Safe in the Arms of Jesus" (1870), "Rescue the Perishing" (1870), and "Though Your Sins Be as Scarlet" (1887).

Doane also was impressed with how quickly she worked. Once when he was about to leave her house to catch a train, he asked Fanny if she could write some words for a hymn he was composing, thinking that she could prepare something for the next time they met. She started to work immediately, and before he left 15 minutes later, she had finished the words to the hymn "Safe in the Arms of Jesus."

Fanny Crosby wrote hymns with many different composers. One of them was the Reverend Robert Lowry, pastor of a church in Brooklyn, where Fanny lived. Lowry was active in the gospel song movement and composed many hymns. Together they wrote "All the Way My Savior Leads" (1875) and "Hide Thou Me" (1880). Another composer was Ira D. Sankey, an associate of evangelist Dwight L. Moody, with whom she wrote "Tenderly Calling." With **Phoebe Knapp** she wrote "Blessed Assurance." Fanny Crosby was still writing hymns in her eighties when she and Mrs. Knapp wrote "Open the Gates of the Temple" (1903).

Fanny Crosby's personal life had periods of sunlight and shadow. She married a fellow teacher, Alexander Van Alstyne, who also was blind. They had a child who died in infancy. After this the couple drifted apart, and Van, as he was called, died in 1902. In later years Fanny moved to Bridgeport, Connecticut, to live with a widowed sister. It was there that she died on February 12, 1915, at the age of 94.

> Blessed assurance, Jesus is mine!
> O what a foretaste of glory divine!
> Heir of salvation, purchase of God,
> Born of His Spirit, washed in His blood.
> This is my story, this is my song,
> Praising my Saviour all the day long.
> —"Blessed Assurance" words by Fanny Crosby

SOURCES
Claghorn, Gene. *Women Composers and Hymnists.*
Crosby, Frances. *Fanny Crosby's Life Story.*
Foote, Henry. *Three Centuries of American Hymnody.*
Hughes, Charles. *American Hymns Old and New.*
James, Edward. *Notable American Women.*
Mattfeld, Julius. *Variety Music Cavalcade.*
Reynolds, William. *Hymns of Our Faith.*
Rodeheaver, Homer. *Hymnal Handbook for Standard Hymns.*
Root, George. *Story of a Musical Life.*
Ruffin, Bernard. *Fanny Crosby.*
Spaeth, Sigmund. *History of Popular Music in America.*

DAVIS, KATHERINE (1892–1980)   "The Little Drummer Boy"

Katherine Kennicott Davis was born in St. Joseph, Missouri, on June 25, 1892. She was educated at Wellesley and then studied composition at the New England Conservatory of Music. After this she went to Paris to study privately with Nadia Boulanger. Katherine Davis returned to Wellesley to teach music from 1916 to 1918. She later taught voice and piano in private schools in Concord and Philadelphia. In 1929 she left teaching and from then on worked as a composer, editor, and arranger of music.

Undoubtedly Katherine Davis's best-known work was "The Little Drummer Boy," which is still frequently performed every year at Christmas time. It was first published as "Carol of the Drum" in 1941 with words and music by Katherine Davis. In 1958 the title was changed to "The Little Drummer Boy" and two names were added as collaborators, Henry Onerati and Harry Simeone. Simeone subsequently recorded the song with his chorale.

"The Little Drummer Boy" has had phenomenal success. By the mid-1970s it was the sixth best-selling song in worldwide sales. ("White Christmas" was first.) Up to the 1970s "The Little Drummer Boy" had sold more than 25 million recordings worldwide.

Over the years Katherine Davis composed more than 800 pieces. She wrote books of music for piano and for choir; she also wrote a book of Christmas carols. Her longer works include a folk operetta, *Cinderella* (1933), a Christmas cantata, *This Is Noel,* and a one-act opera, *The Unmusical Impresario,* written with Heddy Root Kent. Among the hymns that she wrote were "Leaning Last Night" and "Let All Things Now Living."

Katherine Davis died in Concord, Massachusetts, on April 20, 1980.

SOURCES

Claghorn, Gene. *Women Composers and Hymnists.*
Craig, Warren. *Sweet and Lowdown.*
Jacques Cattell Press. *ASCAP Biographical Dictionary.*
Shapiro, Nat. *Popular Music.*
Simon, William. *Reader's Digest Merry Christmas Songbook.*
Who's Who of American Women, 1970.

DUNGAN, OLIVE (1903–)   "Thy Loving Kindness"

Born in Pittsburgh, Pennsylvania, on July 19, 1903, Olive Dungan was a child prodigy. She made her debut as a concert pianist with the Pittsburgh Festival Orchestra when she was seven. Later she studied music at the Pittsburgh Institute of Musical Art, the Miami Conservatory, and the Universities of Miami and Alabama.

After that she taught and composed music. Two collaborators who wrote the words for her hymns were Florine Ashby and Ada Morley. Some of the hymns Olive Dungan composed are "The Christ Child," "Eternal Life," "Be Still and Know That I Am God," and "Thy Loving Kindness."

SOURCES

Claghorn, Gene. *Women Composers and Hymnists.*
Lynn Farnol Group. *ASCAP Biographical Dictionary.*

EDDY, MARY BAKER (1821–1910)   "Satisfied"

Mary Baker Eddy, the founder of the Christian Science Church, was born on July 16, 1821, in Bow, New Hampshire. She was the youngest of six children.

Because of her own health problems, she became interested in the art of healing. When she was treated by Dr. Phineas Quimby, she was drawn to his philosophy that the cause and cure of disease is mental.

The healing of her own physical injury in 1866 convinced her that she was on the right course. She began to lecture and establish schools to teach her philosophy based on the ideas contained in her book *Science and Health.* By 1890 she had established 20 churches and 33 teaching centers across the United States. In 1908 she founded *The Christian Science Monitor,* a newspaper that continues to be published today.

In addition to her other activities, Mary Baker Eddy also wrote hymns. Among them are "Shepherd Show Me How to Go," "Blest Christmas Morn, though Murky Clouds," "Brood o'er Us with Thy Shelt'ring Wing," "O Gentle Presence, Peace and Joy and Power," "O'er Waiting Harpstrings of the Mind," "Saw Ye My Saviour? Heard Ye the Glad Sound," and "Mother's Evening Prayer," with music by Frederick C. Atkinson.

Mary Baker Eddy married three times and had a son. She died in Chestnut Hill, Massachusetts, on December 3, 1910, at the age of 89.

> It matters not what be thy lot,
> So Love doth guide
> For storm or shine, pure peace is thine,
> What-e'er betide.
> —"Satisfied," words by Mary Baker Eddy

SOURCES

Christian Science Hymnal, 1937.
Claghorn, Gene. *Women Composers and Hymnists.*
Foote, Henry. *Three Centuries of American Hymnody.*
Hughes, Charles. *American Hymns Old and New.*
James, Edward. *Notable American Women.*

FULLER, MARGARET (1810–1850)
"Jesus, a Child, His Course Begun"

The remarkable author, teacher, feminist, and intellectual Sarah Margaret Fuller was born in Cambridgeport, Massachusetts, on May 23, 1810. Before her untimely death she penned the hymn "Jesus, a Child, His Course Begun."

Given a classical education by her father, a Harvard graduate and lawyer, she became a prodigy. She taught languages in Bronson Alcott's school in 1835 and established her famous discussion groups in Boston in 1839.

She joined Ralph Waldo Emerson and others in producing *The Dial* magazine. Subsequently she was hired by Horace Greeley as literary critic for the *New York Tribune*. In addition to her newspaper work, she wrote several books.

It was on her 1850 return journey from Europe, where she had been a correspondent for the *Tribune*, that she, her husband, and her child drowned when their ship sank off Fire Island, New York.

> Jesus a child, his course begun:
> How radiant dawned his heavenly day!
> And those who such a race would run
> As early should be on their way.
>
> —"Jesus a Child, His Course Begun,"
> words by Margaret Fuller

SOURCES
Christ-Janer, Albert. *American Hymns Old and New.*
Claghorn, Gene. *Women Composers and Hymnists.*
Hughes, Charles. *American Hymns Old and New.*
James, Edward. *Notable American Women.*

HANAFORD, PHOEBE (1829–1921)
"Cast Thy Bread upon the Waters"

Phoebe Ann Coffin was born on May 6, 1829, on Nantucket Island, where her father was a businessman and shipowner. She was a cousin of feminist Lucretia Mott. Shortly after Phoebe's birth her mother died.

As a child Phoebe Ann Coffin was interested in writing, and by 13 she was being published in the newspaper. Her education included the study of Latin and mathematics, which was unusual for girls at that time. For a few years she taught school.

In 1849 she married Dr. Joseph H. Hanaford and went to live in Reading, Massachusetts, where they had two children. Phoebe continued to write, and over the years she wrote 14 books of poetry, children's stories, antislavery essays, and biographies. Her biographies were particularly successful. The one on Abraham Lincoln sold 20,000 copies.

In her middle years, she found religion more important to her than anything else. She worked as an editor of a Universalist magazine and Sunday-school paper. During this time she separated from her husband. In 1868, encouraged by a woman minister, Reverend Olympia Brown, Phoebe Hanaford became a Universalist minister. She became the pastor for several different churches in Massachusetts, Connecticut, and New Jersey. During the last 20 years of her life she lived in New York City with Universalist author Ellen E. Miles.

Of the hymns Phoebe Hanaford wrote, the best known is "Cast Thy Bread upon the Waters," with music by Thomas Whittemore. Another of her poems, "The Empty Sleeve," about a Civil War soldier, was set to music by the Reverend John W. Dadum.

In 1921, at the age of 92, Phoebe Hanaford died in Rochester, New York.

> Cast thy bread upon the waters,
> Thinking not 'tis thrown away.
> God himself saith, thou shalt gather
> It again some future day.
>
> —"Cast Thy Bread upon the Waters,"
> words by Phoebe Hanaford

SOURCES
Christ-Janer, Albert. *American Hymns Old and New.*
Claghorn, Gene. *Women Composers and Hymnists.*
Hughes, Charles. *American Hymns Old and New.*
James, Edward. *Notable American Women.*

HAWKS, ANNIE (1836–1918)   "I Need Thee Every Hour"

Annie Sherwood Hawks was born in Hoosick, New York on May 28, 1836. After she married, she and her husband lived in Brooklyn and attended the Hanson Place Baptist Church, where the Reverend Robert Lowry was pastor. Lowry composed music for hymns and was always looking for a text to set to music. He found that his parishioner Annie Hawks could write the words, so they began collaborating on hymns. Their best-known hymn was "I Need Thee Every Hour."

In addition to caring for a husband and three children, Annie Hawks continued to write hymns, completing more than 400 during her lifetime.

She lived out the latter days of her life with her daughter and son-in-law in Bennington, Vermont, where she died on January 3, 1918.

> I need Thee every hour, most gracious Lord
> No tender voice like thine can peace afford.
> I need Thee every hour, Every hour I need Thee
> O bless me now, my Saviour, I come to Thee.
>
> —"I Need Thee Every Hour," words by Annie Hawks

SOURCES
Foote, Henry. *Three Centuries of American Hymnody.*
Reynolds, William. *Hymns of Our Faith.*
Spaeth, Sigmund. *History of Popular Music in America.*

HYDE, ABIGAIL (1799–1872)
"Dear Saviour, if These Lambs Should Stray"

The early hymn writer Abigail B. Hyde was born in Stockbridge, Massachusetts on September 28, 1799. Her family moved to Litchfield Hill, Connecticut, where Abigail attended school.

She married Reverend Lavius Hyde in 1818 and had eight children, yet she continued to write poetry as she had since childhood. Some of her poems were published in the *Religious Intelligencer*.

Many of her poems were set to music as hymns. Her poem "Prayer on Behalf of Children" became "Dear Saviour, if These Lambs Should Stray" (1824), with music by William Batchelder Bradbury. The hymns "And Canst Thou, Sinner, Slight" and "Behold the Glorious Dawning Brought" also have words by Abigail Hyde. The 1851 edition of Asahel Nettleton's *Village Hymns* contained 34 of Abigail Hyde's hymns.

She died in Andover, Massachusetts, on April 7, 1872.

> Dear Saviour, if these lambs should stray,
> From thy secure enclosure's bound,
> And lured by worldly joys away,
> Among the thoughtless crowd be found.
> —"Dear Saviour, if These Lambs Should Stray,"
> words by Abigail Hyde

SOURCES
Christ-Janer, Albert. *American Hymns Old and New.*
Claghorn, Gene. *Women Composers and Hymnists.*
Foote, Henry. *Three Centuries of American Hymnody.*
Hatfield, Charles. *Poets of the Church.*
Hughes, Charles. *American Hymns Old and New.*

KNAPP, PHOEBE (1834–1908)   "Open the Gates of the Temple"

The parents of composer Phoebe Palmer Knapp were Methodist evangelists. Her mother, Phoebe Worrall Palmer (1807–1874), was a deeply religious woman who wrote hymns, such as "O When Shall I Sweep through the Gates." Her mother also held a weekly women's prayer meeting in New York City; the meeting flourished for 37 years.

Like her mother, Phoebe Palmer Knapp had a great love of sacred music. Born in New York City on March 8, 1834, she married Joseph F. Knapp, founder of the Metropolitan Life Insurance Company. They were members of the same church as **Fanny Crosby** with whom Phoebe Knapp wrote some of her best-known hymns.

In later years as the widow of Joseph Knapp, she was enormously wealthy and could afford to have a pipe organ installed in her apartment at the Hotel Savoy. Her son, Joseph Palmer Knapp, was the head of Crowell-Collier Publishing Company and helped his mother publish the more than 500 hymns that she wrote. Her best-known hymns were "Blessed Assurance" and "Open the Gates of the Temple," with words by Fanny Crosby.

Phoebe Knapp also composed the music for some of her mother's hymns. Two by this mother-daughter team are "The Cleansing Stream" and "Welcome to Glory."

Phoebe Knapp died in Poland Springs, Maine, on July 10, 1908.

SOURCES

Claghorn, Gene. *Women Composers and Hymnists.*
Hughes, Charles. *American Hymns Old and New.*
Reynolds, William. *Hymns of Our Faith.*
Spaeth, Sigmund. *History of Popular Music in America.*

LATHBURY, MARY (1841–1913)   "Day Is Dying in the West"

Born in Manchester, New York, on August 10, 1841, Mary Artemesia Lathbury was the daughter of a Methodist preacher. She became a writer and editor for the Methodist Sunday School Union, editing the *Sunday School Advocate* and other periodicals. Much of her poetry appeared in these publications. In later years she wrote *The Children's Story of the Bible* (1898).

While at Chautauqua for a summer conference, Mary Lathbury was asked by the founder, Dr. John H. Vincent, to write a vesper song for evening services. She wrote "Break Thou the Bread of Life" (1877). It became the well-known hymn "Day Is Dying in the West" (1877), which is often used as a communion hymn. The music was written by William Fiske Sherwin, who was also associated with the Chautauqua conference.

Another of her hymns is "O Shepherd of the Nameless Fold" (1881). Mary Lathbury died in East Orange, New Jersey, on October 20, 1913.

> Day is dying in the west
> Heaven is touching earth with rest
> Wait and worship while the night
> Sets her evening lamps alight
> Through all the sky.
>   —"Day Is Dying in the West," words by Mary Lathbury

SOURCES
Claghorn, Gene. *Women Composers and Hymnists.*
Foote, Henry. *Three Centuries of American Hymnody.*
Hughes, Charles. *American Hymns Old and New.*
Reynolds, William. *Hymns of Our Faith.*
Rodeheaver, Homer. *Hymnal Handbook for Standard Hymns.*

LEECH, LYDIA (1873–1962)   "When the Veil Is Lifted"

Born in Mayville, New Jersey, on July 12, 1873, composer Lydia Shivers Leech was educated at Columbia Conservatory and Temple University.

She became a church organist and traveled widely as accompanist for evangelical services.

She composed approximately 500 hymns, among them "God's Way," "I Have Redeemed Thee," "When the Veil Is Lifted," "Some Day He'll Make It Plain," and "No Fault in Him."

Lydia Shivers Leech died in Long Beach, California, on March 4, 1962.

SOURCES
Claghorn, Gene. *Women Composers and Hymnists.*
Lynn Farnol Group. *ASCAP Biographical Dictionary.*
Reynolds, William. *Hymns of Our Faith.*

POUNDS, JESSIE (1861–1921)   "Beautiful Isle of Somewhere"

Jessie Brown Pounds was a professional hymn writer married to a minister.

She was born on August 31, 1861, in Hiram, Ohio. As a teenager she had her writings published in religious magazines. When she was older, she wrote hymns for the Fillmore Brothers Music House in Cincinnati. She wrote music for them for more than 30 years, writing more than 400 hymns and numerous cantatas.

Some of her best-known hymns were "The Touch of His Hand on Mine," "I Know that My Redeemer Liveth," "I Must Needs Go Home by Way of the Cross," "Anywhere with Jesus I Can Safely Go," written with Mrs. C. M. (Helen) Alexander, and "Beautiful Isle of Somewhere," with music by J. S. Fearis.

She died in 1921.

> Somewhere the sun is shining
> Somewhere the song-birds dwell
> Hush, then, thy sad repining,

God lives, and all is well.
> —"Beautiful Isle of Somewhere," words by Jessie Pounds

SOURCES
Claghorn, Gene. *Women Composers and Hymnists.*
Mattfeld, Julius. *Variety Music Cavalcade.*
Reynolds, William. *Hymns of Our Faith.*

SIGOURNEY, LYDIA (1791–1865)   "Blessed Comforter Divine!"

Poet, writer, vocalist, and hymnist Lydia Sigourney was born Lydia Howard Huntley in Norwich, Connecticut, on September 1, 1791.

She was the only child of a hired man and his wife. The woman for whom her father worked saw that the child was talented and helped with her education and literary career, making it possible for Lydia to publish her first book in 1815.

Although she would have preferred earning her living as a writer, Lydia found it necessary to open a young ladies' school in Norwich to support herself. In 1819 she married a widower, Charles Sigourney, who had three children, and with him she had two more. Even with a large family, Lydia Sigourney was able to continue writing. At first she gave the profits to charity, but later her earnings helped support her family. She became a prolific writer of poetry, short stories, and biography. Her works comprise 56 volumes, including more than 2,000 magazine articles.

In addition Lydia Sigourney was a popular vocalist in Connecticut. She was known as the "Sweet Singer of Hartford."

She also wrote hymns, some of which appeared in Asahel Nettleton's *Village Hymns* in 1824. Among her hymns are "Fill the Fount with Roses," "As Thy Day, So Shall Thy Strength Be," "Go to Thy Rest Fair Child," and "Blessed Comforter Divine" with music by Timothy Olmstead.

Lydia Sigourney died in Hartford on June 10, 1865.

Blessed Comforter Divine!
Whose rays of heavenly love
Amid our gloom and darkness shine,
And point our souls above,
And point our souls above.
> —"Blessed Comforter Divine," words by Lydia Sigourney

SOURCES
Claghorn, Gene. *Women Composers and Hymnists.*
Hatfield, Edwin. *Poets of the Church.*
Hitchcock, H. Wiley. *New Grove Dictionary of American Music.*

Hughes, Charles. *American Hymns Old and New.*
James, Edward. *Notable American Women.*

STOWE, HARRIET BEECHER (1811–1896)

"Still, Still, with Thee"

Harriet Beecher Stowe is known primarily as the author of *Uncle Tom's Cabin.* In addition to writing books, however, she also authored hymns.

She was born on June 14, 1811, in Litchfield, Connecticut. Her mother died when Harriet was four years old. Her father, Lyman Beecher, and her brother, Henry Ward Beecher, were both dynamic preachers, and Harriet's early life was spent in an atmosphere of intense Calvinism.

In 1836 she married Calvin Ellis Stowe, a professor of Biblical literature, and with him she had seven children. In her early years she wrote for her own enjoyment, and after her marriage she continued writing, partly to supplement the family income.

Her book, *Uncle Tom's Cabin* (1852) was the result of her strong anti-slavery feelings. It was her way of preaching against slavery, as her father had. Sales of the book were astronomical, second only to those of the Bible. The book had enormous influence and aroused the conscience of the nation, but it did not change the United States peacefully, as Harriet Beecher Stowe had hoped.

Harriet Beecher Stowe also wrote hymns, among them "Still, Still, with Thee," with music from Felix Mendelssohn-Bartholdy; "When Winds Are Raging o'er the Upper Ocean," with music by Uzziah C. Burnap; and "Abide in Me, O Lord, and I in Thee." Her hymns were published in the hymnal, *Plymouth Collection* (1855), used in her brother's church.

> Still, still with Thee, when purple morning breaketh,
> When the bird waketh, and the shadows flee
> Fairer than morning, lovelier than daylight,
> Dawns the sweet consciousness, I am with Thee.

SOURCES
Christ-Janer, Albert. *American Hymns Old and New.*
Foote, Henry. *Three Centuries of American Hymnody.*
Hughes, Charles. *American Hymns Old and New.*
James, Edward. *Notable American Women.*

WARNER, ANNA (1820–1915)

"Jesus Loves Me"

Anna Bartlett Warner was born in New York City on August 31, 1820. She grew up on Constitution Island in the Hudson River opposite West

Point. The family had moved there from New York City after some severe financial losses.

Anna and her older sister, Susan, tried to help support the family through their writings. Susan became a successful and prolific writer, publishing one or two books every year for 30 years. Under the pseudonym Amy Lothrop, Anna wrote poetry, children's stories, and books about gardening.

Anna Warner also wrote hymns. Her best known is the familiar Sunday school hymn "Jesus Loves Me," written in 1859 and set to music by William B. Bradbury in 1862. Her other hymns include "Jesus Bids Us Shine," "One More Day's Work for Jesus," "A Mother's Evening Hymn," "A Child Pilgrim," and "Evening," the latter written with Robert Lowry. One hymn begins with the graceful line "We would see Jesus, for the shadows lengthen across this little landscape of our life."

For more than 50 years, the Warner sisters gave Bible classes for the West Point cadets, and it is at West Point that the Warner sisters were buried, Susan in 1885 and Anna on January 15, 1915. It was their wish that Constitution Island be given to West Point, and so it was.

> Jesus loves me! this I know,
> For the Bible tells me so
> Little ones to him belong,
> They are weak but he is strong.
> Yes, Jesus loves me,
> Yes, Jesus loves me,
> The Bible tells me so.
>
> —"Jesus Loves me," words by Anna Warner

SOURCES
Claghorn, Gene. *Women Composers and Hymnists*.
Hughes, Charles. *American Hymns Old and New*.
Julian, John. *Dictionary of Hymnology*.
Reynolds, William. *Hymns of Our Faith*.
Rodeheaver, Homer. *Hymnal Handbook for Standard Hymns*.

WILSON, JENNIE (1857–1913)
"Hold to God's Unchanging Hand"

Jennie Wilson was a prolific writer of poetry and hymns.

Born near South Whitley, Indiana, in 1857, she contracted a spinal disease as a child that left her confined to a wheelchair the rest of her life.

Despite her affliction, she wrote unceasingly, producing more than 2,000 poems and hymns.

Among her best-known hymns are "Hold to God's Unchanging Hand,"

"Jesus Is Calling the Children," "There Will Be Light at the River," "Is It Well with Your Soul?," and "Christ Is Calling You Tonight."

Jennie Wilson died on September 3, 1913.

SOURCE

Claghorn, Gene. *Women Composers and Hymnists.*

X | GOSPEL

INTRODUCTION

African-American gospel music began to develop in the late nineteenth century after a period of religious revivalism. Its development corresponded with the rise of the Pentecostal "holiness" and "sanctified" churches. Combining hymns with popular, folk, blues, and jazz elements, gospel music tended to be more joyful, uplifting, and exuberant than traditional church music.

One of the first hymnals to include gospel songs was *The Harp of Zion* (1893), which was used by the National Baptist Convention for more than two decades. An early composer of many popular gospel songs was the Reverend Charles Albert Tindley of Philadelphia. Many of his songs are contained in the 1921 Baptist hymnal *Gospel Pearls*, together with songs by Thomas A. Dorsey and Lucie Campbell.

Dorsey was another pioneer of gospel music. He came from a career in popular music where at one time he was an accompanist for **Ma Rainey.** Dorsey wrote gospel hymns for a church choir he directed. To popularize his music, he and singers Sallie Martin and Mahalia Jackson toured the country performing his songs in churches and concert halls. He and Sallie Martin organized the National Convention of Gospel Choirs and Choruses, which taught groups how to sing gospel. Pianist Roberta Martin and gospel singer Willie Mae Ford Smith were also active with this organization and influential in the gospel movement.

Gospel songs were recorded as early as the 1930s. Since then radio, television, records, and live concerts have brought gospel music into the secular world, where it has had considerable influence on American popular music.

CAMPBELL, LUCIE (1885–1963)
"He'll Understand and Say Well Done"

Lucie Eddie Campbell was a teacher and also one of the early gospel songwriters.

She was born on April 30, 1885, in Duck Hill, Mississippi. Her family moved to Memphis when she was a child. After she graduated from Booker T. Washington High School in 1899, she became a teacher there. During summer vacations she earned her master's degree at the State University at Nashville. She continued teaching at the same high school for 40 years. In addition she directed the choir at her church and actively participated in the National Baptist Convention for more than 30 years. She was president of the National Baptist Choral Society and music director of the National Baptist Training Union.

As a songwriter Lucie Campbell is best known for the hymn "The Lord Is My Shepherd." She also composed "Footprints of Jesus," "Just as I Am," "A Sinner like Me," "Heavenly Sunshine," "I Need Thee Precious Lord," "He'll Understand and Say Well Done," "End of My Journey," and "Just to Behold His Face." She wrote "Something within Me" for the singer Connie Rosemond. Her songs have been recorded by many of the top gospel singers.

Lucie Campbell was still writing gospel songs at 76. She died on January 3, 1963, in Nashville, Tennessee.

SOURCES
Heilbut, Tony. *Gospel Sound.*
Hitchcock, H. Wiley. *New Grove Dictionary of American Music.*
Jackson, Irene. *Afro-American Religious Music.*
Southern, Eileen. *Biographical Dictionary of Afro-Americans.*
Southern, Eileen. *Music of Black Americans.*

COATES, DOROTHY (1928–   )   "That's Enough"

Singer and songwriter Dorothy McGriff Love Coates was born Dorothy McGriff in Birmingham, Alabama, on January 30, 1928. As a child she sang gospel and in her teens sang with a family group, the McGriff Singers. She did not finish high school because she had to go to work to help support her family.

In 1945 she began singing with a local group, the Original Gospel Harmonettes. She toured and recorded with them until the early 1950s, performing many of her own songs.

Her personal life has had many difficulties. She was first married to gospel singer Willie Love and later to Carl Coates. The marriages didn't last. Her daughter was born with cerebral palsy. To try to support her daughter and also continue her gospel singing, she worked days and sang nights until she finally drove herself to physical collapse. Nevertheless, when she was able, she participated in the civil rights marches with Martin Luther King, Jr.

Dorothy Coates is well known for her songwriting as well as her singing. The first song she wrote, "He's Right on Time," was so successful that it has become a gospel standard. Since then she has written hundreds of gospel songs, among them "Get Away Jordan," "Lord, You've Been Good to Me," "There's Always Somebody Talking about Me," "I Won't Let Go of My Faith," "How Much More of Life's Burden Can We Bear?," "You Must Be Born Again," "Every Day Will Be Sunday," "I'm Trying, Lord," "Come On in the House," "That's Enough," and "Hide Me, Jesus."

Dorothy Coates has performed at gospel festivals throughout the United States as well as the Newport Jazz Festival. She makes her home in Birmingham, Alabama.

> There's always somebody talking about me,
> Really I don't mind.
> They're trying to block and stop my progress,
> Most of the time.
> The mean things you say don't make me feel bad,
> I can't miss a friend I've never had,
> I've got Jesus and that's enough.
>
> —"That's Enough," words and music
> by Dorothy Love Coates

SOURCES

Claghorn, Gene. *Women Composers and Hymnists.*
Heilbut, Tony. *Gospel Sound.*
Hitchcock, H. Wiley. *New Grove Dictionary of American Music.*
Southern, Eileen. *Biographical Dictionary of Afro-Americans.*

MARTIN, ROBERTA (1907–1969)   "Brighten the Way"

Gospel singer, pianist, and composer Roberta Evelyne Martin was born on February 12, 1907, in Helena, Arkansas. Her family moved to Chicago when she was ten years old. She took piano lessons when she was young, planning to be a concert pianist. Later she studied music at Northwestern University.

Starting in 1931 and for many years after she was the accompanist for the Ebenezer Baptist Church gospel choir, which had been organized by Theodore Frye and Thomas A. Dorsey. Together with Frye she helped organize the Junior Gospel Chorus at the church, which grew into the Martin–Frye Singers and later the Roberta Martin Singers.

In the 1940s Roberta Martin formed the Martin and Martin Singers with **Sallie Martin** (no relation), and toured the United States and Europe performing gospel music.

For years she worked with Thomas A. Dorsey's National Convention of Gospel Choirs and Choruses. She was accompanist there for **Willie Mae Ford Smith** in the Soloists Bureau of the convention. She was also accompanist for Mahalia Jackson and the Barrett Sisters.

Roberta Martin was an accomplished musician—one of the few gospel musicians who could read, write, and arrange music. She was a brilliant pianist whose piano work set the standard for all gospel pianists who came after her.

From 1956 on she became minister of music at Mount Pisgah Baptist Church in Chicago. During this time she continued to give concerts and work in community activities.

Among the approximately 100 songs she wrote are "Brighten the Way," "He Never Said a Word," "Try Jesus, He Satisfies," "God Is Still on the Throne," "Let It Be," "Just Jesus and Me," "He's Always Giving," "Walk On (One Step at a Time)," and "Savior Lead Me On." Her songs were published through her own company, the Roberta Martin Studio of Music, which she established in Chicago in 1939.

Roberta Martin died on January 18, 1969, in Chicago.

SOURCES

Heilbut, Tony. *Gospel Sound.*
Hitchcock, H. Wiley. *New Grove Dictionary of American Music.*
Jackson, Irene. *Afro-American Religious Music.*
Southern, Eileen. *Music of Black Americans.*

MARTIN, SALLIE (1895–1988)
"He Has Gone to Prepare a Place for Me"

Sallie Martin was one of the pioneers of black gospel music and had great influence on its development.

She was born in Pittfield, Georgia, on November 20, 1895. Her mother was a gospel singer who toured the small-church circuit in the South. Sallie Martin's parents died, and at 16 she moved to Atlanta, then Cleveland, and finally Chicago. In 1929 she began singing in the chorus of the Pilgrim Baptist Church led by Thomas A. Dorsey.

Coming from a background of popular music and blues, Dorsey undoubtedly found traditional church hymns very solemn and restrained. He believed that sacred music should express deep feelings and emotions the way the blues did, and he began composing what later became known as gospel music. Many church goers were enthusiastic about it, but some thought the music lacked proper dignity and prohibited it from being sung inside their church.

For Dorsey, it was an uphill battle to have his music performed. Sallie Martin was enthusiastic about gospel music and helped him sell his songs by traveling with Dorsey throughout the country singing the gospel songs he composed. She also helped organize and teach choirs how to perform his music. In 1932 Sallie Martin joined Dorsey in organizing the National Convention of Gospel Choirs and Choruses, where vocalists and choir groups could be trained to sing gospel and where gospel choirs came together each year to perform.

In 1940 Sallie Martin left Dorsey to tour as a soloist, with Ruth Jones as her accompanist. Ruth Jones later became the well-known singer **Dinah Washington.** Sallie Martin also established a gospel music publishing house with Kenneth Morris; the resulting Martin & Morris Publishing Company prospered. Then with **Roberta Martin** (no relation), Sallie formed the Martin and Martin Singers. When the group broke up, she organized her own Sallie Martin Gospel Singers. She sang on tours throughout the United States, Europe, and Africa. In Los Angeles she recorded with the St. Paul Baptist Church choir, which sang gospel on television.

In 1970 she retired, but nine years later she returned to play an extended engagement in Paris in *Gospel Caravan,* which also featured the gospel singer **Marion Williams.**

At the age of 88 Sallie Martin appeared with **Willie Mae Ford Smith** and Thomas A. Dorsey in a television documentary about gospel music, "Say Amen, Somebody" (1982), which was shown on Public Television.

Many of Sallie Martin's songs were written with Thomas A. Dorsey, among them "The Sweetest Name I Know," "Just a Few Days to Labor," "He's Come Again," "Nearer Oh Lord to Thee," "He Has Gone to Prepare a Place for Me," "Wonderful Is His Name," and "Speak Lord Jesus."

Sallie Martin was married to Wallace Martin.

SOURCES

Cloyd, Iris. *Who's Who among Black Americans.*
Hitchcock, H. Wiley. *New Grove Dictionary of American Music.*
Jackson, Irene. *Afro-American Religious Music.*
Southern, Eileen. *Biographical Dictionary of Afro-Americans.*
Southern, Eileen. *Music of Black Americans.*

SMITH, WILLIE MAE FORD (1904–   )   "If You Just Keep Still"

Willie Mae Ford Smith was one of the great early gospel singers. She was born on June 23, 1904, into a poor family of 14 children in Rolling Fork, Mississippi. Her father was a railroad brakeman and a church deacon. When Willie Mae was 12, her family moved to St. Louis, Missouri. In the eighth grade she had to quit school in order to help her mother run a restaurant. In later years she was employed as a social service worker in a mental hospital.

Her first important appearance as a gospel singer occurred in 1922 when the family group in which she sang, the Ford Sisters Quartet, performed at the National Baptist Convention and received much acclaim. Although she enjoyed singing, she believed she had a "calling" to preach the gospel. Therefore, in the late 1920s she went to a seminary school and became an ordained minister.

In 1936 she formed the Soloists Bureau of the National Convention of Gospel Choirs and Choruses, where she taught gospel singing and was the director for many years. As soloist at the convention the following year, she received an ovation for singing her own gospel song, "If You Just Keep Still." For many years Willie Mae Ford Smith sang at churches and revival meetings with her powerful contralto voice; at these gatherings she also gave her sermonettes, as she called them. In 1939 she left the Baptist Church and joined the Church of God Apostolic.

She has sung at the Newport Jazz Festival and at Radio City Music Hall in New York, but she has made only a few recordings.

Among the songs Willie Mae Ford Smith has written are "A Sword in His Right Hand," "If You Just Keep Still," and "My Mind's Made Up and My Heart Is Fixed."

In 1982 she was featured in a PBS-TV documentary about gospel music, "Say Amen, Somebody," along with Thomas A. Dorsey and Sallie Martin. There, she talked about the conflict women feel in trying to pursue their calling as gospel singers, which often involves being away from home to sing in other cities. It was often difficult to decide between their family's needs and their religious obligations. She told how she had wanted to be a minister but that her church disapproved of women ministers. In the end it was necessary for her to leave her church to follow her calling. It was often a lonely road that Willie Mae Ford Smith trod, but because of her efforts, the way was made easier for others.

In 1988 she received a National Heritage Fellowship from the National Endowment for the Arts for her contribution as an outstanding American folk artist.

SOURCES

Claghorn, Gene. *Women Composers and Hymnists.*
Heilbut, Tony. *Gospel Sound.*
Hitchcock, H. Wiley. *New Grove Dictionary of American Music.*
Jackson, Irene. *Afro-American Religious Music.*
Lanker, Brian. *I Dream a World.*
Southern, Eileen. *Biographical Dictionary of Afro-Americans.*
Southern, Eileen. *Music of Black Americans.*

WARD, CLARA (1924–1973)   "How I Got Over"

Clara Ward came from a family of gospel singers. Her mother, Gertrude Mae Murphy Ward, and her sister, Willa Ward Moultrie, were both professional gospel singers. Clara was born on April 21, 1924, in Philadelphia, Pennsylvania.

She sang in her church choir as a child. As she grew older, she, her mother, and sister formed the Ward Trio. Later they added two other singers—Henrietta Waddy and **Marion Williams**—and formed the Famous Ward Singers. They were a tremendous success at the National Baptist Convention in 1943. Later they toured the country with the Big Gospel Cavalcade.

In 1957 they performed at the Newport Jazz Festival. Four years later Clara made the controversial decision to take gospel music into the secular world of nightclubs and theaters. The group subsequently played Las Vegas and Disneyland.

All of this was distressing to those who believed that gospel music belonged only in church. They felt night clubs degraded the sacredness of the music, and that the music itself was being destroyed through "jazzed up" contemporary arrangements. That religious singers should be willing to do this for money was the final blow. There were many singers who refused commercial offers and continued to sing only in the church. Those who moved on to Las Vegas could console themselves with the fact that they were bringing the music to a wider audience, spreading the word, and creating a greater appreciation for gospel music.

In the 1960s the Famous Ward Singers, the most successful pop-gospel group, split up. Willa Ward had her group, the Willa Ward Singers, and Mother Ward formed the New Ward Singers. Clara and her singers went on to perform at Radio City Music Hall in New York in 1963—the first gospel group to do so. She also took the leading role in Langston Hughes's *Tambourines to Glory* and appeared in the film *It's Your Thing*.

In addition to singing, Clara Ward wrote over 200 gospel songs, among them "How I Got Over," "Great Is the Lord," "God Is God," "He's Watching over You," "King Jesus Is All I Need," "We're Going to Have a Time," "I Just Can't Make It by Myself," "In His Arms," and "Trying to Get Home."

Clara Ward and her mother moved to Los Angeles in the 1960s. Clara had a stroke in 1967. In time she recovered and was able to return to performing and recording. She also toured Europe and Japan. But on January 16, 1973, Clara Ward died in Los Angeles at the age of 48.

SOURCES

Jackson, Irene. *Afro-American Religious Music.*
Mapp, Edward. *Directory of Blacks in the Performing Arts.*
Southern, Eileen. *Biographical Dictionary of Afro-Americans.*
Southern, Eileen. *Music of Black Americans.*

WILLIAMS, MARION (1927–   )   "I Shall Wear a Crown"

Gospel singer and songwriter Marion Williams was born on August 29, 1927, in Miami, Florida. She sang in the church choir and at revival meetings when she was a child.

In 1947 she joined the Ward Singers, becoming their lead singer. She remained with them for 12 years. Then she left the Ward Singers to form the Stars of Faith. In 1961 she starred on Broadway with Alex Bradford in Langston Hughes's gospel musical *Black Nativity*. After a successful engagement in New York, the production company took the show on tour throughout Europe and Australia. At Christmas time in 1963 *Black Nativity* was produced on national television.

Marion Williams began performing solo in 1965. She toured widely during the 1960s and 1970s, including the United States, Europe, and Africa. She sang at the Newport Jazz Festival in 1975. In 1980 she played an engagement at the Cookery, a night club in New York City. And in 1990 she appeared in the Bill Moyer's program "Amazing Grace," telecast on Public Television.

In addition to singing gospel, Marion Williams has written and arranged gospel songs. Her songs include "Holy Ghost Don't Leave Me," "I Shall Wear a Crown," and "We Shall Be Charged."

SOURCES

Claghorn, Gene. *Women Composers and Hymnists.*

Hitchcock, H. Wiley. *New Grove Dictionary of American Music.*

Jackson, Irene. *Afro-American Religious Music.*

Pareles, Jon. "Gospel Praises the Lord." *NY Times,* February 18, 1990, Section 2, p. 27.

BIBLIOGRAPHY

BOOKS

Albertson, Chris. *Bessie*. New York: Stein & Day, 1972.

Anderson, E. Ruth, comp. *Contemporary American Composers*. Boston: G. K. Hall & Co., 1982.

Anderson, Robert, and Gail North. *Gospel Music Encyclopedia*. New York: Sterling Publishing Co., 1979.

Arnold, Elliott. *Deep in My Heart*. New York: Duell, Sloan, 1949.

Baggelaar, Kristin, and Donald Milton. *Folk Music More Than a Song*. New York: Thomas Y. Crowell, 1976.

Baxter, Ian, Christine Baxter, and Robert E. Finley, eds. *Who's Who in the Theatre*. Detroit: Gale Research, 1981.

Benzinger, Barbara, and Eleanor Dickinson. *That Old-Time Religion*. New York: Harper & Row, 1975.

Berendt, Joachim. *The Jazz Book*. New York: Lawrence Hill & Co., 1975.

Block, Adrienne Fried, and Carol Neuls-Bates, comp. and eds. *Women in American Music*. Westport, Conn.: Greenwood Press, 1979.

Block, Maxine. *Current Biography*. New York: H. W. Wilson, 1940.

Bloom, Ken. *American Song: The Complete Musical Theatre Companion*. New York: Facts on File Publications, 1985.

Bogle, Donald. *Brown Sugar*. New York: Harmony Books, 1980.

Bordman, Gerald, *Jerome Kern: His Life and Music*. New York: Oxford University Press, 1980.

———. *The Oxford Companion to American Theatre*. New York: Oxford University Press, 1984.

Bronson, Fred. *Billboard Book of Number One Hits*. New York: Billboard Publications, 1985.

Brooks, Edward. *The Bessie Smith Companion*. New York: Da Capo Press, 1982.

Burgess, Dorothy. *Dream and Deed: The Story of Katharine Lee Bates*. Norman: University of Oklahoma Press, 1952.

Burke, W. J., and Will D. Howe. *American Authors and Books, 1640 to the Present Day*. New York: Crown Publishers, 1972.

Burton, Jack. *The Blue Book of Broadway Musicals*. New York: Century House, 1952.

———. *The Blue Book of Hollywood Musicals*. Watkins Glen, N.Y.: Century House, 1953.

Candee, Marjorie Dent. *Current Biography*. New York: H. W. Wilson, 1956, 1958.

Charabati, Victoria France. *Contemporary Newsmakers*. Detroit: Gale Research, 1988, pp. 441–43.

Chase, Gilbert. *America's Music*. Rev. 2nd ed. New York: McGraw-Hill, 1955.

———. *America's Music*. Rev. 3rd ed. Urbana: University of Illinois Press, 1987.

Chilton, John. *Who's Who of Jazz*. New York: Chilton Book Co., 1970.

Christ-Janer, Albert, Charles W. Hughes, and Carleton Sprague Smith. *American Hymns Old and New*. New York: Columbia University Press, 1980.

Christian Science Hymnal. Boston: Christian Science Publishing Society, 1937.

Claghorn, Charles Eugene. *Biographical Dictionary of American Music*. West Nyack, N.Y.: Parker Publishing Co., 1973.

Claghorn, Gene. *Women Composers and Hymnists: A Concise Biographical Dictionary*. Metuchen, N.J.: Scarecrow Press, 1984.

Clarke, Donald, ed. *Penguin Encyclopedia of Popular Music*. New York: Viking Penguin, 1989.

Cloyd, Iris, ed. *Who's Who among Black Americans*. New York: Gale Research, 1990.

Cohen, Aaron I., ed. *International Encyclopedia of Women Composers*. New York: R. R. Bowker, 1981.

Cohen-Stratyner, Barbara, ed. *Popular Music, 1900–1919*. Detroit, Michigan: Gale Research, 1988.

Collier, James Lincoln. *The Making of Jazz*. New York: Dell Publishing Co., 1978.

Collins, Judy. *Trust Your Heart*. New York: Fawcett Crest, 1987.

Cook, Bruce. *Listening to the Blues*. New York: Charles Scribner's Sons, 1973.

Craig, Warren. *The Great Songwriters of Hollywood*. New York: A. S. Barnes, 1980.

———. *Sweet and Lowdown: American Popular Song Writers*. Metuchen, N.J.: Scarecrow Press, 1978.

Crosby, Frances Jane. *Fanny Crosby's Life Story*. New York: Every Where Publishing Co., 1903.

Dachs, David. *Anything Goes: The World of Popular Music*. New York: Bobbs-Merrill, 1964.

Dahl, Linda. *Stormy Weather: The Music and Lives of a Century of Jazzwomen*. New York: Pantheon Books, 1984.

Davis, Sheila. *The Craft of Lyric Writing*. Cincinnati: Writer's Digest Books, 1985.

Davis, Tracy. "Close-up of Cynthia Weil and Barry Mann." In *Song Writer's Market*, edited by W. Brohaugh. Cincinnati: Writer's Digest Books, 1983.

Dellar, Fred. *The Illustrated Encyclopedia of Country Music*. New York: Harmony Books, 1987.

Dellar, Fred, Roy Thompson, and Douglas B. Green. *The Illustrated Encyclopedia of Country Music*. New York: Harmony Books, 1977.

Dixon, Robert, and John Godrich. *Recording the Blues*. New York: Stein & Day, 1970.

80 Years of American Song Hits. New York: Chappell and Company, 1973.

Emurian, Ernest K. *Living Stories of Favorite Songs*. Boston: W. A. Wilde Co., 1958.

Engel, Lehman. *Words with Music*. New York: Macmillan, 1972.

Evans, Mark. *Soundtrack: The Music of the Movies*. New York: Da Capo Press, 1979.

Evory, Ann, and Peter M. Gareffa, eds., *Contemporary Newsmakers, Issue 2*. Detroit: Gale Research, 1985.

Ewen, David. *American Popular Songs*. New York: Random House, 1966.

―――. *American Songwriters*. Bronx, N.Y.: H. W. Wilson, 1986.

―――. *Complete Book of the American Musical Theater*. New York: Holt, Rinehart & Winston, 1958.

―――. *The Life and Death of Tin Pan Alley*. New York: Funk & Wagnalls, 1964.

―――. *New Complete Book of the American Musical Theater*. New York: Holt, Rinehart, & Winston, 1970.

―――. *Panorama of American Popular Music*. Englewood Cliffs, NJ: Prentice-Hall, 1957.

―――. *Richard Rodgers*. New York: Henry Holt, 1957.

Feather, Leonard. *The New Encyclopedia of Jazz*. New York: Horizon Press, 1960.

Feinstein, Elaine. *Bessie Smith*. Harmondsworth, Middlesex, England: Penguin, 1985.

Foote, Henry Wilder. *Three Centuries of American Hymnody*. New York: Archon Books, 1968.

Friedman, Myra. *Buried Alive*. New York: Bantam Books, 1974.

Fuld, James J. *The Book of World-Famous Music*. New York: Crown Publishers, 1975.

Furia, Philip. *The Poets of Tin Pan Alley*. New York: Oxford University Press, 1990.

Futrell, Jon. *The Illustrated Encyclopedia of Black Music*. New York: Harmony Books, 1982.

Gareffa, Peter M., ed. *Contemporary Newsmakers*. Detroit: Gale Research, 1986, 1988, 1989.

Gertner, Richard, ed. *International Motion Picture Almanac*. New York: Quigley, 1984.

Gleason, Ralph. *Celebrating the Duke*. Boston: Little, Brown, 1975.

Gourse, Leslie. *Louis' Children*. New York: William Morrow, 1984.

Green, Stanley. *Encyclopaedia of the Musical Theatre*. New York: Dodd, Mead, 1976.

―――. *Encyclopedia of the Musical Film*. New York: Oxford University Press, 1981.

―――. *The World of Musical Comedy*. New York: Ziff-Davis Publishing Co., 1960.

Hamm, Charles. *Yesterdays: Popular Song in America*. New York: W. W. Norton, 1979.

Hammond, John. *On Record*. New York: Ridge Press, 1977.

Handy, D. Antoinette. *Black Women in American Bands and Orchestras*. Metuchen, N.J.: Scarecrow Press, 1981.

Hanson, Patricia King, ed. *The American Film Institute Catalog of Motion Pictures Produced in the United States. Feature Films, 1911–1920*. Berkeley: University of California Press, 1988.

Harker, David. *One for the Money: Politics and Popular Songs*. London: Hutchinson, 1980.

Harris, Sheldon. *Blues Who's Who*. New Rochelle, NY: Arlington House, 1979.

———. *Blues Who's Who*. New Rochelle, NY: Da Capo Press, 1989.

Hatfield, Edwin Francis. *The Poets of the Church*. Detroit: Gale Research, 1978.

Heilbut, Tony. *The Gospel Sound: Good News and Bad Times*. New York: Simon & Schuster, 1971. Revised 1985.

Hentoff, Nat. *Jazz Is*. New York: Random House, 1972.

Herbert, Ian, Christine Baxter, and Robert E. Finley, eds. *Who's Who in the Theatre*. Detroit: Gale Research, 1981.

Hitchcock, H. Wiley, and Stanley Sadie, eds. *The New Grove Dictionary of American Music*. New York: Grove Dictionaries of Music, 1986.

Hoffmann, Frank, ed. *The Cash Box: Singles Charts, 1950–81*. Metuchen, N.J.: The Scarecrow Press, 1983.

Holiday, Billie, and William Dufty. *Lady Sings the Blues*. New York: Avon Books, 1956.

Hughes, Charles W. *American Hymns Old and New: Notes on the Hymns and Biographies of the Authors and Composers*. New York: Columbia University Press, 1980.

Jackson, Irene V. *Afro-American Religious Music*. Westport, Conn.: Greenwood Press, 1979.

Jackson, Katherine, and Richard Wiseman. *My Family the Jacksons*. New York: St. Martin's Press, 1990.

Jacques Cattel Press, comp. *ASCAP Biographical Dictionary*, 4th ed. New York: R. R. Bowker, 1980.

James, Edward T., Janet Wilson James, and Paul S. Boyer, eds. *Notable American Women, 1607–1950*. Cambridge, Mass.: Belknap Press of Harvard University Press, 1971.

Janis, Elsie. *The Big Show: My Six Months with the American Expeditionary Forces*. New York: Cosmopolitan Book Co., 1919.

———. *So Far, So Good*. New York: E. P. Dutton, 1932.

Jasen, David A., ed. *Alexander's Ragtime Band*. New York: Dover Publications, 1987.

Jones, Hettie. *Big Star Fallin' Mama: Five Women in Black Music*. New York: Viking Press, 1974.

Jones, Leroi. *Black Music*. New York: William Morrow, 1970.

———. *Blues People*. New York: William Morrow, 1963.

Julian, John, ed. *A Dictionary of Hymnology*. New York: Dover Publications, 1957.

Kanter, Kenneth Aaron. *The Jews on Tin Pan Alley*. New York: Ktav Publishing House, 1982.

Kaplan, Mike, ed. *Variety Who's Who in Show Business*. New York: R. R. Bowker, 1989.

Kinkle, Roger. *The Complete Encyclopedia of Popular Music and Jazz, 1900–1950*. New Rochelle, N.Y.: Arlington House, 1974.

Kislan, Richard. *The Musical: A Look at the American Musical Theater*. Englewood Cliffs, N.J.: Prentice-Hall, 1980.

Krafsur, Richard P., ed. *The American Film Institute Catalog. Feature Films, 1961–70*. New York: R. R. Bowker, 1976.

Krythe, Maymie R. *Sampler of American Song*. New York: Harper & Row, 1969.

La Blanc, Michael L., ed. *Contemporary Musicians*, vol. 5. Detroit: Gale Research, 1991.

Lanker, Brian. *I Dream a World*. New York: Stewart, Tabori & Chang, 1989.

Lawless, Ray M. *Folksingers and Folksongs in America*. New York: Duell, Sloan & Pearce, 1965.

Lax, Roger, and Frederick Smith. *The Great Song Thesaurus*. New York: Oxford University Press, 1989.

Lee, Peggy. *Miss Peggy Lee*. New York: Donald I. Fine, 1989.

Lewine, Richard, and Alfred Simon. *Songs of the American Theater*. New York: Dodd, Mead & Co., 1973.

———. *Songs of the Theater*. New York: H. W. Wilson, 1984.

Lieb, Sandra R. *Mother of the Blues: A Study of Ma Rainey*. Amherst: University of Massachusetts Press, 1981.

Locher, Frances, ed. *Contemporary Authors*, vol. 105. Detroit: Gale Research, 1982.

Logan, Mary S. *The Part Taken by Women in American History*. New York: Arno Press, 1972.

Lynn Farnol Group, comp. and ed. *The ASCAP Biographical Dictionary of Composers, Authors and Publishers*. New York: ASCAP, 1966.

Lyons, Len. *The Great Jazz Pianists*. New York: William Morrow, 1983.

Mainiero, Lina, ed. *American Women Writers*. New York: Frederick Ungar, 1979–1982.

Mantle, Burns. *American Playwrights of Today*. New York: Dodd, Mead, 1929.

———. *Contemporary American Playwrights*. New York: Dodd, Mead, 1938.

Mapp, Edward. *Directory of Blacks in the Performing Arts*. 2nd ed. Metuchen, N.J.: Scarecrow Press, 1990.

Mattfeld, Julius. *Variety Music Cavalcade, 1620–1961*. Englewood Cliffs, N.J.: Prentice-Hall, 1962.

May, Hal, and Susan M. Trosky, eds. *Contemporary Authors*, Detroit: Gale Research, 1984–1988.

McClary, Susan. *Feminine Endings: Music, Gender and Sexuality*. Minneapolis: University of Minnesota Press, 1991.

McNamara, Daniel I. *The ASCAP Biographical Dictionary of Composers, Authors and Publishers*. New York: Thomas Y. Crowell, 1948.

Millett, Fred. *Contemporary American Authors*. New York: Harcourt, Brace, 1940.

Mooney, Louise, ed. *Contemporary Newsmakers*. Detroit: Gale Research, 1990.

Moore, Carman. *Somebody's Angel Child: The Story of Bessie Smith*. New York: Thomas Y. Crowell, 1969.

Moritz, Charles, ed. *Current Biography*. New York: H. W. Wilson, 1953–90.

Morthland, John. *The Best of Country Music*. New York: Doubleday, 1984.

Munden, Kenneth W., ed. *The American Film Institute Catalog of Motion Pictures Produced in the United States. Feature Films, 1921–1930*. New York: R. R. Bowker, 1971.

Nash, Jay Robert, and Stanley Ralph Ross. *The Motion Picture Guide*. Chicago: Cinebooks, 1986.

New York Times Film Reviews, 1913–1968. New York: New York Times & Arno Press, 1970.

New York Times Theater Reviews, 1920–1970. New York: New York Times & Arno Press, 1971.

Oakley, Giles. *The Devil's Music: A History of the Blues.* New York: Harcourt Brace Jovanovich, 1978.

Oliver, Paul. *The Blackwell Guide to Blues Records.* Cambridge, Mass.: Basil Blackwell, 1990.

———. *The Story of the Blues.* Radnor, Penn.: Chilton Book Co., 1969.

Oliver, Paul, Max Harrison, and William Bolcom. *The New Grove Gospel, Blues and Jazz.* New York: W. W. Norton, 1980.

Placksin, Sally. *American Women in Jazz: 1900 to the Present.* New York: Seaview Books, 1982.

Pollock, Bruce, ed. *Popular Music: An Annotated Index to American Popular Songs.* Vols. 9–13. Detroit: Gale Research, 1986–1990.

Reynolds, William Jensen. *Hymns of Our Faith.* Nashville: Broadman Press, 1964.

Richards, Laura E., and Maud Howe Elliott. *Julia Ward Howe, 1819–1910.* New York: Houghton Mifflin, 1915.

Rigdon, Walter, ed. *The Biographical Encyclopedia and Who's Who of the American Theatre.* New York: James H. Heineman, 1966.

———. *Notable Names in the American Theatre.* Clifton, N.J.: James T. White and Co., 1976.

Rodeheaver, Homer A. *Hymnal Handbook for Standard Hymns and Gospel Songs.* Philadelphia: Rodeheaver Co., 1931.

Rodgers, Richard. *Musical Stages.* New York: Random House, 1975.

Root, George F. *The Story of a Musical Life.* 1891. Reprint. New York: AMS Press, 1973.

Rothe, Anna, ed. *Current Biography.* New York: H. W. Wilson, 1945, 1946.

Rublowsky, John. *Popular Music.* New York: Basic Books, 1967.

Ruffin, Bernard. *Fanny Crosby.* Philadelphia: United Church Press, 1976.

Salem, James. *A Guide to Critical Reviews,* Part 2, *The Musical, 1909–1974.* Metuchen, N.J.: Scarecrow Press, 1976.

Scobey, Lola. *Dolly Parton, Daughter of the South.* New York: Kensington Publishing Corp., 1977.

Shapiro, Nat, and Nat Hentoff. *Hear Me Talkin' to Ya.* New York: Dover Publications, 1955.

Shapiro, Nat, ed. *Popular Music: An Annotated Index of American Popular Songs.* 6 vols. New York: Adrian Press, 1964–73.

Shemel, Sidney, and M. William Krasilovsky. *This Business of Music.* New York: Billboard Publications, 1977.

Shirley, Kay, ed. *The Book of the Blues.* New York: MCA Music, 1963.

Sicherman, Barbara, and Carol Hurd Green, eds. *Notable American Women, The Modern Period: A Biographical Dictionary.* Cambridge, Mass.: Belknap Press of Harvard University Press, 1980.

Siegel, Alan H. *Breakin' in to the Music Business.* Port Chester, N.Y.: Cherry Lane Books, 1983.

Silverman, Jerry. *Folk Blues.* New York: Oak Publications, 1968.

Simon, George T. *The Best of the Music Makers.* Garden City, N.Y.: Doubleday, 1979.

Simon, William. *Reader's Digest Merry Christmas Songbook.* Pleasantville, N.Y.: Reader's Digest Assoc., 1981.

———. *Reader's Digest Treasury of Best Loved Songs.* Pleasantville, N.Y.: Reader's Digest Assoc., 1972.

Skowronski, JoAnn. *Black Music in America.* Metuchen, N.J.: Scarecrow Press, 1981.

Slide, Anthony. *The Vaudevillians.* Westport, Conn.: Arlington House, 1981.

Smith, Sharon. *Women Who Make Movies.* New York: Hopkinson & Blake, 1975.

Southern, Eileen. *Biographical Dictionary of Afro-Americans and African Musicians.* Westport, Conn.: Greenwood Press, 1982.

———. *The Music of Black Americans.* New York: W. W. Norton, 1971. Revised 1983.

Spaeth, Sigmund. *A History of Popular Music in America.* New York: Random House, 1948.

Stambler, Irwin, and Grelun Landon. *Encyclopedia of Folk, Country, and Western Music.* New York: St. Martin's Press, 1969. Revised 1984.

Stambler, Irwin. *Encyclopedia of Pop, Rock and Soul.* New York: St. Martin's Press, 1974. Revised 1989.

Steward, Sue, and Sheryl Garratt. *Signed, Sealed, and Delivered.* Boston: South End Press, 1984.

Stewart-Baxter, Derrick. *Ma Rainey and the Classic Blues Singers.* New York: Stein & Day, 1970.

Stuessy, Joe. *Rock and Roll: Its History and Stylistic Development.* Englewood Cliffs, N.J.: Prentice-Hall, 1990.

Taylor, Deems. *Some Enchanted Evenings.* New York: Harper & Brothers, 1953.

Taylor, Paul. *Popular Music since 1955.* Boston: G. K. Hall, 1985.

Truitt, Evelyn Mack. *Who Was Who on Screen.* New York: R. R. Bowker, 1984.

Tyler, Don. *Hit Parade.* New York: Viking Penguin, 1989.

Vaughan, Andrew. *Who's Who in New Country Music.* New York: St. Martin's Press, 1989.

Warfel, Harry R. *American Novelists of Today.* New York: American Book Co., 1951.

Waters, Edward N. *Victor Herbert: A Life in Music.* New York: Macmillan, 1955.

Wenner, Hilda E., and Elizabeth Freilicher. *Here's to the Women.* Syracuse, N.Y.: Syracuse University Press, 1987.

Whitcomb, Ian. *After the Ball: Pop Music from Rag to Rock.* New York: Simon & Schuster, 1972.

Whitman, Wanda Willson, ed. *Songs That Changed the World.* New York: Crown Publishers, 1969.

Who Was Who in America, vol. 3, *1951–1960.* Chicago: Marquis Who's Who, 1966.

Who Was Who in the Theatre, 1912–1976. Detroit: Gale Research, 1978.

Who's Who in America, Wilmette, Ill.: Marquis Who's Who, 1932–1990.

Who's Who of American Women. Chicago: Marquis Who's Who, 1958–1991.

Wilder, Alex. *American Popular Song: The Great Innovators, 1900–1950.* New York: Oxford University Press, 1972.

Wilk, Max. *They're Playing Our Song.* New York: Atheneum, 1973.

Witmark, Isidore, and Isaac Goldberg. *Story of the House of Witmark: From Ragtime to Swingtime.* New York: Lee Furman, 1939.

Woolery, George W. *Children's Television: The First Thirty-Five Years, 1946–1981.* Metuchen, N.J.: Scarecrow Press, 1985.

PERIODICALS

Allen, Bonnie. "Hot Voice, Cool Head." *Ms,* June 1989, pp. 42–45.

Anderson, Nancy. "Here Come the Judds!" *Good Housekeeping,* June 1988, pp. 38–45.

Arrington, Carl Wayne. "Madonna in Bloom: Circe at Her Loom." *Time,* May 20, 1991, pp. 56–58.

Bennett, Helen Christine. "The Woman Who Wrote 'Mother Machree.' " *American Magazine,* December 1920, pp. 34–185.

Fried, Stephen. "Bulletproof Waif." *Gentleman's Quarterly,* May 1990, pp. 91–95.

Gates, David. "Starting Out at No. 1: A 20-year-old's Hot Debut." *Newsweek,* August 6, 1990, p. 63.

Givens, Ron. "Suzanne Vega's Vision." *Stereo Review,* July 1990, p. 79.

———. "The Pick of the Crop." *Newsweek,* October 16, 1989, pp. 65–66.

Gleason, Holly. "What's Hot: Country Women." *Ladies Home Journal,* November 1988, pp. 142–46.

Hirschberg, Lynn. "The Misfit," *Vanity Fair,* April 1991, pp. 158–68.

Hubbard, Kim. "When Suzanne Vega Peeled Away Her Folkie Label, Fans Found a Pop-Rock Star." *People,* June 8, 1987, p. 71.

"In Person: Mariah Carey." *Seventeen,* October 1990, p. 64.

Jerome, Jim. "In the Best Family Tradition, Carlene Carter Gets on Track and Steams Her Way to a Country Hit." *People,* November 12, 1990, pp. 169–70.

Jones, Malcolm, Jr. "Country's New Traditionalist, a Carter Comes Home." *Newsweek,* August 17, 1990, p. 58.

Leland, John. "You Gotta Pay Respect." *Newsweek,* January 6, 1992, pp. 50–51.

Lyons, H., and C. O'Haire. "Gretchen Cryer: Friends and Lovers." *Ms,* December 1978, p. 49.

McGuigan, Cathleen, and Todd Barrett. "Suzanne Vega, Ethereal Girl." *Newsweek,* August 3, 1987, p. 69.

Morganstern, Dan. "Hall of Fame Winner." *Downbeat,* August 24, 1967, p. 22.

"A New 'Comedy Gift.' " *Literary Digest,* October 27, 1917, p. 27.

O'Neal, Jim. "Victoria Spivey, Brooklyn's Blues Queen Dead at 60." *Rolling Stone,* November 18, 1976, p. 26.

"Pop's New Vision." *New York,* May 28, 1990, p. 26.

Sanderson, Jane. "Fighting to Cast Off Death's Shadow." *People,* November 26, 1990, pp. 90–94.

Sanz, Cynthia, and Sanderson, Jane. "Goodbye, Sunshine: A Car Crash Claims Dottie West on Her Way to the Opry." *People,* September 16, 1991, pp. 38–39.

Scott, V. "Bette." *Good Housekeeping,* March 1991, p. 64.

NEWSPAPERS

Brady, James. "In Step with Reba McEntire." Parade, *Oakland Tribune*, October 27, 1991, p. 14.

"Country's '80s Lady, K. T. Oslin Makes Her Mark after 25 Years as a Singer." *San Francisco Examiner-Chronicle*, Datebook, July 30, 1989, p. 35.

Hilburn, Robert. "Tracy Chapman's Next 'Crossroads.' " *San Francisco Examiner-Chronicle*, Datebook, July 1, 1990, p. 39.

Pareles, Jon. "Gospel Praises the Lord and Sings the Blues." *New York Times*, February 18, 1990, Section 2, p. 27.

Plaskin, Glenn. "Carly Simon Fights Fear." *San Francisco Chronicle*, August 29, 1990, p. B5.

"Renovated New York Palace to Reopen Today." *San Francisco Chronicle*, April 1, 1991, p. E4.

Selvin, Joe. "Rosanne Cashes in on Her Humanity." *San Francisco Chronicle*, December 17, 1990, p. F3.

"Songwriters Carole Bayer Sager, Burt Bacharach to Be Divorced." *San Francisco Chronicle*, July 13, 1991, p. C8.

Tannenbaum, Rob. "Building the Perfect Diva." *Rolling Stone*, August 23, 1990, p. 33.

"Transitions." *Newsweek*, January 2, 1989. p. 55.

Zailian, Marian. " 'Funny Face' Fabulous Feet." *San Francisco Examiner-Chronicle*, December 24, 1989, p. 20.

NEWSPAPER OBITUARIES

"Alma Sanders." *New York Times*, December 16, 1956, p. 83.

"Anne Caldwell." *New York Times*, October 24, 1936, p. 17.

"Carolyn Leigh." *New York Times*, November 21, 1983, p. 20.

"Catherine Cushing." *New York Times*, October 21, 1952, p. 29.

"Dorothy Donnelly." *New York Times*, January 4, 1928, p. 25.

"Dorothy Fields." *New York Times*, March 29, 1974, p. 38.

"Elsie Janis." *New York Times*, February 28, 1956, p. 1.

"Ethel Waters." *New York Times*, September 2, 1977, p. 1.

"Florence Reece." *New York Times*, August 6, 1986, II, p. 4.

"Joan Edwards." *New York Times*, August 29, 1981, p. 11.

"Rida Johnson Young." *New York Times*, May 9, 1926, p. 9.

"Rosetta Duncan." *New York Times*, December 5, 1959, p. 23.

"Sylvia Fine Kaye." *New York Times*, October 29, 1991, p. B5.

"Willie Mae Thornton." *Oakland Tribune*. July 28, 1984, p. B6.

GENERAL INDEX

SONG INDEX

About the Author

VIRGINIA L. GRATTAN is the author of *Mary Colter: Builder Upon the Red Earth*. She also taught secondary school English for twenty years.